girlfriends
Talk About Men

Sharing Secrets for a Great Relationship

CARMEN RENEE BERRY AND TAMARA TRAEDER

WILDCAT CANYON PRESS
A Division of Circulus Publishing Group, Inc.
Berkeley, California

girlfriends Talk About Men: Sharing Secrets for a Great Relationship
Copyright © 1997 by Carmen Renee Berry and Tamara C. Traeder
Cover photograph © 1997 Stephanie Rausser
Special thanks to A La Carte Restaurant in Berkeley, California, for
allowing us to shoot the cover photograph on their premises.

Publisher: Julienne Bennett
Editor: Roy M. Carlisle
Copyeditor: Priscilla Stuckey
Cover and Interior Design: Gordon Chun Design
Typesetting: Holly A. Taines
Typographic Specifications: Body text set in Cochin 11/14. All heads and
italics are Cochin.

Printed in the United States of America
Library of Congress Cataloging-in-Publication Data
Berry, Carmen Renee.
    Girlfriends talk about men : sharing secrets for a great relation-
ship / Carmen Renee Berry and Tamara Traeder.
        p. cm.
Includes bibliographical references.
ISBN 1-885171-21-8 (pbk. : alk. paper)
1. Man-woman relationships. I. Traeder, Tamara, 1960- . II. Title.
HQ801.B48   1997
306.7 — dc21   97-29944   CIP

Distributed to the trade by Publishers Group West
99 98 97 ∾ 10 9 8 7 6 5 4 3 2 1

girlfriends
Talk About Men

Other books by
Carmen Renee Berry and Tamara Traeder

girlfriends: Invisible Bonds, Enduring Ties
(Wildcat Canyon Press, 1995)

The girlfriends Keepsake Book:
The Story of Our Friendship
(Wildcat Canyon Press, 1996)

To all the good men out there.

Contents

Acknowledgments

First, we thank the women who allowed us to record conversations we women have all the time about men — conversations that men rarely, if ever, get to hear. Without these personal stories, this book would never have been possible.

For life-long encouragement, we are grateful to our parents, Dr. David A. Berry and Mary Ellen Berry and Gus Traeder and Fern Traeder. We extend a warm "thank you" to Julie Bennett for creating the initial concept for this book and for her insightful suggestions throughout the writing process. As the song says, no one does it better . . . than Roy M. Carlisle whose editorial brilliance, humor, and emotional support kept us focused all the way to the end. Priscilla Stuckey deserves a special thanks for going beyond copyediting by sharing her own thoughtful insights with us, bringing more depth and diversity to the project. And what could we have done without Summer Laurie, our official "keep-everything-straight" person who transcribed interviews, followed up on permissions, and kept track of who said what to whom? Lastly, we are indebted to Holly A. Taines who came into the office before anyone else and stayed long into the night laying out the manuscript in time to meet our printing deadline. To all who work on the Circulus team, thanks, thanks, and more thanks.

What Are We Really Saying Behind Closed Doors?

For most women, the language of conversation is primarily a language of rapport: a way of establishing connections and negotiating relationships.

—DEBORAH TANNEN
You Just Don't Understand

Do you not know I am a woman? When I think, I must speak.

—WILLIAM SHAKESPEARE

As You Like It

When we started this project, we planned to ask women about the best advice they could give to other women about one of our favorite topics—men. Most women, however, quickly demurred, insisting that they "had no idea," they "didn't understand men at all," they were not able to give advice, and they were reluctant to express an opinion. Could this be? Both of us have given, and received, endless advice about the opposite sex; surely we were not the only ones?

We also found, as we started interviewing women, that as women got older, they were less eager to give advice to other women about their decisions. As one fifty-three-year-old woman put it: "I think when you're young, you're absolutely sure what your friend should do with her relationship. Very strongly you say what you believe and this is what she should do. You don't think of ramifications. You're going by what you feel. I think that as an adult, when a friend has a relationship, you're less inclined to go in like a bull. You know that advice freely given might be freely ignored or later remembered and thrown back at you. When a woman is having trouble in

3

a relationship, I'm the kind of person who gives an ear, a shoulder, and lets her say all she wants to say. But I don't give advice."

We finally realized something that we should have known from writing our earlier book, *girlfriends*: most women do not offer what we consider "advice." Instead, women tend to be empathetic, eager to listen to a problem that we share with them, and reflect back to us what they are hearing. Unlike many men, who may be eager to tell us how to fix a problem or to give their opinion, many women instead will want to frame your problem in light of your particular circumstances. Or, when advising someone, we may talk about our own experiences, using our own stories to illustrate a point. When we changed the focus of our book from "advice" to "talking about men," therefore, women started opening up.

The seeming need of many women to talk about men indicates that perhaps we do not understand them, that we consider *them* different from *us*. Well, at the risk of severe generalization, *are* they? We wanted to hear what women really think, so we frequently asked women, "Are men and women really different from each other?" Most women thought so, but many of their attitudes have shifted in one direction or another over the years. For instance, twenty-four-year-old Reva found more differences as her five-year relationship with Jeff continues: "I used to always get really annoyed when people said men and women are different. I insisted, 'No they're not!' My feel-

4

ing was, 'We're all just humans; there's no difference.'

"But since I've been in this relationship, I've seen that there are differences. I used to dismiss the idea as a cliché, but a lot of times the clichés end up being right. For instance, it's pretty obvious to me that I'm a lot more in touch with my emotions than Jeff is. He is a very emotional person with me. In our relationship he has no trouble showing how he feels about me and he definitely knows when I'm not happy. But I can tell easily if someone else is upset, and he just doesn't have that kind of empathetic thing. He can tell when I'm upset, but with other people he has a harder time."

Conversely, some women's attitudes were shifting the other way. When we talked to a forty-year-old woman who had been married for fifteen years and divorced for five, she found that the differences became less noticeable to her as she got older: "I do see differences between men and women, but you know what? They're getting less and less as the years go by. I saw them a lot clearer when I was twenty than I do at forty. At twenty, I thought that men wanted sex and women wanted intimacy. I don't see that at all anymore. Not at all. The guys I go out with are looking for intimacy just as much as the women I know. I've been amazed at the degree to which I had to let that old prejudice go. The men I've met are looking for physical closeness—hugging and snuggling—and emotional openness.

"These are men who have been influenced by the

better aspects of the men's movement, so they're in men's groups, or they're therapists, or they've been in therapy for a number of years. They've been changed by all those things. They're now looking for basic human things that we girls always thought we were looking for—and always gave ourselves credit for being the ones who wanted those things. A couple of guys that I've met have been in the same men's group for six years, and another one has been meeting with the same guys for eight years, and I see this as wonderful, because they view these groups as places to get together and share their feelings as men. They're not getting together to display their prowess. They're getting together to share their feelings and be human with one another. In effect, they're turning to men to do some of the work that in the past men have turned to women to do, because our roles are socialized more differently now than they were years ago."

Of course men vary widely from one another, as do women. Whether we believe men and women are different from each other because we are different genders or merely because we are different individuals, regardless of gender, becomes irrelevant. Why and how we are different from the men we love, and how we cope with or celebrate these differences, is an assessment only each of us individually can make for ourselves. What we hope to accomplish in this book is to share other women's stories with you about their experiences with men and how they reacted and what they thought. Perhaps these stories will help us deal with a problem we are having with the opposite sex or help us look at a situation from a different perspective.

We suspect that many will search these pages for male-bashing stories told by bitter, unhappy women who are never satisfied with the men in their lives. We are sorry to disappoint you. The women we interviewed had an extremely high regard for men.

When discussing their husbands, friends, and lovers who were kind, reliable, vulnerable, strong, and sexy, smiles came to women's faces and tales of respect were told. But when the focus was on adult males who were immature, unable to follow through on their word, unfaithful, and domineering, the talk was radically different. Even though this book is entitled *girlfriends Talk About Men*, from time to time we found ourselves including "boys" in our discussions as well. When referring to males under the age of eighteen, *boys* is an appropriate term to use. However, men who have yet to grow up and assume adult responsibilities can also be called boys, and when we heard negative comments about men, it was this kind of "boy-man" who was targeted.

We heard stories from women who, usually through painful experiences, realized that they needed to leave these boys behind, and we also heard stories about how girlfriends came to their aid, helping them move away from and beyond these relationships. As if each girlfriend has an internal "boy alert" detector, we can sniff out males who may at first appear to be men but who turn out to be boys—and boys, in our experience, spell trouble.

If there has been any bashing done in this book, it has been "boy bashing." Boys, we women are on to you. We know the difference between a good man and a bad boy, and we're spreading the word woman to woman, girlfriend to girlfriend. Boys are those we pass by on our way to men, with whom we are willing to share our love and our respect.

And if you are a woman still trying to love a boy, hoping he'll change, we hope you learn from the wisdom of other women and realize that you are worthy of a man's love, not a boy's neediness. Living life with a man you love is a journey well taken. We hope our collective experiences offer some guidance along a loving path. Many of us have experienced the help that our girlfriends can provide, when we need to sort through a problem or make a decision, merely by providing a sympathetic ear. They frequently do more as well, providing us with examples of what they have done in similar situations, and sharing insights about ourselves that help us to see the right actions to take. As you read about other women's thoughts about and experiences with the opposite sex, know that you are not alone! We can learn to rely on our trusted girlfriends, both our own and the girlfriends who have spoken in this book, to help us with our relationship issues. As we proceed, perhaps we will be blessed with new and helpful ways of thinking about our own lives.

Making
Connections

Love is an exploding cigar which we willingly smoke.

—LYNDA BARRY

Big Ideas

Where the Men Are

It appears that each one of us is compulsively searching for a mate with a very particular set of positive and negative personality traits.

—HARVILLE HENDRIX

Getting the Love You Want

The first challenge in our relationships with men is meeting them. We have heard many women talk of being frustrated by the lack of available men, especially as we move past our early twenties and all the "good ones" seem to be "taken." We may find ourselves complaining with our friends about how the only men "left" are those who are emotionally handicapped or just not interested in women because they are gay, they hate women, or they are just afraid of relationships (for whatever reason).

The heartening news is that we don't have to solve the problem of the unavailability of "all men." We only need to find one "good one" to begin the adventure of a relationship—and we can each find *one*.

When we find a man who appeals to us, we then need to determine whether that person is a "good one" for us. What may work for one woman in a relationship may not work for another, and a man who appeals to us in one period of our life may not be right for us in another. We will discover a lot about ourselves in this journey toward finding the right person for ourselves.

Meeting the Man of Your Dreams

If you want to meet men, you must either be approachable or take the initiative. It is much easier to be approachable.

—MARGARET KENT

How to Marry the Man of Your Choice

How do you meet the man of your dreams? When we asked women who are not with a mate how to meet men, we found various levels of sarcasm, despair, hopelessness, or just shrugged shoulders and hands raised, palms up, with comments such as, "If you find out, please let me know."

Many books are available to women telling us that we can "make love happen." We are encouraged to "get out there" (wherever that is) and find our man. Maybe the problem with some attempts to meet men is that we place ourselves in an unfamiliar setting and then wonder why nobody compatible shows up, like a woman going to a baseball game to meet men when she has no interest in sports. Anyone who has ever been to a singles' event knows how awkward it can feel; everyone is there for the same reason, and everyone is similarly self-conscious. Even when singles' events are dressed up to look like something else, they can still be difficult. Andrea, a single, thirty-something professional woman, told us, "Karen and I were determined to find romantic relationships for each of us, and being young enough to assume that we could control this process, we decided to attend a singles' group that was formed ostensibly in support of the arts but that was really a thinly disguised attempt to meet people and be pretentious at the same time. Karen now insists that I dragged her to this event, but we are still in dispute about that one.

"It was an art exhibit, and it was awful. Everyone was either too cool—lots of all-black outfits—or too embarrassed to talk to anyone else. We dutifully took a tour of the exhibit and had to keep a straight face when the tour guide solemnly pointed out a display including a broom and a pile of garbage and explained how this expressed Western angst, or something equally unbelievable. Of course we may have been too cynical or youthfully arrogant, but we had a horrible time. We never went back to another event for the group, which we came to call 'Yuppies for the Arts,' but of course we enjoy referring to the evening when it comes to the subject of 'horrible things you made me do.'"

This is not to imply that sitting at home every night will open the door to meeting a potential mate. Our interviews uncovered a similarity among the women who were enjoying long-term relationships: they met their beloved in the process of living. They attended an art exhibit because they actually enjoyed art; they took dog training classes because their dogs actually needed to be trained; they joined a ski club because they actually loved to ski—and along with doing the things they enjoyed, they met men who shared their interests. For example, Claudia took a beginners' ice skating class because she felt the need for more exercise. She met another beginning student in her class named Corey who, a year-and-a-half later, became her husband.

We heard time and again that meeting their husbands seemed natural, if not fated. As Barbara, married to her second husband for twenty years, states, "What's going to happen is going to happen. Don't put yourself into an atmosphere that is foreign to you, because why would you want to meet someone in an unnatural setting? Let it grow out of whatever interests you. Why go on a cruise because you think that maybe you'll meet Mr. Right on a cruise when you don't even like sailing? I'm not opposed to trying new things; I think that's a really good idea. My strongest advice is just to be who you are, and someone will find you and you will find somebody. I truly believe that."

When we asked Barbara if that philosophy had proven true in her own life, she explained, "After I was divorced (and I did not want to be divorced), I was a teacher and spent my evenings working on the school yearbook. Everybody said, 'You can't just go to your little house and you can't just be at school; nothing will ever come of it. Well, it did! A man at the school who I hadn't spoken to the first seven years that I worked there asked me to help chaperone a group of seniors on a five-day science trip. I did, and I knew that I would die if he didn't ask me for a date before we got home. And now we're married. Although everyone said nothing would happen unless I went places and did things, I just kept to my own life and thought, 'Something will happen.' You never know how it's going to happen and how it's going to play out."

We've observed that keeping to one's own life does not imply being so focused on your tasks that you never look up and notice that available men may be in the room. As Margaret Kent points out in her book *How to Marry the Man of Your Choice*, "Many men surround you in your daily life, but you do not even know they exist. Some of these men may be looking at you with great longing, but they are afraid to speak to you because you don't seem approachable."[1] We may not seem approachable for a variety of reasons, such as we're too busy climbing the corporate ladder, secretly fearful of relationships and unwilling to make eye contact, or emotionally connected to a past love and not yet ready for Mr. Next.

When a woman is genuinely interested in a romantic liaison, Kent advises that you "say hello to every man where you live, where you work, where you shop, where you conduct your business, and where you go for recreation. Say hello to every man you are reasonably sure is not a felon." We are not suggesting that you say hello in situations that could put you in harm's way. Rather, it's intended to remind us to look up from our responsibilities and notice the men who are around us.

If we are not sure whether we are open to meeting men or not or what messages we are portraying to the men around us, we may want to ask our girlfriends. They notice a lot about us, just as we observe a lot of valuable information about them. What we learn from them may be surprising. And if we find that we are rushing around with our eyes averted from the available men in our lives, we may want to slow down a bit, long enough to say a friendly hello, and open our eyes (and maybe even our hearts) to the kindness of male attention and the potential of romance.

Sport Dating

*A girl can wait for the right man to come along,
but in the meantime that still doesn't mean she can't have
fun with all the wrong ones.*

—CHER

What Women Say About Men

Sport dating is regular dating without any concern for long-term romance—dating for the sheer fun of it. As Carolyn, a lawyer in her late thirties, describes her sport dating in the past: "It was a kick, back in the days when all my friends were dating and it was the societal norm. If you didn't have a date one Friday night, you'd probably have one the next Friday night or Saturday night or

Sunday afternoon. It was just the idea, 'More dates are better'—not so much an ego thing as just the urge to get out there and meet a lot of people and have different experiences with different guys. Some want to go to the symphony, and some want to go rock climbing; others want to go skiing. And then you meet their friends, and that opens up a whole other group. It's how I met a lot of my girlfriends, because they were friends of a guy I was dating. It just opens up your world."

Not every woman is ready to invest in a long-term relationship at this very moment. You may be one of these women, wanting, temporarily or permanently, to have relationships with attractive men for the sheer fun and glamour of it. That's okay, too. Just know what you want and know what to expect. Laura, a California resident, told us this story: "I had broken up with my boyfriend and met Keith at a friend's house on the East Coast. It was one of those instant sparks, and the next thing I knew, he got on a plane to Los Angeles to see me. He picked me up from work in a limousine, and we went off in a helicopter on a tour around the bay. He hung out in the city all week while I was working, so of course I was sneaking off at lunch. We spent the weekend at a bed-and-breakfast and went hiking and bike riding. Then I flew to New York, and it was the same sort of thing—a limousine-and-champagne kind of a romance. He always had an idea of something fun to do. Instead of fantasizing about it, he would make it happen.

"One day I remember getting a delivery of a huge box at the office. In it was a ski suit and a ticket to Denver to meet him in Aspen. That was really great. I loved every minute of it, and it wasn't about the money. It could have been a bottle of wine and a weekend in the country. It was the spirit of adventure and coming up with these fantasy rendezvous and acting them out."

When we asked what happened with that romance, Laura replied, "Well, like most champagne romances, we got tired after a while. It was a little too much of the fast life. It wasn't that we didn't care for each other, it just wasn't meant to be a long-term relationship. It was meant to be fun. We lived on different coasts, so it was more stimulating than secure. I saw him on and off for about nine months, and then we just got busy with other things. It was fun. I'd do that again."

While the concept of quantity dating may seem overwhelming or even impossible for sheer lack of men, one quality of sport dating may help everyone who is frustrated in finding a satisfactory relationship. A positive aspect of sport dating is that it is fun. It may seem that if you are not sure "he's the one," then you cannot spend time with him. However, as one grown woman was told by her mother, "Lighten up! When I was dating, my friends and I went out with several men, and no one demanded that you be exclusive right away. This doesn't have to be so deadly serious. Have some fun!"

One woman told us that she once took this advice to

the extreme and dated seven different men in seven days. Halfway through the week she started confusing the names and offending her dates! But taken at a reasonable speed, sport dating can be smorgasbord of fascinating men and a spectrum of experiences.

Since we could all use a little more fun in our lives, we need to ask whether we are enjoying ourselves or whether dating just seems like another task to check off our to-do list. If we are not having fun, we might get some pointers from our girlfriends who are enjoying their dating experiences and find out their secrets. Perhaps they are taking the process more lightly, or they are only dating men with whom they share interests. We all need to ask how we can have more fun. It may be as simple as changing our attitudes. For instance, if we are inspecting every man we meet to see if he is "the one," enormous pressure will be placed on our first dates!

We work hard and have what seems to be an ever-growing list of responsibilities. Take a page from the sport dating manual and have some adventures. Life begins now, not after you are engaged or married. Enjoy living today!

Blind Dates

My heart sank when I opened the door.

—ANONYMOUS

Every woman has had the experience of spinning her own wheel of fortune, otherwise known as going on a blind date. Usually arising from a spirit of adventure ("Oh, what can it hurt?") or determination ("I will have a date this year!"), these experiences can range from truly inspiring to mildly interesting to downright awful.

Sheila tells this story: "My husband grew up in a small town about four hours southwest of my big city, and his high school class was only one hundred people. His close group of friends became my close group of friends at college, thanks to a wonderful girl in his group who was also in my college dorm. Even though we had all these friends in common, my husband and I never met all through college.

"Finally, the timing must have been right for our mutual friend to introduce us. It was one of those lightning bolt experiences. He proposed on the second date, and within three months we were married. This past August we celebrated our twenty-eighth anniversary with—who else?—our dear friend who introduced us. She not only has become a soul mate of mine, she is also like a sister to my only-child husband. Our families have become one family. Indeed, I have become part of his original close group of friends — almost like I always belonged."

Of blind dates that worked, many seemed to be set-ups that were engineered by a close friend. Like Sheila, Rhonda also had a friend who arranged a date for Rhonda with Rhonda's future husband. Of course, girlfriends know us better than anyone, and if anyone can spot a good match for us, they probably will be the ones. As Rhonda explained about her girlfriend, "I appreciated her understanding of me and what I wanted in a man. She also knew some things about my past, and she put me together with a very kind and caring guy."

Hope, married for the past thirteen years, met her husband on a double blind date arranged by college room-mates. She told us, "Bart showed up in a clunker car, which was quite a change from my previous boyfriend. My ex was really into his car. He had a brand new sports car, and at times I thought he loved the car more than me. So here's this new guy, Bart, in a really horrid car. We parked on campus and were walking toward the the-ater when someone yelled, 'Hey, isn't that your car?' We looked back to see smoke billowing out of the hood. Bart just smiled and said, 'I'll deal with it tomorrow,' and he kept walking with me. I was blown away! I thought, 'He's not overly concerned with his car. He'd rather be with me.'"

Blind dates can be good ways to meet new people, maybe even a man you could love. However, things may go awry if the person introducing you to each other has an unconscious agenda. For example, Victoria was talking with a married friend who raved about her teenage daughter's piano teacher. She tells the story: "My friend said, 'Oh, he would be perfect for you!' so the date was arranged. While the man was physically attractive, we had next to nothing in common, and the conversation slowed to a near crawl before the coffee arrived. I thought his jokes were silly, he found my one-liners dull. In fact, at one point he said to me in a disapproving tone, 'You think you're really funny, don't you?' And I said in a monotone, 'Yes, I'm hilarious.' After an extremely long forty-five minutes, the painful experience came to an end. As I walked gratefully through my own door, the phone rang with my married friend on the other line, wanting to hear all the details about the date. I realized that he was perfect for her, not me. She was attracted to him, and, since she was married and could not pursue him, she sent me in her place."

But when friends truly have our best interests at heart, they can bring together two people who are perfect for each other even though these two are as resistant as two mules. Susan and Craig, both talented writers and artists, had been told about each other by their two wily friends, Roy and his daughter Vanessa, for a year before each was persuaded to venture to a party that the other would be attending. Susan told us, "We couldn't believe the press we were hearing about each other. I was told he was the male version of me, and I thought, 'I can't even deal with the female version of me, so why would I want the male version?' He was thinking, 'How could anyone be this good? She must be weird looking or really neurotic.' He had this whole image of me with long hair up in a bun and chopsticks, wearing some kind of muumuu, with twenty cats trailing behind me. To me, he was Dorky Craig from Pasadena. I don't like the name Craig, and I don't like Los Angeles, so on both counts he was this weird friend of Roy's and Vanessa's who they were trying to push off on me. I thought he would be really nerdy looking.

"I was coming up the back stairs to the party, and, wouldn't you know it, I saw him first thing. My first thought was, 'Uh-oh.' Because I didn't know he would be attractive. He, on the other hand, was shocked when he saw me in a black miniskirt wearing a glowing neon eye between my breasts. I felt an amazing kinship instantly and did something very uncharacteristic. After a brief meeting, I rushed away from him and didn't speak to him for the rest of the party. He did the same. We didn't talk for four months after that party. We were really freaked out."

Undaunted, their friends got them together again for a big celebratory lunch: "So here was this brunch, and for me it was early, like at 11 A.M., and usually I don't move before 4 P.M., so this was a major investment on my part. I just came into the room and saw him, and he had on this purple jacket and was smiling. I had the same

24

'uh-oh' feeling. The seat next to him, of course, was empty at this big round table. We proceeded to turn away from each other, to concentrate on the table and not each other. I invented a game, which was to have everyone tell how they sleep, neat or messy—what does the bed look like when they get up in the morning? We get to Craig and he says, 'Neither neat or messy; you just know that a dance has taken place.'

"Well," Susan breathed in sharply, "I was trying to be subtle, but I was completely speechless. Then there were crayons and butcher paper on the table, and Craig started to draw. When I looked over, I realized he was using all the colors I never use, the tertiary colors. He was making this gorgeous portrait, and I noticed he was left-handed and had a silver bracelet on. I looked over and said to myself, 'I am going to marry him.' Now, that thought had never before crossed my mind—I thought I would never be married. I decided immediately that I would never tell anyone and told myself to put that thought away somewhere.

"We arranged to have tea the following day. I was terrified and told my assistant, 'Find his hotel, I want to cancel.' But he had already checked out and we were supposed to meet at the restaurant, so I had no way to reach him. My assistant then called and said, 'You had better see this fax that just came.' So I went to the office, and this fax is like a poster. It says 'Craig and Susan, 4 P.M. at the Ritz, Can't Wait.' I knew there was destiny.

I saw it and I thought, 'I have to go.'

"I suddenly became about thirteen years old, trying on seventeen different outfits, including a stupid black skirt that didn't fit. I tried to squeeze into it, and thought to myself, 'I've got to be nuts.' I thought the only way to help myself was to get there early and get the best table. There is a wonderful table at the Ritz—it's by the window. So I got there half an hour early, and he was sitting there waiting at *that* table, drawing in his sketchbook, wearing these shoes that I loved, and again I knew I was going to marry him. We sat down for a four-hour tea, and two hours into it we were discussing our marriage."

In the search for true love, we sometimes are willing to risk the possible annoyance of a blind date, and sweet unions such as Susan's and Craig's keep our hope alive that blind dates can work. So if you decide to spin the wheel of blind fortune, learn from other women's experiences and lessen the risk of having a miserable time by following some basic principles: Make the meeting low-key enough that you are not required to spend several hours with someone you may loathe (we suggest meeting for coffee or lunch); only allow people to fix you up that have no power over you (politely decline your boss's urge to fix you up with someone he or she just adores); do not allow someone to set you up with one of their relatives (they tend to be a little biased, and it is very awkward telling someone what a jerk his or her brother is); be cautious if one of your relatives has met your perfect mate (relatives have funny ideas about what is good for you); and, finally, make sure the person fixing you up has more invested in you than in the person with whom you're being fixed up. In other words, limit the matchmakers to your very best girlfriends — someone who is more devoted to your happiness and the longevity of your friendship than she is to you marrying her cousin Fred.

Dating on the Internet

Blonde bombshell seeks warm-hearted man for own private fireworks.

—PERSONAL AD

For many years, men and women have been searching each other out through the personal advertisements in classified sections of newspapers. Placing ads on the Internet is a new take on the personals. While some roll their eyes in fear ("but you could meet an ax murderer!") or in disgust ("Are you *that* desperate?"), many women we interviewed found the Internet a viable way to meet quality men. Since more men than women have home computers, the Internet is one of the few places where the men outnumber the women. As one woman told us laughing, "At least a man on the Internet has to be able to read, type, and earn enough money to pay his phone bill. That's a step up from some of the guys I've dated."

In a more serious tone, she added, "You can tell a lot about a man by the way he expresses himself in writing. I usually assume men are making themselves sound a bit better than they really are, but that's okay. I write a man off if he asks for my phone number quickly, makes crude sexual comments, or seems obsessed with knowing what I look like. If he is interested in getting to know me on-line to see if there's any chemistry, then he makes points with me. I'm not attracted to desperate men."

Wendy claims to have met "some wonderful men over the Net. One guy, in particular, has caught my eye because he seems genuinely interested in me. We've been chatting over the Net now for about four months about books we're reading, about stresses in our work, sharing our opinions about this and that. I think I'm finally ready to meet him in person, which will be fun and strange at the same time. On the one hand, it seems like I know him so well, and on the other, I've never even heard his voice."

Like Wendy, Gail's experience on the Internet has been very positive. In fact, she met the man she has been dating for the past four months over the Net. She told us, "I've met several men on-line, but Jake really caught my eye. He was very articulate. In addition to being able to express his opinions about things, he was also interested in what I had to say. What a nice change from some men I've dated who only like to hear themselves talk."

"Jake and I traded pictures over the Net, and I thought he was a real cutie. So we met and hit it off right away. We've been dating steadily ever since. I feel like I know him better than other men I've dated longer because we had that time on-line to get to know each other's minds. It's more complicated once the physical attraction kicks in, so I'm glad we had that time before we met face-to-face."

While the Internet can seem like a lush garden full of fruit to pick, beware of the rotten apples. One woman told us about a man she had been getting to know on-line and was interested enough to ask him to e-mail her a picture. Eagerly she waited for the image to come on-screen, only to see a picture on him sitting on a couch with his arm around another woman. As if that weren't bad enough, he had scratched out the eyes of the woman in the photograph so she looked mutilated. Needless to say, that was the last on-line conversation she had with him!

Not only is it advisable to be discerning regarding the men you meet on-line, it's also important to be computer literate enough not to do something unintended. A forty-something businesswoman laughed at herself when she told us, "I was having the best time flirting with one man through e-mail. Things were steaming up between us, he sending me passionate messages, and I returning them sizzling over the phone lines. After I had written an especially seductive message, I accidentally hit 'reply all' rather than 'reply.' Without realizing it, I'd sent this very private message to everyone in my e-mail address book! After I got a strange e-mail from my teenage niece, teasing me about what I'd accidentally sent her (don't you just hate how smart kids are these days?), I frantically went through my message board hitting 'unsend' to all the e-mails I could before my friends, family, and business associates read my mail! Ugh! I'm much more careful now."

Dating through classified ads or on the Internet is not for everyone, and whoever chooses this route needs to exercise the appropriate caution. We advise never giving out your address, and giving out your phone number only to someone that you wish to meet. If you feel comfortable meeting a man in person, it is safest to do so in a public place, during the daytime, with a lot of people around. If you wish to exercise extra caution, you may even want to enlist a couple of girlfriends to come with you and sit nearby to make sure you are safe.

Careful seems to be the word that is used again and again by the women who are investigating romance over the Internet, whether you're considering meeting a particular man who pushes your buttons or considering which buttons you're going to push on the keyboard. But by exercising a reasonable amount of caution, you can meet men through the Internet whose paths you may not otherwise cross, and perhaps discover that special one.

Romantic Dates Long Remembered

We love because it's the only true adventure.

—NIKKI GIOVANNI

Reader's Digest

What's romantic to you? Dinner by candlelight? A midnight walk along the beach? Cuddling by a roaring fire? We asked women what they found romantic, and the themes we found centered around thoughtfulness and simplicity.

Remembering her first love, Trish told us, "Vance always wore T-shirts and jeans. But this one time he came over with a shirt that was unbuttoned partway down. He brought homemade chocolate chip cookies and brandy with two glasses. I thought, 'Oh, my! This is very exciting and out of the ordinary!' I smiled at him and asked, 'Do you have something in mind?' He just smiled and nodded. I loved being surprised by something so simple and yet so romantic."

Simple surprises, if thoughtfully created, caught the attention of many of the women we interviewed. For some women, even cleanliness can be romantic. Agnes told us about an easy, relaxed, and romantic date she had with a man named Ramon who was not known for his domestic cleanliness. "He invited me over for dinner, and when I arrived, I was amazed to see the place spotless. I knew that he'd spent the entire day cleaning up for our evening together. That kind of effort meant a lot to me."

Similarly, consideration when we most need it can prove to be extremely romantic. Debbie told us that when she was sick, her boyfriend, who lived twenty miles away, would take the train to see her, and would bring her a box of soft tissues for her nose, a can of soup, and an orange. Little things go a long way.

Spontaneity, even if there's more than just the two of you, can create a romantic, never-forgotten memory. Jane told us about a double date she went on when she was living in San Francisco. At dinner, the group started talking about how much fun Disneyland can be. On the spur of the moment, the group hopped a cheap midnight plane to southern California, had a slumber party in the same room at a budget hotel, spent the day gallivanting around Disneyland, and flew home that evening! The result? Fun and romance on a moment's notice.

Some women we spoke with wondered whether men and women have different ideas of what constitutes romance. One woman, a West Coast psychotherapist, said her and a boyfriend's idea of romance coincided: "He was in Atlanta, so we had a bicoastal relationship and only saw each other every three months. One night after dinner in Atlanta, he found an estate out on the edge of the city where no one had lived for years. It was just acres of green meadow, surrounded by trees. We went out at midnight and took a blanket and a tape deck and a basket with wine, cheese, French bread, cookies, glasses, and candles and spread it out in the middle of this beautiful meadow. I lay in his arms while he quoted this incredible poetry and stroked my face. We looked at the stars and there were fireflies. I thought it was a movie set. It was wonderful."

Other women did not believe that men and women thought of romance as the same. Victoria told us, "The difference between my husband's view of romance and mine is that he views romance as foreplay, with sex being the grand finale. An experience can be romantic for me, whether or not we end up in bed. In fact, sometimes, sharing a romantic moment that doesn't include sex is all the more wonderful for me. My husband has learned that about me, although he doesn't quite understand it. For him, romance and sex are connected."

Gregory J. P. Godek, in his book *1001 Ways to Be Romantic,* confirms this observation by giving men "a word to the wise: *Don't equate romance with sex.* It's one of the quickest ways to foster resentment and miscommunication. Equating the two tends to turn romance into barter." Godek goes on to write, "Romance is *always* about love, but only sometimes about sex. Got it?!"[2]

As with all things, romance is in the eyes of the beholder. Everyone has her idea of gestures and situations that she finds romantic. Colleen, a hair stylist in her early forties, even found that being alone in a sensual, quiet setting was romantic and that another person wasn't always necessary: "For me, romance isn't always about the opposite sex, and it isn't always with another person. It can be light that hits the water at sunset. It can be the lights off in your living room with a fire and some music going and a nice glass of wine and you thinking 'this is good.' One of the senses is involved usually." While many of us may not think of being alone as romantic, a setting where we are restful and not required to speak or do anything, where we can soak up the atmosphere and feel that we are valuable just for being ourselves, can evoke the same peaceful joy that we associate with a romantic situation with a man we love.

Women's ideas of romance may differ. For some women, activities involving the senses, such as the sight of a flickering fire or the feeling of walking in a foggy night, is romantic, while for others romance may involve some sexual play. The women who seemed the most satisfied with their romantic experiences were clear about what they did not want, and found ways for both partners to enjoy the moment.

We found in our interviews that the best romantic experiences are not necessarily the most expensive occasions, but those opportunities to enjoy each other, to get to know a new aspect of the other person's personality. It is often in the midst of laughter, adventure, or simple kindness that a man and a woman discover there is something special between them, something worth pursuing.

Spotting the Good Ones

A woman has got to love a bad man once or twice in her life, to be thankful for a good one.

—MARJORIE KINNAN RAWLINGS

The Yearling

Once we meet someone to whom we are attracted, we begin the process of getting to know him. Sometimes this process goes slowly, when we are not sure this is the right person for us, and sometimes it is accompanied by the experience of "falling in love," the sensation of unquenchable attraction to the other person. While falling in love can make us feel euphoric (as scientific research suggests, naturally occurring amphetamines are produced in our bodies that help make us feel giddy and perpetually excited), it may also produce some discomfort.

Debbie tells us: "I was thinking about the 'first blush' stage and how I remember the first two weeks we were dating we were both going into work at 11:30 every morning. I just didn't go in at the usual time. I don't know why or how I got away with it, but I remember we couldn't separate, there was so much to know. We would sit I don't know where for hours talking about I can't imagine what. I was so tense when I wasn't with him. I sort of needed to be touching him all the time, a physical assurance that he was right there. So we talked and held hands, and we couldn't ever leave, and it was torture when we weren't together."

While every television show or movie reinforces the idea that falling in love is the best possible thing that could happen to us, these cultural messages, along with the chemical changes in our bodies, may blind us to the realities of someone's character. We tend to find all attributes adorable in someone with whom we are in love. But the "blind love" phase eventually passes for the vast majority of people, and we have to sort out who each other really is and whether we want to be together. And those of us who are not head over heels when we start dating someone can already be looking at those questions. The early phase of a relationship is a good time to take a clear-eyed look at someone who may become a long-term mate. This period of time provides an opportunity to learn a lot about ourselves, what is important to us, and what we enjoy about this other person in our lives.

Red Light, Green Light

If your head tells you one thing and your heart tells you another, before you do anything, you should first decide whether you have a better head or a better heart.

—MARILYN VOS SAVANT

The Wit and Wisdom of Women

We all know about those butterflies in our stomachs as we anticipate meeting a man or going on that first date. Hoping to make a good impression, praying that this guy's not a weirdo, we venture out with a man who has some glimpse of potential. Maybe before we even get to the car or at some point during dinner, we get signals indicating either this guy is someone we could be interested in, or this date is a big mistake!

Gail, a public health nurse and self-avowed dating expert, wrinkled her nose when she told us about her first (and last) date with a man she'd met through a dating service. She said, "I'd seen his picture and his biographical profile. He had the look of someone worth knowing, so I agreed to go out with him. We were at the restaurant having dinner. I was feeling optimistic, even though the beginning of the date had the flavor of an interview. Maybe an hour and a half into the dinner, he abruptly said, 'Oh, I see you've had a lot of dental work done.' I was flabbergasted that he would actually comment on that. Now I laugh about it, but that comment changed the experience for me. I lost any interest in dating him again."

Granted, one of the hazards of a first date is that neither person has adequate information about the other to put such comments into context. What might be a harmless comment in one context is quite offensive in another. So, for the men who might be browsing through this book for some pointers, we recommend that you choose your words carefully, especially during those initial fragile hours of the first date. According to the women we interviewed, these are some of the first-date behaviors that turn women off:

∽ No eye contact: Trish told us that she had looked forward to meeting Frank, a man she'd met through a dating service and with whom she'd enjoyed an hour-long phone conversation. She found his voice "very sexy" and was expecting to respond well when they met face-to-face.

To her disappointment, Frank was unable to look her in the eye as they sat sipping their coffee. Instead he stared at the floor, at the ceiling, or at other women who were walking by. She told us, "I thought it was a sign when my head started pounding. When he told me he was a 'loner,' I took that as the final clue, this was not the man for me."

∽ Being compared with his mother: Energetic and fun loving, Sara told us she nixed a man after one date when he told her, "'You know, Sara, you remind me a lot of my mother.' At that point I thought, 'Gosh, too much information, and I don't even know if it's a good thing or not.' At the very least, I didn't want to be seen as a mother figure."

∽ Aggressive talk: What some men might regard as a sexual compliment, might come off like a threat to a woman who does not know a particular man very well. Such was the case of Marsha, whose first-time date "told me he wanted to rape me. And then he asked if he could come up to my apartment! I said, *'No!'* and never went out with him again. I couldn't relax after that, whether it was meant harmlessly or not. All I knew was that I wanted to get away from him."

∽ Being followed: Chris, a child care specialist, rolled her eyes when she told us about a man she knew in college who followed her from class to class evidencing his interest in her. He never even made it to the first date. As Chris put it succinctly, "Stalking is not attractive."

The consistent advice we received in our interviews was to trust yourself when you feel apprehensive or turned off by a man. Remember, this man is not your last chance for happiness. If there's a little red flag waving, we recommend that you take your leave. Better safe than sorry.

On the other hand, some women told us about little signs given by men in their first encounters that indicated these men were worth taking a closer look at, sometimes literally! For instance, Andrea, a thirty-five-year-old nurse, told us that she met her current boyfriend of two years "in a bar, which is the last place I thought I would meet anyone worth dating. A man from the next table started a conversation with me, but I was not being very friendly, as I had just dated two men in a row who seemed friendly at first and then turned into really insecure, and frequently arrogant, boys. I was not interested in starting a new relationship until I could figure out where I had gone wrong. However, he persevered and finally asked me if I would consider going to lunch with him.

"For some reason, I felt that for once, I should really take a few moments before answering the question, and I was determined to do exactly what I wanted to do without being pressured. So I just looked at him intently to see what my instincts told me about him. I literally stared at him for about ten seconds, really looking into his eyes to see what kind of character I saw there.

"What impressed me the most was that he let me stare at him and didn't fidget or interject with another comment or look down or appear nervous. I thought, 'This guy must have a real sense of who he is for him to let me just take my time responding.' He just looked back at me without moving or without assuming a pose. I said, 'Yes, I would like to have lunch with you.' Then he gave me *his* phone number to call him if I still felt that way later! I was so impressed that he gave me so much power in the relationship and actually opened himself up to rejection so that I could feel safe. I liked his sense of self-confidence without his appearing too cocky or overly impressed with himself. He was being courteous, realizing that it may feel unsafe for me to hand him my phone number in a bar. We have been together ever since, and his easy confidence has continued to impress me."

Another woman, a business owner who had been dating men and not finding the right one, was impressed by a man's casual approach to his own appearance: "I had dated a man who put an enormous amount of effort into how he looked. While that in itself is not a bad thing, I found that he was quite self-absorbed and much too interested in himself to pay attention to me. He always talked about himself, his opinions, his job. You know the type, always performing and trying to impress. After we broke up, I wanted to find someone who would have some time for and interest in me.

"When I met Paul, who was in my line of business, I loved the fact that he just had on a plain blue button-down shirt, a so-so tie, and a standard-issue beige raincoat. His collar was even kind of sticking up. I thought it was a good sign that he was just a *guy* guy and didn't spend a lot of time thinking about his appearance. He was the kind of man I was looking for."

When we asked Jody, a twenty-eight-year-old marketing executive, if there were any details that she noticed right away, she answered immediately, "He was genuinely considerate. Before we dated, we were just friends and would see each other only occasionally. However, when I received a job promotion, it happened that he was the first person I told. The next time I visited his home, he was wearing a shirt that I had told him that I liked earlier, he had a radio station on that he rarely listened to but knew I liked, and he had a small bottle of champagne ready to celebrate my promotion. I couldn't believe he paid attention to all of those details. That characteristic has held true for all of the time that I have known him, even after we were married."

These signals are important to notice when we first meet someone who might become that special one. Of course, noticing positive signs is no guarantee that we will walk straight to the altar and live happily ever after. However, these kinds of details are all we have at the very beginning, and they are a good place to start our observations.

Your girlfriends can help you identify important signs and decode the details that you may not notice. You may want to ask a girlfriend what characteristics she thinks you should avoid, and if you have been in an unsatisfying pattern with men, she will probably be able to tell you quickly what those characteristics are and how they manifest themselves! And she may also be able to point out what kind of man she thinks would make you the happiest.

If one of your women friends is around for an initial meeting with a man, go ahead and ask her what she thinks. Sue, a forty-year-old artist, was surprised when her friend made this observation about a man that they had both just met and who had shown interest in Sue: "I asked Lisa what she thought about Mack, and she said that she liked that Mack had made an effort to talk to her and to make sure that she, Lisa, liked him, too. It not only showed some politeness, it also showed Lisa that I was important enough to Mack that he wanted to make sure that she approved of him, too. I was really touched that she put it that way."

Good girlfriends, who are genuinely invested in your happiness, want the best man for you and can be fiercely protective and unnervingly insightful when it comes to letting new men in your life. So take advantage of their love and perspective before you invest too much energy in the wrong guy or let a really good one get away.

See How He Lives

Housekeeping ain't no joke.

—LOUISA MAY ALCOTT

Little Women

One of the ways we women can glean information about a man we may suspect has romantic potential is to check out his living space. When asked what a woman would not want to see when she walks into a man's place, we got answers like:

    ∿ Other women

- Farrah Fawcett's 1970 poster pose
- Piles of dirty laundry

Marsha described the first time she visited her boyfriend's apartment, finding a large, framed picture of a woman on his coffee table. "I asked, 'Who's this?' He told me it was his exgirlfriend. I said, 'Why do you still have a picture of her?' He said, 'She gave it to me.' I pressed further and asked, 'Why is it still out?' He shrugged and said he hadn't gotten around to putting it away. Now that we've broken up, I keep wondering if other women are going into his apartment now and seeing pictures of me!"

According to the women we talked with, some of the men they've dated seem to be able to live with minimal creature comforts: living rooms furnished with an old couch and a packing crate for a chair, and bedrooms with foam rubber pads on the floor serving as beds. Jenny, a psychology student, dated a man whose bedroom had three items: a computer, a table, and a chair.

Wasn't there a bed? we asked. She responded, "He didn't sleep on a bed. He pulled out some bedding from the closet at night. The arrangement wasn't even up to futon status. So it was not very inviting to me to imagine spending the night there with him. I sleep on a waterbed at home and have very comfortable furniture. The sparseness was unnerving to me."

Marsha echoed Trish's observations when she described her last boyfriend's living situation as a "closet off from the garage. It was big enough to fit a twin-sized bed and one dresser in it, and that was it. Do you know any women who would live like that? I don't."

One woman we interviewed cleans houses for a living, thereby having more than average access to the living quarters of the male species. She told us, "I clean for a lot of single men, and I notice what magazines they choose. They have anything from girlie magazines to shelves of magazines that have to do with stereos of all kinds and cars and gadgets.

"What is odd to me is that they collect these magazines, like medical journals. Stacks and stacks of them, neatly arranged. They leave the magazines opened with things circled, like they're always looking for something they're going to buy. The stereo magazines are beautifully kept, in mint condition, while the girlie magazines are all torn up. Even my most compulsive clients. One man I clean for keeps his place in perfect order, and his girlie magazines are all trashed. When I first start cleaning for a man, he usually puts those magazines away before I get there. But after a while, he relaxes and leaves them around the house."

In addition to noticing a man's reading material, women might assume that a man will treat her the way he treats his surroundings. Gail told us, "I like to look around a man's apartment for signs of warmth and nurturing. Recently I went into a man's apartment that was full of plants, healthy, growing, lots-of-leaves plants.

45

There was also wood and lots of books and several candles burning dimly. It seemed really warm and inviting, like it was natural to curl up, snuggle up. When I saw the plants, I thought, 'These plants aren't like chia pets where you just water them once and they do their own thing. This man must be able to nurture, since you have to take care of plants to have them be that healthy.'" A man who regularly demonstrates that he has the ability to nurture may very well be a keeper.

Depending on what is important to us, we may find heartening the lack of furniture and interior design. One woman told us, "When I went into his apartment, I saw blank walls, minimal furniture, lots of vitamin bottles and healthy food and piles of clothing. These told me a lot of things, all of which turned out to be true. The piles of clothing meant he didn't find neatness to be an important issue, so that may be difficult if we got married. That has been true. On the other hand, the blank walls and sparse furniture indicated to me that he was not fussy and opinionated about design (whereas I have definite opinions), so that we would not have a lot of conflict about that. We haven't. And, finally, the vitamins and healthy food indicated that he cared about his health and would probably care about mine. That has been true as well. I got lots of information on my visit to his apartment!"

You can find out his living style, however, only if he invites you to his home. If the man you are seeing does not invite you to his home at first, it simply may mean that he is embarrassed because his home needs straightening up or the magazines need to be cleaned out. However, if weeks go by and he makes it clear that he does not want you there, beware. He may be hiding something—at worst, a wife and kids and, at best, a fear of intimacy with another person (because our homes reveal a lot about ourselves) or a lack of desire to make the place hospitable to you. If the man in your life won't invite you home, ask your friends what their experience has been and whether they think his behavior is fishy. If you come to the conclusion that something else is going on, we advise presenting him with your conclusions and giving him a chance to respond, rather than assuming your suspicions are reality. Once you find out his side of the story, you can decide if this relationship is worth your time or not.

Listen to What He Says,
Notice What He Does

*There are very few human beings who receive the truth,
complete and staggering, by instant illumination. Most of us
acquire it fragment by fragment, on a small scale, by succes-
sive developments, cellularly, like a laborious mosaic.*

—ANAÏS NIN

The Wit and Wisdom of Women

Okay, so you're attracted to a man. How do you know he's a good match for you? Well, listen carefully, because he will tell you almost everything you need to know right away if you are paying attention. But don't just listen with your ears, listen also with your eyes. Many a woman has been fooled by the words of a man, but it's hard to lie with the way you live your life.

Joan saw something special in Sam one afternoon that made her think, "This is a man I could marry. I didn't think 'this is the *only* man I could marry,' but 'I could really marry this man.'" There were three of us in his car— Sam, me, and a young friend of mine, a thirteen-year-old who I was taking around for the day in the city. We were stopped at a stoplight where Sam was dropping us off. There was a bus lane to the right of us, and as we were getting out I opened the door without looking, unaware of the bus lane. A bus came up and hit his car door and bent it. It didn't fall off, but it was clearly a serious problem, and it was totally my fault. Sam looked at the door, and I said, 'Oh my gosh, I can't believe it.' He immediately said, 'Don't worry about it. You go have a good time, and I'll get it fixed. Don't even think about it.' I thought, 'Here's someone with whom I can do something really stupid that destroys a piece of his property, and he's not going to yell at me!'

"Perhaps his reaction meant all that much more to me because the last man I'd been involved with would have told me in a voice loud enough for people in the next block to hear that I was the biggest idiot on the face of the earth. Sam showed me that I could be with a man who behaved very differently."

By watching a man's behavior, you may learn just enough to know that this is one fish that needs to be thrown back into the sea. One professional woman told us, "When I first met Johan, I was impressed by his good looks, advanced degrees, and seeming sophistication. On one of our first dates, we started talking about where we grew up and went to college and so forth. When I told him that I had gone to a college located in the South, he (who was from the East Coast and went to all of the 'right' schools) was shocked and exclaimed, 'You're kidding! I don't believe you! You are too sophisticated to have gone to school there!'

"Well, I should have known at that point that he was a horrible snob and that we would have a bad time over his attitude. Instead, I was too swept away by how attractive he was, and I ignored the warning signs. It took another year to figure out that he really did look down on people who didn't have his background. I finally realized that snobbishness was covering up a lot of insecurity he had about himself and that he would probably treat me that way in the future. I finally got out of the relationship. I could have saved myself a lot of heartache if only I'd paid attention to that first conversation!"

Some women we interviewed saw warning signs early on but ignored them and got married anyway. In fact, most of the divorced women we talked with said things like, "Looking back, I can see all the signs were there," or "I minimized the craziness because I wanted it to work out so badly." Such is the tale of Cindy who, on the first date, had all the information she needed to pass this one by. He invited her to go to dinner and to the theater, an invitation she accepted. But when it came to discussing the arrangements, he went through all these machinations to avoid driving to her place to pick her up. She said, "I thought, 'Why doesn't he just pick me up? That would be a nice thing to do.'

"When we hung up, I didn't feel good about it. I thought, 'I can't go out with this person! He won't even pick me up for our date!' I talked the right talk, but I'd never been married and didn't want to ruin any chance with an available man. So I went out on the date and eventually married him. I finally had my fill of his selfishness and left him. We've been divorced now for two years, and I regret the years I wasted not admitting what I had known from that very first date."

Paying attention to both a man's actions and his words can reveal potential problems if there's a discrepancy between them. We heard many versions of the same tale, men who talked one way and acted another. A fine example of this was conveyed to us by Janey, who told us that Jerry, a warm, fun-loving man, said on their first date that "he made a great boyfriend but not good husband material. I dismissed it as the usual I'm-afraid-of-commitment line I hear a lot from guys, and I went out with him again.

"We had such a great time together, like we were a perfect match. Before long, we were dating each other exclusively. I'd never been happier. After about six months I initiated the 'where is this going?' conversation. He said he wasn't ready for marriage but wanted to continue dating me. I figured that he'd eventually come around, and so it was business as usual for another six months or so. We repeated this for two years.

"Finally, I was ready to settle down. I wanted to get married and start a family, and I was madly in love with Jerry. We were so well-matched. I brought up the topic again, and he said what he always says, that he's not the marrying kind. When I got upset with him, he said, 'I've never lied to you. I told you from day one that I wasn't going to get married.'

"I was stunned. And then I was furious, first at him

51

for acting like he was such a paragon of virtue by saying one thing verbally but another through his actions. And then at myself, for being such a fool. It's been months now since Jerry and I broke up, and it's still so painful. I've learned my lesson—I'll not invest myself in a relationship again unless the man's words and actions coincide."

When we're feeling desperate, it's easy to make poor choices for ourselves, overlooking red flags, minimizing the warning signs. We may put up with things we shouldn't and settle for less than we deserve. A good woman friend, whose opinion and maturity we trust, will be able to give us an outside view of what she sees. Of course, we all have to make our own decisions in life, but sometimes it helps to have input from the people who love us and know us best, whether we ultimately listen to their viewpoint or not. This is especially the case if we are not feeling good about ourselves and consequently tend to sell ourselves short in all of our relationships. It's our observation that the better we feel about ourselves, the better we take care of ourselves in relation to men, and the more able we are to see and acknowledge the clues that answer the question: Is this a man of character, whose words are supported by his actions?

Watch How He Treats Other People
(and Animals)

*The best index to a person's character is (a) how he treats
people who can't do him any good, and (b) how he treats
people who can't fight back.*

—ABIGAIL VAN BUREN

Syndicated column

How the man you are with treats other living beings,
human and otherwise, indicates wonderfully what kind
of person he is and how you can expect to be treated
when times are rough between you. One important way
to discern a man's character is to watch how he relates to
animals, as these vulnerable creatures can trigger feelings men often feel toward their wives and children.
Teddi, now in her early thirties, laughs when she recalls
her first few dates with an up-and-coming sales man-
ager who she realized was not the man for her. She told
us, "The first time we went out to dinner, he brought up
his desire to own a puppy, which I thought was kind of
sweet. Anyone who loves animals can't be all bad, right?
The next time we went out, he brought it up again but
expressed his fear that he may be away from home all
day and the puppy would be lonely. Well, that was a
legitimate concern.

"Then on the third date, he started talking about his
desire for a puppy yet again. I started wondering why he

seemed so troubled about this issue, and then he said, 'But what if I move? What will I do with the puppy?' All of sudden, I could hear him talking that way about a wife and children: 'But what if I move? What will I do with my wife and children?' I realized that this guy may have some problems with commitment! If he's so tortured about whether he wants a dog, how is he going to decide if he wants a family? I decided that this was not the guy for me, and although we are still friends, I laugh every time I think of those conversations."

Conversely, a man who demonstrates the ability to care for a pet may be a man quite capable and ready for caring for you. Victoria told us how impressed she was with Jim when she heard how he protected his kitten, Sassy. She told us, "We were talking on the phone one afternoon, and he was telling me how he'd recently sprained his ankle playing volleyball. Suddenly he said, 'Oh, no! I'll be right back!' Through the receiver, I heard him bang around the room, yelling 'get away!' and then yelping in pain himself. After a few moments, he returned to the phone and told me, 'My larger cat attacked the kitten, and I had to save her or she'd have been seriously hurt.' I asked him if he was okay and he said, 'Yeah, my ankle took a beating, but I had to protect Sassy.' I knew then and there, here is a man I can trust."

Another test of a man's character is observing how he treats strangers or people who have less power than he in a social interaction. Jenny, a forty-five-year-old real estate agent, told us about a man she dated who provided clear signals of his attitude toward others: "Even though he was always charming to me, he didn't show respect to other people. When we traveled together, he was one of those tourists who would always act as if the rules, whatever they were, didn't apply to him. It always made me extremely uncomfortable, and I always found myself apologizing on 'our' behalf. I remember one time when we were traveling in a more traditional country where tourists had to tread lightly, and he started photographing an old woman begging. However, two very angry men started yelling at us not to do it. I begged him to stop, but he continued on, and they started chasing us. We barely escaped without injury.

"That trip really did it for me. I couldn't believe how little respect he showed for other people. I never felt like he was a bad person, but when we discussed it, he really didn't understand that his behavior was inappropriate. I finally realized that I didn't want to be with someone who was so clueless, at best, and arrogant, at worst. I had to end the relationship."

On the other hand, Hallie could tell that she was with a man who would treat those smaller than he with grace and love: "When I took Stan to meet my sister and her family—she has two boys—he was almost immediately down on the floor with the two boys, who are five and seven years old. He knows how boys like to fight and hit almost everything that moves, so after about fifteen minutes of talking to my sister, he took off his glasses, got down on the floor with his hands over his head, and told them to 'beat him up.' They were delighted and jumped on him and hit him and just generally got out their energy. He was just giggling the whole time. They couldn't wait for him to come back!"

Similarly, Millie, a thirty-year-old legal assistant, says she can tell by how her boyfriend acts toward his friends, as well as hers, that he is someone worth spending time with: "Steve is so generous. He is a programmer who has helped me out with my computer problems, and who is always willing to help my friends when their computers go awry or when they are buying new equipment. He doesn't do it in a way that's invasive. I mean, he doesn't have this psychological need to search out people to help and be everybody's hero, he is just willing to help when one of our friends needs it."

Last, but certainly not least, a man shows his nature by the way he treats your girlfriends, especially when you're not around. Ellen told us that she knew Sid was not the man for her when her close friend, Denise, came to her tearfully saying that Sid had made sexual advances toward her. She told us, "I trust Denise. She's not the kind who would go after a man I cared about, so I knew she hadn't been flirting with Sid. If I couldn't trust him with my girlfriends, then I knew he would go out on me with women who would never think to tell me about it. I broke up with him that same day."

A man's trustworthiness can also be detected by our girlfriends. One of the authors tells the story: "I knew my girlfriend, Cathy, had met a man worthy of her when I met her new boyfriend, Bob. Cathy and I were very close friends, and I was used to men trying to compete with me for her attention or ignoring me altogether. Bob took a completely different course of action. He went out of his way to become my friend, and, beyond that, he actively protected the time Cathy and I spent together. I was amazed and immediately won over. They've been married now over ten years, and I still count her as one of my best friends. She might not still be in my life if it weren't for the way Bob included me in his life and in their lives. It's easy to support a relationship with a man like that."

Our girlfriends can help us see a side to the men we're dating that we will never see on our own. Whether the news is good or painful, listening to a girlfriend's impressions and experiences can help us locate men of proven character, men who are worthy of our trust.

Definitely *Not* Love at First Sight

Mr. Darcy walked off; and Elizabeth remained with no very cordial feelings toward him.

—JANE AUSTEN

Pride and Prejudice

Perhaps we all dream of catching the eye of a gorgeous man across the room and, as violins play in the background, watching him move toward us as our heart says this is the one. In talking to women, we found that some of the most successful marriages began, not with love at first sight, but with a resounding, "Yuk!"

This was certainly the case for Veronica, a thirty-year-old massage therapist, who told us, "When I first met my husband, Frank, I couldn't stand him. In fact, he drove me nuts. I met him in college when we both rented rooms from a family near campus. We were expected to have dinner together, and because there were young children in the family, the meal was scheduled early in the evening, at about the same time I returned home from work each afternoon. I would walk in the door and head straight for my spot at the table.

"When I'm tired, I like to decompress alone before I talk to people. But Frank wouldn't let me sit there quietly and eat. Instead, he'd tease me and try to make me talk a little more. He'd go on and on, and I'd think, 'Who is this guy? I wish he'd just leave me alone.'"

Veronica's dislike for Frank continued until one weekend when the two of them were left in charge of the children for a couple of days. Together they fed, bathed, dressed, and cared for the children, which allowed her to see another side of Frank. After that experience, they became good friends.

But romance didn't bloom quickly. Nearly two years later they decided to "pursue the relationship. Actually, I had gone to Colorado and he'd gone to Minneapolis. He was dating another woman, so I thought, 'Oh, well, maybe that's it.' But we kept in touch. His other relationship didn't work out, and ours did."

Not judging a book by its cover can prove to be valuable in matters of the heart. Evelyn, who recently celebrated her twenty-sixth anniversary, also reacted negatively to her first encounter with Martin, her future husband. Evelyn met Martin in college, soon after she had come to the States after growing up in Africa, a child of a missionary family. She told us, "I thought he was conceited and arrogant. He thought I was another ugly missionary kid. Neither one of us liked the other, even though he was also a missionary kid. He grew up in South America in a family that was very aloof, even a bit strange.

"He realized he didn't know much about how to interact with people, so he started studying body language. I'd be sitting there with a book, and he'd get real close to my face and ask me what time it was, just to see if I'd pull away. I started liking the attention because he came around all the time doing this. We had our first date on Valentine's Day, although I found out later that he only asked me because he thought I had to work and would say no. But I arranged someone else to cover for me and so he had to take me out. When I got back to the dorm that night, I jumped on my girlfriend's bed and said, 'I don't know about this guy. He's so weird.'

"But as time went on, I felt more and more comfortable with him. We'd both been raised in similar subcultures. We both felt like outsiders here in the States. And he treated me with a great deal of respect. I was overwhelmed by most of the guys I met here, all wanting to get me in the back seat of their cars as soon as possible. But Martin didn't do that. He told me, 'If I ever try that on you, know that I care more about myself than I do you.' So I felt very safe with him. Eventually what seemed weird to me turned into interesting, even fascinating. We've been married twenty-six years, and I can assure you they've not been dull."

If we feel both intrigued and a bit put off by a man, we have the freedom to take our time in deciding what to do. But if someone intrigues us, even if our interest is hooked through annoyance, and we are ready to be in a relationship, we owe it to ourselves to take some time to look at the individual. As the previous stories show, we frequently have a negative reaction to men who end up making a good match for us. The important factor is that we had a *reaction,* and someone caught our attention. If we find ourselves in this situation, we may want to check in with our girlfriends to ask them what they think about this guy. Our friends may have some interesting observations.

The same goes if we notice our girlfriend's attention has been ensnared by a man who irritates her but whom she clearly has noticed. If this is someone you think might be a good match for *her,* a girlfriend's duties include pointing out his positive characteristics. An indirect way to initiate the conversation is to get together with her and watch a movie called *Crossing Delancey Street,* where a character played by Amy Irving finds herself curious about a man who her grandmother tries to fix her up with, a man from a neighborhood that the Irving character thought she had left behind. This woman, like the women in the earlier stories, finds that her irritation was based on the assumptions that she made about the man instead of on the man himself.

Bye, Bye, Bad Boy . . . Hello, Love

Yes, it's true. Women are perverse. We like trouble. . . . Someone who doesn't need us is a lot less scary than someone who needs us too much.

—CYNTHIA HEIMEL

Get Your Tongue Out of My Mouth, I'm Kissing You Good-bye!

Many women thrill at the scene in *Gone with the Wind* where Rhett Butler sweeps a belligerent, but secretly desiring, Scarlett off her feet, up the stairs, and into bed — with assumed fireworks going off overhead. Often the fireworks are triggered by men who stir us up unconsciously but who aren't necessarily good for the long run. Most women admit that they've dated "bad boys" and "good guys," and both have their appeal and their own set of problems. Some women we talked to help us identify the types and the sets of problems you might expect from either type. Ursula said that bad boys are different from grown-up men, that they are "more attentive but prefer form over function. The bad boys were attentive to being romantic and doing sweet things, so there was never any complaint about the 'trimmings.' Whether they were good people or whether I trusted them was the question. A bad boy is the one you want to pick up at the bar. High on charisma, low on commitment."

Such was the experience of Irene, a student in her twenties, who was engaged to marry a man with whom she was madly in love. When she saw him, she was immediately attracted to him. She told us, "I had a strong sense of wanting to marry him from the beginning. Right away. Even before we started dating I was dreaming about him. I was really out of control and things moved very fast. I even believed that God was telling me that 'this is the one for you,' so I had a lot of confidence in my decision to accept his marriage proposal. But it moved so fast that he freaked out, and I soon saw that the man I thought I'd fallen in love with wasn't the man he genuinely was. It was very painful to face that."

Trying to learn from her mistakes, Irene is now dating a man she is getting to know at a much slower pace. She said, "It's been really refreshing to be with a man that I like some days and don't like on others. He's more down to earth, someone I really appreciate. He isn't someone I feel fireworks for, but I appreciate his kindness. I like feeling grounded, without all the craziness. There aren't as many surprises, not as many disappointments."

The pain of disappointment often becomes a price too high to pay, and some women, once they are genuinely ready for a lifelong relationship, trade in the thrill of the bad boys for the stability of a good guy. Ursula told us, "I fell in love with a man whom I trust and love, but it's different." Her "good guy" husband has a romantic side to him, but even when he sends her roses, "it doesn't have the zing" that she's experienced with others. Many women have experienced the secret or not-so-secret thrill of being the woman chosen by the man that is so hard to get. However, Ursula stated the advantage of marrying the good man quite succinctly: "But the good thing is that I don't have to worry about finding someone else's underwear in my car, so it's a trade-off I'm willing to make."

Similarly, Dierdre had dated a lot of guys accompanied with fireworks and excitement. She told us, "It was too manic. But with me and Wilt, it was so solid. He started out as a buddy. We met in college, and he was the type of guy on campus that no woman would have thought of romantically. He was the big brother, the teddy bear. When our relationship started turning a bit more romantic I thought, 'Oh, no. This is such a good friendship. I don't want to mess it up with sex.' He felt the same way and was afraid of making it romantic, so he didn't kiss me for months and months. At first I was glad because I was tired of guys who tried to get me in the back seat after the first date. Usually I was the one trying to slow things down. But after a while, I started thinking, 'Why isn't this guy kissing me?' It was a complete role reversal!

"The clincher for me came around six months into the relationship when he was in California and I was in Indiana. It was Valentine's Day, and I was used to the typical, generic bouquet of flowers. That day, in my little college mailbox, was a slip notifying me that I had a package. I was thrilled to receive a shoe box full of the most delicious chocolate brownies I've ever eaten. He had made them himself! They weighed about twenty-five pounds! I'd never experienced someone going to so much trouble just for me. I knew that he was someone special because he took the time to figure out what I wanted rather than just go through the routine of dating. He figured flowers would have been nice, but they probably wouldn't make much of an impression on me. But chocolate! Now there's something to remember!"

While some women felt there was a trade-off in being in a relationship with a trustworthy man, others found a strong sense of physical attraction and a sense of safety in the same man. Fireworks can happen also with grown-up men, and, if we get lucky, or if we decide to wait for it, we can fall head over heels with someone who turns out to be a keeper. Laurine told us of finding herself "swept away" by the sight of a good-looking man, now her husband of ten years: "I have to admit, I did experience lightning. From the moment I saw him, I went home — I'll never forget this — and said to my roommate, 'I saw the most gorgeous man and I'm madly in lust, but he's a freshman.' We were seniors at a small college, where you knew everybody, so I assumed he was a freshman since I hadn't seen him before. My roommate and I had this great debate about the ethics of being a senior, and do you get involved with a freshman, and so forth. I'll never forget that.

"I saw him across the campus green, and I was just

beginning to need glasses. I wasn't wearing them regularly—too vain, and I didn't have contacts. So I wasn't looking up frequently, and all of a sudden this shape came into view. I sort of saw this big frame walking, and I thought, 'Well, that is a nice shape,' but I couldn't see anything. As he got closer, I was getting him into focus, and literally looking at him from his toes on up, so obviously. I got very embarrassed and walked off. He thought, 'What a snob.' He was trying to meet me, and I had snubbed him.

"In spite of our poor beginning, I found out that he wasn't a freshman, and we started to date. Interestingly, he had seen me two years before and, unbeknownst to me, we had taken a class together. He had been tracking me all those years and had finally found out that I had broken up with a series of boyfriends and was sort of ready. Once I was able to focus on him—literally—it was love at first sight. We're celebrating our tenth anniversary this year."

So, bad boys may be fun for a while (reserved for sport dating as previously discussed), but, according to our interviews, it's the grown-up men who make the best husbands. Perhaps who we are attracted to is more of a reflection of us and where we are in life than an indicator of anything else. If we are in a playful or transitional place in life, some attention from a bad boy may be just what we want. However, expecting more than a lightweight relationship from someone who we know to be trouble, is unrealistic and will only end up hurting us in the end. If we find ourselves continually attracted to bad boys from whom we want a long-term relationship, then we may want to look at the reasons we keep picking men who will never give us what we want. Perhaps we just need some excitement in our lives that we can more safely find elsewhere, such as in more fulfilling work. We don't need to sell ourselves short! But when we are ready for an emotionally mature man, we will most likely find him attractive when we find him or discover our attraction over time, and his attention will create that thrill for us that a bad boy, at another time did. When that time comes, we can enjoy that knowledge that not only is this a man we can trust and depend on as a friend, but someone we can enjoy romantically and sexually as well.

How do you know which category your current interest falls into—the bad boy or the grown-up man? It may take a while to find out, for men who seem like a good match at first may never be around in the moments that you need them. Or a man may start showing resentment at expectations that you have about him, such as expecting him to show up on time—or at all—for dates. One woman told us how a man she had been dating got angry with her for expecting him to call if he was going to come late to their date from his softball practice!

So watch for signs. Is this someone you can trust, who will be able to handle the stress of losing or changing jobs, raising children, facing money problems or perhaps illness? Watching how he deals with roadblocks right now will give you a good idea. And since he may be on good behavior with you, you may want to ask your friends what they have noticed about this man. Would they like to see you with him for the long-term? We suggest getting their input and also paying attention to how safe and secure you feel when you're with him. As one woman told us, she's falling in love with a man she's been dating for the past six months. She said, "He really made me zing at the beginning—and is proving over time to also be self-aware and thoughtful. As my girlfriend said one day, 'You've finally met a grown-up!'"

Safe Is Sexy

Now an even more insidious emotion emerges—attachment.
Liebowitz theorizes that partners in the attachment phase
stage of love trigger the production of endorphins in each other,
giving each the sense of safety, stability, tranquillity. Now
lovers can talk and eat and sleep in peace.

—HELEN FISHER, PH.D.

Anatomy of Love

A certain amount of healthy danger can add fuel to the fireworks of a passionate romance. But when it comes to long-lasting love, safety is a key element. Carol C. Wells, in *Right-Brain Sex*, writes, "What seems to be essential to really great sex is not the state of love but the state of feeling loved. Feeling loved is synonymous with feeling safe."[3]

Helen shared the moment when she knew that her now-husband of ten years was someone safe: "The ultimate moment was this one time we were in a huge, huge fight, and we were living together, and I had run into the bathroom because there was nowhere else to go in this small apartment. So I turned on the shower so that I couldn't hear him. Joe came in, and we yelled at each other. I kicked a shoe, which accidentally flew into the air, and he caught it. He lifted it above his head to throw into the shower, paused, and then said, 'No, I'm not going to do that.' I had thought he was going to hit me. I said, 'Gosh, you were going to hit me with that shoe.' He was stunned that I thought he'd ever hurt me. He said, 'No, I was thinking about throwing it into the shower and then decided the water would ruin it. I was never going to throw it at you.' I realized that this man was never going to hurt me. From then on, I knew."

Laurine mentioned one particularly clarifying moment in her time spent with her boyfriend: "I remember, years after we first met, we had negotiated moving in together, and I was thinking, 'Well, we will try this out and see what happens.' I was asking, 'Do I want to spend the rest of my life with this person?' I remember waking up one morning next to him — his breath smelled, he had a two-day old beard — and he gets up and exclaims, 'Let's just celebrate today!' I thought, 'Wow!' It was really powerful that he was so exuberant on a just an ordinary day. I remember feeling safe and excited. That combination was new to me."

Ursula summed it up with respect to her now husband: "I felt like I'd been trying on shoes that didn't fit all my life. Finally, he fit—it was values, it was trust, it was clear. It wasn't fireworks or a dramatic moment in technicolor. It was a dawning of a realization that came over time that he was the person for me. And that is a deeper, truer passion than a transient, sexual thrill."

Men who become "husband material" are often those who create a sense of safety for the women they love. This does not mean that we should look only at that aspect of our men, because if there is no spark, there is no point to the relationship. All the safety in the world will not make a long-term relationship work if there is no attraction as well.

But if you become attracted (and it may not happen on the first encounter!), keep your eyes open for your sense of security around him. Small things will tell you a lot about who someone is and how he will respond to you and your children, if you have them someday. Or ask a close woman friend if she thinks the man you are with is someone who is safe for you. One woman was reassured by a friend when she was deciding whether or not to marry her boyfriend: "I knew that I was attracted to, and felt safe with, Barry, but I wanted my good friend's opinion. Lisa told me that she thought that Barry would never consciously hurt me, because he loved and respected me too much. She always gave my boyfriends very close scrutiny, so I trusted that she was telling me the truth! Her opinion confirmed what I had been feeling." Lisa knew the truth—that a mate who treats you with respect, who protects and nurtures you, will do the same for you and the children you may raise together.

Coming Together

. . . a relationship has a momentum, it must change and develop, and will tend to move toward the point of greatest commitment.

—CAROLYN HEILBRUN

The Wit and Wisdom of Women

When we have met someone, and enjoy them to the point of thinking about spending our lives with them, both men and women may hit a roadblock. While it is fashionable to complain about men's inability to "commit," we know a lot of women as well who are ambivalent about signing up for marriage, even when both parties say they are in love with the other. What is going on with men and women's reluctance to marry?

But He Said He'd Call . . .

If you never want to see a man again, say, "I love you.
I want to marry you. I want to have children"—
they leave skid marks.

—RITA RUDNER

The New York Times

How many times has a man said, "I'll call you," and you've never heard from him again? Most women know what it's like to hear that phrase at the end of a date and then wonder, "What does that mean? Does that mean he likes me or is that his way of saying goodbye?"

We asked women how they decipher "male code," and we received some helpful insights into the minds of men. Alice, an avid dater and enjoyer of men, told us that she thinks "boy time is different from girl time. When a man says he'll call, he may mean he hopes to get in contact at least once before the end of time. We women assume he'll call first thing tomorrow morning, as soon as he wakes up."

Victoria added to this view by saying, "I've realized that men respond to attraction differently than women do. When I have fun with a man, I want to be with him again as soon as possible. But that's not necessarily true for men. Granted, sometimes they disappear because they aren't attracted to me. But other times, I believe that they pull back because they really think I'm hot. It's the opposite of what I would do."

We found support for Victoria's suspicion from self-declared expert on men's weird behavior, Dave Barry. He explains in his book, *Dave Barry's Complete Guide to Guys*, why men seem to act in total variance with what seems normal to women. He writes, "Guys are born with a fundamental, genetically transmitted mental condition known to psychologists as: The Fear That If You Get Attached to a Woman, Some Unattached Guy, Somewhere, Will Be Having More Fun Than You. . . . So guys are extremely reluctant to make commitments, or even take any steps that might lead to commitments. This is why, when a guy goes out on a date with a woman and finds himself really liking her, he often will demonstrate his affection by avoiding her for the rest of his life.

"Women are puzzled by this. 'I don't understand,' they say, 'We had such a great time! Why doesn't he call?'

"The reason is that the guy, using the linear guy thought process, has realized that if he takes her out again, he'll probably like her even more, so he'll take her out again, and eventually they'll fall in love with each other, and they'll get married, and they'll have children, and then they'll have grandchildren, and eventually they'll retire and take a trip around the world, and they'll be walking hand-in-hand on some spectacular beach in the South Pacific, reminiscing about the lifetime of experiences they've shared together, and then several naked international fashion models will walk up and invite him to join them in a hot tub, and he won't be able to do it."[6]

What's a woman to do in the real world of romance? Try to have horrible dates so a man will come back again? Reverse psychology won't work in this situation, but perhaps patience and a little humor will.

Victoria shared with us her strategy of dealing with this dilemma. She told us, "I figured this out some years back when the guy I was dating would be a real pain on every other date. At first I was hurt and confused, but eventually I saw his pattern: we'd have a fun, warm, and exciting time together in which we'd draw closer to each other, and then, on the next date, he'd be a sour mood or show up late, which would push us apart some. I stopped getting upset about it and just planned for it, since I realized it was his way of handing his ambivalence about connecting to a woman. During dates where there was distance, I said to myself, 'He must have had a really great time with me last weekend, because he's in a real snit tonight.'"

Dr. Judith Sills gives credence to this approach in dealing with the ambivalent male in her book, *A Fine Romance*. She believes that if a man or woman has a relationship pattern in which the other person seems to lose interest, "It could be because you are doing something to make his or her anxiety worse." When we sense a man moving back from us, we may move closer to him, rather than allowing him the space he needs. By pursuing an ambivalent man, so claims Dr. Sills, we can intensify his fears and unwittingly chase him away.

And what is Dr. Sills's advice? She tells us, "Don't fall apart. *Back off.* This is the best advice you'll ever get on courtship and the hardest to put into effect. When you are feeling insecure and rejected, you will need to behave with confidence and serenity. When you are feeling desperate to be with someone, you'll need to loosen up and resist some opportunities to be together. When you are concerned that if you let go, nothing will be there, take the risk of finding out. If it's true, you need to end it.

"Back off means exactly what it says: Stop being so available, stop expressing your interest so dramatically, stop being so accommodating, stop trying to win his or her interest. Start establishing some degree of independence."[7]

We believe this is great advice, but how do we do it? If we are feeling insecure and rejected, it is, as Dr. Sills says, difficult to stay distant. Like Odysseus asking his sailors to strap him to the mast of his ship so that he would not be tempted by the Sirens' call, we need to enlist our girlfriends' help. In the past, our culture expected us to be demure and never take the initiative. However, as we all become more powerful and aggressive in asking for what we want in our jobs or in defending a cause we believe in, we tend to treat our romantic relationships the same. If we want it, we should go after it, right? Much to all of our chagrin, we found that this doesn't seem to work with many men (although there are exceptions). If it doesn't work with the man we are interested in, we have the freedom to determine whether he is the right man for us. However, if he is the guy we want, we will have to determine for ourselves whether to take the initiative.

So when our hearts want to contact the man in our thoughts, but our heads wonder if it's a good thing to do, call a friend and ask her advice: Does she see you wanting to call because you are feeling insecure? or because you are feeling your own power? If the former, maybe it's time to pause and collect yourself; if the latter, enlist her help in getting up your courage! And when we see a girlfriend struggling with the same issue, do the same for her. Help her put herself and the relationship in perspective. We can come to trust ourselves more with the help of our girlfriends.

Do Men Really Have a
Problem with Commitment?

*Do not expect the guy to make a hasty commitment.
By "hasty," I mean "within your lifetime."*

—DAVE BARRY

Dave Barry's Complete Guide to Guys

We hear (and many of us have complained) about the inability of men to make a commitment. "He's afraid of the 'c' word" or "Why doesn't he step up to the plate?" are phrases that are sometimes used. There are definitely people (both men and women) who are off-the-charts terrified of any responsibility to another person. At the other end of the spectrum are those who are so eager to commit they start talking marriage in the first five minutes after learning your telephone number. Most of us, however, are hovering in the middle, respecting the burden of responsibility while at the same time longing for that sense of connection.

According to the women in relationships where ambivalence was resolved by moving on to marriage, we were reminded that men are both similar to us and yet quite different at the same time. At the risk of stereotyping, it seems to us that both men and women have a desire to be married, and yet we want or fear marriage for different reasons. Women, usually socialized to feel more comfortable in intimate relationships, often view closeness as comforting. While men, raised to be competitive, may experience closeness as a threat to their ability to "win" or to survive. Commitment, then, involves an element of fear for the average male, but we've been assured that this fear can be overcome if a man is willing to do his homework and grow in his self-understanding.

This goes for us women too—we feel it's important for both men and women to look at the question of commitment with more emotional maturity. Are you and your man aware of your own fears, and are you both willing to talk about how your feelings impact your choices? Two people who are emotionally mature and willing to look at and talk about their attitudes toward marriage and commitment may learn that their fears can be addressed. While we acknowledge that women can fear commitment, most of the women we interviewed were ready for marriage long before the men they loved.

"Most," but definitely not all. Corinna, a writer and artist, said what she perceived at the time to be a lack of commitment from the man she was seeing, she now sees to be her own problem: "I had a relationship for ten years in which I pinpointed him as the one that could not and would not make a commitment. He lived in a city an hour away, and I saw him once a week. He had children that I wasn't allowed to meet, and I was starved for affection, time, and real relationship stuff. He had problems. His wife had died, and he wasn't ready to make a commitment to me, but I thought maybe he would get ready, so I was always waiting for him to change. It never happened. Years later, I had to look at why I was allowing someone to string me along, why I was not saying that we needed some therapy or whatever it took so that we could spend more time together. I had to look at how, in my own way, I was happy as a clam being the victim who was with a man who was terrified of the commitment. I was just as terrified as he was."

Perhaps if we were honest with ourselves, more stories would be focused on women's fear regarding commitment. And of course not all men fear commitment. Occasionally we heard a story about a man moving toward marriage without any hesitation. Yvonne told us about her son who was married when he was nineteen. She said, "When asked why would he want to marry so young, rather than going out to see the world and then settling down, my son said he didn't want to travel alone and didn't view marriage as 'settling down.' He wanted to share his life with one woman who would travel with him and then, when it was time, to create a home and a family. He couldn't see any good reasons to wait." Most of the women we spoke with, however, said they were ready for commitment long before the men in their lives wanted to move ahead. If you find yourself in this situation, what can you do?

We believe many men need a reason to get married. And why not? If you faced all the expectations that men frequently feel regarding the responsibilities of marriage, and if you faced giving up all the freedoms and pleasures that commitment is thought to entail giving up, would you jump in?

Until forty years ago, men were given one extremely compelling reason to propose marriage: If a man wanted sex on a regular basis, he had to propose. Since the sixties, sex outside of marriage has been readily available. The adage that only "bad girls" have sex prior to marriage may have held in the fifties, but it is not true today. Recently, however, due to a variety of pressures, such as the spreading of the AIDS virus, monogamy has come back into vogue. In addition to the more conservative and usually religious voices calling for sex only within marriage, a surprising number of secular voices are admonishing women to remember the adage, "Why buy the cow if the milk is free?" Pat Allen in her book, *Staying Married . . . And Loving It,* writes, "Most modern, liberated, sexually active women believe they can maintain control over their emotions after making love. What they don't realize is that when a woman gives her body to a man, there's a strong chance that she's going to bond to him—even after only one good sexual encounter."

Allen's position runs counter to the belief that sexual involvement isn't any more bonding to women than it is for men. Some of the women we interviewed claimed to have had non-bonding sexual encounters. However, when a woman is relating to a man in a meaningful, monogamous relationship, often the attachment strengthens through sexual expression.

While exceptions do exist, most men do not bond through sex alone. Rather, Allen asserts that men "bond through the commitments they make and keep."[8] By being sexually available, we risk getting bonded more deeply than the men in our lives. We also weaken one of the forces that have compelled men, through the ages, to face their fears and move toward deeper love and commitment.

But certainly sex isn't the only reason for men to choose marriage. What else would motivate a man to overcome his fears?

For some men, it is time to become a "responsible citizen" in the eyes of one's peers. One woman remembers telling her fiancé's friend of their impending wedding plans: "We had lunch with Steve right after we got engaged, and it was clear that Steve felt it was a personal betrayal to him that we were going to get married—now we were 'over there' and he was 'over here' and he did not want us to be in different places." Steve got engaged to his current wife six months later.

The compelling event may be a feeling of desertion, or it may be a sense of the pieces of one's life falling into place. One woman talked about Jack, who had just become a partner in her husband's business and who was attending his first dinner of the seven partners in the business: "Jack was sitting at that table at the partnership dinner, surrounded by married couples, and he was the only person alone. I think it is true of men that when they get to be a little older, when they have begun their careers, then they have got to prove themselves in that one area of their lives, before they can jump into marriage. I think that was true of Jack, and I think it is true of other men." Jack was engaged to his current wife shortly thereafter.

Similarly, another married woman with two children, now starting her own business, laughs when she tells this story about how proposals come about: "There's something that has to trigger it, I don't know what it is. My husband got accepted to business school, and he couldn't afford to go, which meant he couldn't go. I had a trust fund set up for me earlier and had a little money. All of a sudden he turned to me and said to himself, 'Ah, trust fund baby' and we got married! I mean, the proposal was within the hour of receiving the acceptance letter! We had been dating for a year, it was going to happen anyway, we had been discussing it, but the timing was brilliant!"

Some women said that they had to engineer the reason for their husbands to propose. In one interview with several married women, one woman in her midthirties raised this question: "Is there a woman out there, a married woman who has not in some way or another trapped her husband into marrying her, asking her to marry him? An ultimatum, playing hard to get, acting really mad? It seems as if most of the women I know who are married reached a point when he was never going to push himself over that cliff himself. He needed a shove."

She added: "I definitely had to push my husband over the edge. It had been my birthday, and I thought he was going to ask me to marry him, and he didn't. He gave me a present in a jeweler's box, which was not a ring. Not a good idea. Then we went to a romantic movie that ends with a wedding. We didn't know what it was about before we went. Then we came home and I was sulking. He was asking, 'What's the matter? What's the matter?' and I said, 'Nothing, nothing.' He finally pushed me into admitting that I was feeling angry. 'Well, because we have been talking about getting married, and you won't ask me, and I am mad.' I had to push him over the edge." Clearly her husband's fear of losing her overcame his fear of becoming engaged.

Olivia, a Midwesterner now married for thirty years, let her man know the consequences when he started getting cagey: "When William and I were dating, everybody told me that he was a confirmed bachelor, because he was thirty-three when we started dating and had never been married, and that I should be careful if I really liked him. Anyway, I thought, 'Boy, if he's a confirmed bachelor, he's coming on pretty strong.' We were together six nights out of seven every week. He took me to Florida one time to visit his college buddy, Bobby, who is a nice-looking man, never been married. Bobby and William were very close, and Bobby knew that William was bringing his girlfriend. We were there for four days, and Bobby had a different date every night, and each date was better looking than the last one. So, when we were flying home, I could tell that there was a definite change in William. He told me, and I knew that it was a made-up story, that he was going to be awfully busy because he had a trial coming up and he was probably not going to see a lot of me. I could read right through that—it was like he was thinking about giving up his freedom and he decided that might be a wrong move. So of course it upset me, but, like I told him, 'No problem.' I'd been through a lot worse. There had been a couple guys calling me, but no big deal. I hadn't heard from him, so I went out on a date. As soon as I had a date with someone else, it was fine again. No problem. Then it was like, plan the wedding and go on.

"The biggest point of it all is how his college buddy was doing what he was used to doing and maybe he was giving that up. Anybody would have known what caused the change—it was very obvious that he was giving up his freedom of a different menu every night."

Does this sound like game playing? It depends on your motivation. There is a difference between taking an action to manipulate another person and taking an action because you believe it is the best choice for yourself at the time. This woman knew what she wanted, and if marriage wasn't possible with this particular man, she was willing to move on. She knew her value as a woman and took a stand. However, we don't recommend the approach of breaking up with your boyfriend or dating other people if you are bluffing; you have to be ready to accept the consequences and truly be ready to go down your path without the person to whom you have been so attached. As one woman put it who left her reluctant boyfriend (who showed up a year later to propose): "My friends said I played hard to get, but the truth is I just came up with a lot of other things that I wanted to do. I dated a lot of people, and somewhere in the back of my mind, I thought 'It's really too bad that I haven't met anyone who I connect with the way I connect with Jack. I wish he didn't have this problem.' But I did not think, 'When is that phone going to ring and we are going to get back together?'

"And I did move on, mentally. I think he saw me having a lot of fun without him. That was sort of a revelation to him, and, frankly, it was a little bit of one to me, too. He didn't like being left out, I guess. A year later, there he was, ready to get married."

Some women had to help change the perception of marriage for their then-boyfriends to take the step. Helen tells this story: "I remember my husband not wanting to commit. We were twenty-three when we got engaged, and I remember him saying, 'I don't want to make this commitment because I won't be able to travel the world, I'm going to be held back from doing the things that I could have done.' I would say, 'Why can't we do those things together? I want to travel the world too. I want to do things, too; it's not like I want to stay home and make babies, or I would have made one by now.' I just thought it was so funny that he would think he had plans and that I was going to hold him back. My plans were just as big. When I said, 'Let's do this together,' he thought, 'What an idea! Maybe we *could* do this together.' And we really have seen a lot together and look at the world that way now. I think he had been conditioned by his father to not get into something too heavy. I remember his father saying, 'She's going to get pregnant, she's going to want you to marry her,' as if I was going to trap him and I didn't have goals of my own. . . . It appalled me to think that he would believe he was losing out."

These stories may lead us to the blanket assumption that all men fear commitment. Before we assume that "it is all his fault" or "men are all like that," however, we need to look at our own situation and feelings, as well as our assumptions about men. We may want to ask ourselves and our close friends if we are contributing to the problem, whatever it is. Are we helping to perpetuate an untrustworthy situation? Or we may wish to ask if we are being fair. Are we looking at the situation with this *one* man rather than grouping the entire male population into one stereotype? If we are to approach a relationship as an adult, each man and woman must look at the individual, not the gender, and learn what his or her role in a scenario is.

Additionally, while in our experience many men are still afraid that commitment means "losing out," we have also run across men whose eagerness to commit may hide deeper, and troubling, issues. Joan shares her experience: "There is something very appealing about a man who thinks that you just can do no wrong and that your relationship has mythic proportions. And that was certainly my first husband, who talked me into marrying him. Our relationship was really 'the relationship to end all relationships.' After we got divorced, he went on to try to convince other women that their relationship was that same thing. It was very enticing, but it didn't necessarily reflect the truth. You need to find someone who has appropriate skepticism but who won't run in the other direction when it is right. But there are those people who really want a commitment right away and who don't have the perspective to say, 'This isn't the right person.' If you get enticed by that, then you get into the wrong relationship."

Harriet, a teacher, agrees: "I think you need to find someone who is obviously balanced in the way he behaves, because I have definitely had both types—you know—the guy who practically proposed on the third date, and the guy that I spent fifteen unbelievably intense months with when we were practically living together. With him it was like, 'Oh my god, don't even bring up the *m* word.' Both of them have issues that they need to deal with. Obviously, the person you want is someone who grows to love you over time and gets to realize how special you are and that you are unique, and that he wants to spend his life with you, not the 'Mr.-I-can-check-these-things-off-my-list-and-you-are-all-of-them, so you must be it!'"

So once we find a man who has achieved some balance and maturity with regard to closeness, it may not be a question of commitment, it may be a question of timing. If he is not ready we each have to decide how long to wait before we move on. We may need to rely on our friends to bolster our resolve while we take the difficult step of walking away from a man we care about but who cannot seem to give us what we want. However, if a man is ready to be married and has done his homework, he will not shy away from commitment and you can decide together whether to take the next step.

Who's the Ambivalent One Here?

It is always incomprehensible to a man that a woman should refuse an offer of marriage.

—JANE AUSTEN

What Women Say About Men

Granted, there may be a woman on this planet who has no ambivalence regarding intimacy with men, but we have never met her and we certainly didn't interview her. Every woman we talked with, especially those in the most satisfying relationships, told us about the tug-of-war inside themselves, a struggle that started at the first meeting and lasted long into the marital years.

Katrina told us, "When I was younger, I asked my mother how I'd know the man I should marry. She told me, 'When you meet the right man, you'll just know.' So I kept waiting to meet a man where I felt no ambivalence at all. But it never happened. No matter how great the guy, or how much in love I felt, there were always little nagging questions. As long as I wasn't 100 percent sure, I figured that I wasn't with Mr. Right."

Many of us, like Katrina, have been schooled in this line of thinking—that the mere presence of ambivalence is evidence that this relationship is a mistake. But we found quite the opposite to be true: that the potential for genuine intimacy will most likely intensify the battle within us.

To shed some light on this topic, we turn to Dr. Judith Sills, who defines ambivalence in her book, *A Fine Romance*, as "simultaneous, conflicting feelings, like wanting and not wanting the same thing. . . . It is the irony of the human condition that we crave attachment as ferociously as we hunger for freedom. This essential polarity is the root of ambivalence in courtship."[4]

It is natural for us to vacillate back and forth, thinking at one moment, "Isn't he adorable? How can I live without him?" and wondering the next, "What did I ever see in him? I need to date other men." While we're flipping back and forth, the men are doing the same thing, one moment giving us "I want you and only you" messages and "What was your name again?" messages the next.

At any given time, it is common for one person to feel more intensely about being in the relationship, while the other balances out the ambivalence by wanting more space. Victoria told us that her husband pursued her for a year before she really gave him a chance. She said, "We worked together, and I didn't think it was wise to date in the workplace. But he didn't give up. He'd volunteer for committees I was on, so we spent a lot of time together. He's a really fun guy, so I started liking him more and more. Finally I said, 'Okay, let's go out.' Throughout the relationship, he's always been the one who felt sure I was the woman he wanted. I've always held back a little more."

In many relationships, the partners take turns feeling ambivalent. Hope told us that Bart had pursued her diligently for several years before she agreed to marry him. "Even after we were married, he wanted more from me than I wanted to give. I was going to graduate school and was really into my career, while he was always complaining that he wanted more time with me, more attention. I just kept brushing him off.

"Then one day I came home from studying at the library and found him with his suitcase packed. He said, 'We need to talk.' His voice had never sounded like that before. We sat down, and he told me he'd had it. He was tired of feeling deprived and didn't have strong feelings for me anymore. He wanted to separate for a while.

"I was shocked. I had been so sure that he'd never

leave me. I sat there staring after him as he drove off. The next few days were horrible for me. I never realized how much I needed him, how much I relied on him, how much I loved him. The tables had turned, and now I was the one who wanted to save our marriage, while he was the one who wasn't sure it was worth the effort." Fortunately, Hope and Bart were able to work out their relationship and come to a balance in which they both acknowledged their need for closeness and their need for space. Some couples fall apart when "The Switch" occurs.

The Switch is a phase described by Dr. Sills. She writes, "The most common victim of The Switch is the woman. She was being actively pursued when, suddenly, he turns off just as she turns on. . . . Today, however, sex roles in courtship are much more flexible. It is therefore increasingly likely that she may pursue him until she captures his interest and then—whammo—she pulls a Switch and he is the victim. So, male or female, you will need to be prepared to handle The Switch if you want to enjoy courtship."[5]

During the course of our interviews, we saw women falling into two general categories: women who felt a strong need for attachment and those who wanted more freedom. The more we listened, the more we realized that, generally speaking, the women who were more likely to want closeness were those who felt, to a smaller or larger degree, that they did not get the attention they

93

needed from their fathers. Katrina told us, "I remember as a little girl, trying to get my father's attention. He was one of those stereotypical work-all-the-time dads. When he did have time for us kids, he'd play ball with my brothers. I'd sit on the sidelines wishing he would notice me."

Hope, on the other hand, who needed more space, talked about being the baby of the family, often the recipient of excessive attention. "There were times," she told us, "when, as a little girl, I'd run to the orchard behind our house and hide in the trees. I had a favorite one that was out of view from the house. The branches were really wide so I could keep my dolls and things up there in a box. I'd sit up there for hours playing by myself, happy to be away from my folks."

While our observations are not scientific, we have noticed that many of the women we interviewed who had never married were those who described one or both of their parents as "intrusive" or "controlling." A never-married woman named Sandi told us that her father is intrusive in taking care of her car. Even though she is in her late twenties and fully self-supporting, her father continues to look after her car in ways that no longer feel comfortable to her. She told us, "My dad does a lot of stuff with my car to make sure I'm taken good care of, so I'll feel free to excel in school and in my work. Because I've relied on him in this way, I've never learned how to properly care for my car. When I was younger, I thought it was great. But now, I have mixed feelings because it's so easy just to let him take care of things. If something goes wrong, he'll say, 'Oh, just trade cars with me and I'll get it fixed.' But I'm realizing that's his way of keeping control over me.

"One time the car needed tires, and I had decided that I would buy them on my own when I got back from a business trip. But when I returned, there were new tires on my car. When I was out of town, he went ahead and bought me new tires to surprise me. I didn't know how to react, because on one hand I was really angry; it didn't feel like he respected me or my space. But on the other hand, it was such a relief to have it over with. So, in the end, I kept the tires." The price to be paid for these tires may be much greater than their monetary value, as women like Sandi may find themselves unwittingly keeping men at arm's length.

Ambivalence is a normal and healthy state for anyone contemplating making a lifelong commitment. If we are feeling ambivalent, we may want to look at our family patterns to see what the terms marriage and commitment mean to us. Generally their meaning will be a reflection of what we learned while growing up. For instance, if love meant suffocation, we will tend to keep from getting too close. The important thing is that each of us does her homework to find out what our ambivalence means for us.

Sometimes there are good reasons for ambivalence, as it may signal some fundamental incompatibility. For example, one person may want to have children while the other doesn't, or one may be drawn to life in the country while the other craves the perks of an urban executive. These are obvious reasons to back away from commitment, and we may have to ask ourselves whether something basic like this is triggering our ambivalence. A good test of whether something concerns us was suggested by Jody, a twenty-seven-year-old publicist: "I knew at one point that something was wrong in a relationship because I stopped telling my friends about the bad things happening. I knew they wouldn't approve of the relationship. When you are used to sharing everything with your friends and then you stop, it is a sign that something is bothering you about a guy." There may be a good reason to be ambivalent, one to which we need to pay attention.

The issue of ambivalence—which side of the seesaw we tend to ride, and how we resolve this tension—may determine whether or not we'll successfully connect to and be able to maintain relationships with the men we love. Often we claim to want marriage before the man in our life does, but is that true? It may be easier to rely on the stereotype of men as "commitment-phobic" than to admit our own ambivalence, for recognizing our own ambivalence may mean we need to make some difficult decisions.

If we have mixed feelings about a connection but honestly cannot find a particular attribute of our partner's that bothers us, then we may simply be ambivalent about the prospect of making a lifelong commitment. Are we being honest with ourselves about who is hesitating? We may want to ask our friends what they see us doing in the relationship: Does it seem to them that we are ready to be married? Are we giving mixed signals to our men? Of course, we need to ask our "truth tellers," the women who will tell us what they really think even if they know we may not enjoy hearing it.

Are We Involved?

The hardest thing to explain is the glaringly evident which everybody had decided not to see.

—AYN RAND

The Fountainhead

One of the less obvious and more humorous ways we women can act out our ambivalence is by denying we are in a relationship at all, even though we may be getting together regularly with someone. Conversely, men can act out their ambivalence by ending a relationship before it begins! Whether resulting from a man's or a woman's reluctance to be in a developing relationship, we discovered a number of women who were unaware that they were dating a particular man or in a relationship until the man in question formally broke up with them. Betty described how, through a singles' group at her church, she met Brent, a young architectural student. After church, the group often met for dessert, and Betty and Brent often sat together and talked. She told us, "One afternoon I received a phone message from him. I thought, 'How nice, he's calling just to say hi.' So, I called him back. I could tell as soon as I heard his voice that something was wrong. He abruptly said, 'I need to end our relationship. I can't see you anymore.' I said, 'Okay,' immediately feeling sad. I thought, 'Oh, no. He's breaking up with me.' And then I thought, 'Hey, wait a minute. We're not even going together!' I realized he saw our times talking when we were with the group as 'dates.' I just thought we were talking together.

"Once he ended our so-called dating relationship, I'd alternate between feeling hurt because he was leaving me and amused because I really didn't care. I think most of all I felt foolish for not realizing that something had been going on between us."

Carolyn told us that she had a casual date with a man that she enjoyed, "but not anybody that I was going to get too deeply involved with—it was just fun. One night, around Christmas, he called me up and said, 'We can't see each other anymore.' I said, 'Okay,' thinking, 'Why is he breaking up with me? We've only gotten together two or three times.' He went on to tell me he felt it was moving along way too fast and that one of us couldn't go to a party the next night thrown by a mutual friend. On one hand this was no big deal to me. But then

I thought, 'Hey, I'm getting broken up with by someone I wasn't even involved with. I didn't know we were seriously dating!' So I go to this party and what was nothing became this horror story of having to go through an evening with everyone whispering, 'Did you hear he broke up with her?' It was so ego deflating."

While none of the women we talked to had any regrets about living their lives without these particular men, all mentioned a bruise to the ego when they realized they were being rejected. Perhaps it's even a bit more humiliating to be left by someone you don't even care about. At least if you know you were in a relationship, you get the enjoyment of missing what you had. Carolyn summed up her experience with a smile when she added, "Now that I think about it, more people have broken up with me than I've had boyfriends!"

If something like this has happened to you, know that you are not alone. These situations can be especially awkward when they occur in a small community or within our particular social circle. Unfortunately, not much can be done when someone else has built up an entire scenario in their head about us. Any protest by the one being dumped is sure to be taken as a defensive measure. However, as friends we can help one another in this situation. First, we can all have a good laugh about it and assure our friend that this is the man's problem, not hers. And further, if we see that our friend is suffering embarrassment from the situation, we, as loyal supporters, can do our part to defend her reputation by telling the real story.

If you find that you have a pattern of being left by men you didn't know you were dating, you might ask a girlfriend to join you in examining the situation. She may be able to help you notice the clues you overlooked. She may actually have a theory about why you seem to be the last to know. After all, it's hard to be successful in a relationship you don't even know you're in!

Will You Marry Me?

But with young bachelors—ah, that was a different matter. . . .
Sometimes, but not often, you did let them kiss you. (Ellen and
Mammy had not taught her that but she learned it was
effective.) Then you cried and declared you didn't know what
had come over you and that he couldn't ever respect you again.
Then he had to dry your eyes and usually he proposed, to show
just how much he did respect you. . . . Oh, there were so many
things to do to bachelors and she knew them all.

—MARGARET MITCHELL

Gone with the Wind

After a couple's passionate discovery or quiet realization that they have each found the right person for themselves, the moment may arrive where one person is asked by the other, "Will you marry me?" Often it was the man who did the proposing, although many couples had already discussed marriage prior to the actual proposal.

Surprise or no surprise, marriage proposals come in all forms, from public offers on television, billboards, or skywriting to private moments gazing at the sunset. The proposal reflects the couple.

Irene, married for over three decades and the mother of two grown boys, told us about her very traditional wedding proposal. She told us, "I was eighteen, living in a small town, and Joe was a sophisticated city boy. He drove up to where I lived each time we went out, because in those days a girl would never even consider driving herself to meet a man for a date. Joe was everything I had dreamed of, and I was hoping he'd ask me to marry him. But he never mentioned marriage directly to me.

"One afternoon, before we were to go out, he and my dad went for a long walk together. I didn't know what they were talking about and waited anxiously for them to return. Joe was asking my father for my hand in marriage, and my dad was grilling him about his plans for the future. During that walk, Joe promised my father, man to man, to always take care of me, no matter what happened.

"They walked into the kitchen where I was sitting, and my father said to me, 'Joe wants to propose marriage to you. How do you feel about that?' I told him I wanted to marry Joe, and so the date was set. Looking back, Joe never did actually ask me directly. My father negotiated the entire arrangement.

"When Joe and I walked out of the church as husband and wife, we were greeted at the door by Joe's father. He held out his arms to me and said, 'Welcome to our family. You have entered in the proper way.' Joe's dad was very religious, and marrying in the church was of the highest importance to him."

The involvement of parents to this degree rarely happens in this day and age. But Irene attributes the longevity of her marriage to this approach to marriage. She told us, "After our sons were born, Joe and I had difficulties for a time. But even though we were having problems, he always made sure I was taken care of. He said time and again, 'I promised your father, and it's a promise I will keep.' We're back stronger than ever now, doing better than ever. I think seeing our marriage as the combining of two families, rather than two people, has helped us work through our problems rather than give up and look for someone else."

Other women receive less traditional proposals that may not be so fully planned. Jody told us this story: "Bruce and I were dating for a little over a year, a year and three months, to be exact. We were in Yosemite National Park, and we were going on a cross-country ski trip. It was a beautiful day, there was snow on the ground, blue skies, it was just perfect. He was skiing up ahead of me, which was unusual, because he would usually wait for me, but he seemed really preoccupied. He was ahead, doing his own thing, and I was huffing and puffing behind him. We went to this place called Mirror Lake, right below Half Dome. It was beautiful. We found a little clearing, and we had brought some lunch — bread and meat and fruit.

"We were sitting on this rock, and he was sitting below me. I looked down at him, his hair was all messed up, but I still thought he looked handsome, and I remember thinking, 'I will never forget the way he looks right now.' I said, 'It's beautiful here,' and he looked up at me and said, 'I'm just surrounded by beautiful things.' I just kind of nodded and didn't know what to say. . . . We pulled out our lunch, and it was really dry, we didn't have any condiments. I took a bite and started gagging, I had too much in my mouth, and we both began to laugh, and he looked at me and said, 'Will you marry me?'

"I looked back at him and thought, 'He can't be serious, because he just asked me when I took a bite of food. He wouldn't do that.' So I just started laughing and choking, and I asked him for a sip of his drink so I could get this food down. I was still laughing, and he looked at me and said, 'Well, will you?' and I said, 'So you're serious!' Still it didn't click in that he really was asking me to marry him, and I jokingly said, 'Well, don't you have a ring or something?' He pulled out an antique ring holder with two old rings in it — one had little diamonds on it, and the other was a sapphire, very delicate, in silver.

"He said, 'I brought these along, they are heirlooms

from my grandmother.' I said, 'Oh, oh,' finally understanding that he meant it. So he said again, 'Well, will you?' And I responded, 'Of course!' It was so natural, and I surprised myself that I said it so easily.

"After that everything changed for us. He was calling me his 'wife-to-be' and fiancée, and it was like my whole world changed in a second, because we had never really talked before about getting married. It was out of the blue, but it felt so natural. He told me later that he was really nervous and was just waiting for the right moment to ask, and when he saw me take that bite of food, he thought it would be a good time because I would be forced to think about it for a few seconds! It was really cute."

Sometimes proposals don't go as planned at all but are memorable nonetheless. Felicia, now married to Roger, told us about his proposal: "I knew he was going to propose, we had talked about it before, and I knew I would accept. He was the only guy who didn't put the moves on me right off the bat. It was at the time of the Vietnam War, and we had known each other for several years through college. Roger expected to be called to Vietnam, and we didn't want to get married at that time, if he was going. He was called several times, but his orders kept getting rescinded because he was training all of the mountaineering and ski troops and reconnaissance groups in the mountains of Colorado. So we got engaged my senior year of college.

"We were going to go up to Lookout Mountain,

which looks out over the city of Denver. Up there is a place where you can make out, and that is what we were going to do, but it started raining like crazy. Then he couldn't find the ring and was fumbling around. Finally he found the ring in the car, and he says, without making eye contact, 'Do you want to, uh, uh, uh . . . ?' He choked on the *m* word. So he proposed in the parking lot in the rain overlooking the city of Denver. Then the police came by and said, 'You need to move from here.' That was it! We have been married for twenty-eight years."

Perhaps the most romantic proposal we heard about took place while a couple, Jim and Angie, was on a trip to Scotland. They stayed at a castle that had been turned into an inn. Jim, being Scottish, got into the surroundings. Unbeknownst to Angie, he met with the owner where they were staying and told him he was going to propose, and they worked out this whole scenario. They ate dinner that night at the inn, and the meal was fantastic. Candlelight, the finest food. Then Jim excused himself, and returned dressed in an authentic kilt that he'd borrowed from the owner of the inn. He escorted Angie upstairs to the roof of the castle, where they were greeted with bagpipe players. It was raining, so Jim held an umbrella over her head, and with the wind whipping around them and the bagpipes playing, he asked her to marry him. It took her breath away, but she still managed to say yes!

While we usually think of men proposing marriage,

women have also been the ones to ask, "Will you marry me?" One couple, now in their mid-fifties, grew up in Winnipeg and knew each other from kindergarten on up. They even went out together a few times when they were both students at a local community college. But they were never serious about each other, and eventually each went on to marry someone else. Jessica married and moved to California, while Bob married and stayed in Winnipeg, but his relationship floundered. Decades later, Jessica was finally getting out of a difficult marriage and staying with her parents, who lived just down the street from Bob's parents in Winnipeg. Jessica and Bob ran into each other and renewed their friendship. After their divorces were final, they started a relationship and eventually moved to California together.

One weekend they took a trip to Reno just to relax and saw all the wedding chapels there. As they were strolling down the sidewalk, all of a sudden Jessica turned to Bob and asked, "So, do you want to marry me?" Bob grinned and said, "I should have married you twenty years ago."

Jessica appreciates that Bob gave her the space and time she needed to make up her own mind. Bob "always had a thing for Jess, all those years," They just celebrated their sixth anniversary, and on their mantel is a photo of the two of them in third grade together.

One couple who live in the Midwest, now married nearly twenty years, realized during their courtship they were moving toward commitment. They decided to ask each other at the same time. So together they turned to each other and asked in unison, "Will you marry me?" And they responded in unison, "Yes!"

The women we interviewed did have two suggestions to offer: Never make a big decision in bed, and do not treat a proposal as serious unless, as one woman put it, "you are both fully clothed and in a public place." Nothing like a girlfriend to put it bluntly! While this may sound like facetious advice, there is truth to it. If a man proposes in the heat of passion, we may want to make sure he feels the same way outside of that intimate context.

One may get engaged in a carefully orchestrated setting or one that feels intuitively right or one that goes *not* according to plan. Whichever party is doing the asking, man or woman or both, he or she will think long and hard before making a lifetime commitment. When he or she is ready to (gulp!) take the big leap, the details of the proposal will undoubtedly form a lifetime memory.

Girlfriend Guidelines

*Few comforts are more alluring for a woman than the rich
intimate territory of women's talk. A woman friend will say,
"You are not alone. I have felt that way, too."*

—ELSA WALSH

The Kinship of Women

In the final analysis, each woman is the only one who knows what is right for herself. But we have gleaned some wisdom from our interviews with women and want to pass these guidelines onto you so that you can apply them to your specific situation.

Listen to Your Body

Bodies cannot lie.

—AGNES DE MILLE

The Wit and Wisdom of Women

When you are around a man you have just met or even one you have known for a long time, how does your body feel? Does it feel tense, do you feel a knot in your stomach, a catch in your back? Do your shoulders move up closer to your ears? Listen to what your body has to say about someone—our bodies frequently pick up on feelings faster than our minds do, possibly because our minds are distracted by how attractive someone is, how eligible or charming he is, and so forth.

One woman described it this way: "I met Stephen at a business meeting in which our two companies were planning to do a research project together. He was in charge of the finance side of the project on his company's side, and I was in charge of the regulatory matters on behalf of my company, so we actually had a lot of contact with each other. He was considerably older than I was but incredibly handsome in a distinguished, gray-suit kind of way. Anyway, I was surprised after our first meeting when he called me up and asked me to dinner. I was not really comfortable with the idea because of our business relationship, but I consulted with other members of my work team, and they seemed to think that there was nothing inappropriate about my dating him (and the women thought I shouldn't pass up the opportunity).

"Well, he was very impressive—really knew all the right things to do—took me to a wonderful dinner, handled all of the details, showered me with attention. But I felt slightly uncomfortable with him, my body was just a little tense, and I always felt a bit on guard when I was around him. We dated for several weeks before I started noticing that his sarcasm level increased ever so slightly when he was drinking, and I realized that his drinking took up quite a bit of his free time. A couple of months more, and I realized that he was capable of being abusive and mean. Finally I got out of the relationship, but I could have saved a lot of time and abuse if I had paid attention to that hesitant feeling my body had when I first dated him."

Margaret, a forty-two-year-old editor, has learned to listen to her "gut feeling": "Over the years of meeting a lot of people, and having my heart broken, and trying to learn from each of the things that have happened, I pay a lot of attention now to the information that I get in the first moment. My first impressions, if I'm paying careful attention to all the information coming in, are usually right. I look in his eyes the first instant, and I can see certain possibilities. That's one of the main indicators.

"I've been finding that often I don't have reasons for the 'sense' I have about somebody, but if I go down the road and let the friendship or relationship play itself out, my initial impressions will have more than a grain of truth to them. That's been a real confidence builder, so I don't feel anymore that I can be easily fooled by people. However, while it's a resource, I don't follow it slavishly. I always give somebody at least three chances. I may be seeing things more negatively one day or more positively another, so I always get together more than once with somebody that I have any slight interest in. But, so far, my instincts have been right."

When we asked how her intuition exhibits itself, she replied, "It's a body signal. I check muscles all up and down my body. Am I tense anywhere with this person, if so, where? What does that tell me about the kind of conflict I might have with that person down the road? Is the tension in my upper shoulders? Is it a protective thing? Is it in my stomach? Is it a control thing? Is it a competition thing? So I analyze what kind of tension I get in my body. And then I listen to how I talk with this person. Do I talk easily? Do I find anything upsetting?

"I've been in situations where I was a lot more attracted the second or third time we got together, so the trick became not to forget my first take on him. I might have thought at first, 'He looks a little grumpy,' or, 'He sounds like he has a little bit of a suspicious edge to him.' Then later I've discovered that I was really attracted to him and decided to forego those initial impressions and just dive in, and uh-oh! I usually pay for it if I don't listen to myself."

So when you are thinking about getting involved with someone, romantically or otherwise, listen to what your body is telling you during your initial encounters. If you find yourself holding your breath, clenching your jaw, or feeling a knot in your stomach, your body may be telling you to exercise caution. If you find yourself breathing and laughing easily (not nervously), and your muscles feel relaxed when you see a person coming, your body may be giving you signals that this person feels safe and can be trusted. If you practice paying attention to your interactions with all people—everyone's signals are different—you will learn what your own body signals mean to you. How do you feel when you are with people you love and who you know love you? Take note, and see if you get those feelings with the next man you date.

Listen to Your Heart

The heart outstrips the clumsy senses, and sees—perhaps for an instant, perhaps for long periods of bliss—an undistorted and more veritable world.

—EVELYN UNDERHILL

Mysticism

Committing yourself to love another human being is one of the most important decisions you'll ever make. Only you can be the final authority on what works or doesn't work for you. It can require a lot of courage to be honest with yourself and figure out what is truly important to you in a relationship with a man.

Knowing your own preferences and priorities is important before you move in with a mate or marry. As Nancy notes, "If you find that you are often annoyed by things that the man does or does not do on a regular basis (always being late, not picking up clothes, not offering to help with domestic duties, and so forth), remember that you will be even more annoyed by these things once you are married."

Once you have figured out what is important in your heart of hearts, let the rest go. Martha, a thirty-two-year-old marketing director for a large company, told us that she had always dated men who were "highly pedigreed." "I came from a family that didn't have much money, and I was one of the few members of my family who had a college degree as well as an advanced degree. I think I was always fighting my insecurity about my family background, and so I found I would date men who went to Ivy League schools, with very expensive degrees. If they were from prominent families, even better. I had this impression that I had to be with someone who had accomplished more than I had. Unfortunately, I seemed to choose men who were arrogant and very aware of their value among the female population. In other words, they usually thought they were 'God's gift to women,' which only fueled my own insecurities about myself.

"After breaking up with yet another of this type, and swearing to myself that I would try something different in the man department, I met Alan, an artist who was completely unlike all of the men whom I had dated. He was not as educated as I was, and I wondered if that would bother me. He marched to the beat of a different drummer but did it in a quiet, matter-of-fact way. He wasn't out to impress anyone. I started realizing how confident and intelligent he was. The more I got to know him, the more I realized that he was truly interested in me as a person and not as an ornament. We have been together for two-and-a-half years, and when I am with him, I felt safe, loved, and listened to like I have never been before. The importance of the number of degrees he possesses has fallen away, as I realize this is someone I could be with for a very long time."

No one is going to satisfy our image of the ideal man. Among the women we interviewed, not one married woman, or woman who had been committed to a man for a long time, thought that her man was perfect. But each was able to see the good and to know what was important to her. The rest of her needs she learned to satisfy elsewhere. Once we know in our hearts what is important to us personally, whether it is patience, confidence, intelligence, warmth, the ability to talk about feelings, or other characteristics, then we can figure out what we can let go in a relationship with a man.

Listen to Your Girlfriends

Talk between women friends is always therapy.

—JAYNE ANNE PHILLIPS

Road Trip: The Real Thing

Girlfriends are women who have seen you in more than one relationship and may be more aware of patterns you fall into than you are yourself. They can provide a lot of insight and point out positive and negative aspects of your chosen man more clearly than you can when you are in your love-besotted state.

Laney tells the story of how her friend and sister made the correct call on two of her former boyfriends: "I have come to rely on my sister's reaction to boyfriends to get clear about whether relationships are right for me. We have similar patterns with men, and she, as the outside observer, seems to have clearer vision than I. More than once I have been with a man whom she realized was not 'all there' or who was treating me less than well. Naturally, I didn't appreciate my sister's assessment, and got mad at her while I was still emotionally involved with these men, but I learned a great deal from her insight and eventually began holding potential mates up to different standards.

"Two boyfriends serve as good examples. The first one was self-centered, wanted sex on demand, and expected me to do the majority of the housework and cooking. My sister was very vocal about her disdain for him, but I refused to throw in the towel because I wanted to give it a chance. When I finally broke up with him, she let her truest feelings be known: 'Ugh! Good riddance!'

"Another boyfriend seemed to cast a spell on me with his good looks (short, dark, and handsome) and sensitive, 'wounded' nature. However, my sister was not as impressed. She didn't like the way I tried to hide any signs of imperfection when he was around and how I got obsessed with whether I looked okay. When after five months he bailed out of the relationship, citing the fact that he panicked at the idea of getting close (a pattern he had with women he dated before and after we went out), my sister again congratulated me.

"She pointed out to me that he had not been responsive to me and I deserved better. 'Yeah, yeah,' I said, not really understanding what she had said to me until months later, when I had dinner with him. I looked beautiful, yet he never seemed to notice and didn't comment. For the first time, I clearly saw that while I was with him I had been 'starving' myself of male affirmation because my eyes were clouded by a fantasy based on his looks, our physical chemistry, and my plans for us to ride off into the sunset. Once I saw what I had been doing, I became more interested in finding a man who really wants to be with me, one who thinks of and treats me like the gem that I am.

"While I sometimes get tired of my sister critiquing

the men I date, and I still sometimes disregard her advice, I'm grateful for the viewpoint she's not afraid to share. My cardinal rule now: run all potential boyfriends by her. If she chews them up, I think twice."

We heard various stories of how women felt they needed to step in to stop a good friend from making what they viewed as a serious mistake. Virginia, a marketing executive, stepped in with another friend when they saw their mutual friend, Tracy, getting involved with a man whom they thought was using Tracy: "When Tracy was going through a divorce, she met a man several years her junior, and after running into one another several times in their small town in the Northwest, they started seeing each other. Well, the physical chemistry was great. Tracy was thrilled to be with a young man who loved sex and who wanted to spend a lot of time enjoying it. Another friend, Janet, and I had dinner a few times with Tracy and Randy, and although Randy was a nice enough guy, he was not much of a conversationalist. Although he talked about taking business courses at the university, he hadn't done much since high school but drift from job to job and was then living with his parents.

"This relationship continued for months. Randy was spending more time at Tracy's house than at his own. They went dancing. They went to concerts. They had sex. They watched movies. Tracy cooked. He sometimes went out to play pool and drink with his friends, then would ring Tracy's doorbell at 2 A.M. Tracy, who was working as well while finishing her college degree, needed to get up at 6 A.M. to get everything moving and get to work. Some evenings she needed to study, but Randy would hang around, drinking beer and teasing her.

"Finally, Janet and I started getting annoyed with Randy and thought he was using Tracy's house as a crash pad. He wasn't looking for work. He wasn't helping her out. You couldn't even have a conversation with him except about football, whereas Tracy didn't even know what a quarterback was and spent most of her time studying anthropology. This did not look like a good option for Tracy's love life.

"One thing we finally did, which may have been heartless, was hide a tape recorder under the couch. We had all shared a pizza at Tracy's house and when Janet and I were ready to leave, Janet distracted Tracy and Randy in the kitchen while I set up the recorder. It didn't work very well, but we did play it back for her later. Randy, by this point in the evening, was pretty drunk and stupid sounding. We left, and they sat on the couch with the stereo on. Mostly the conversation was incoherent.

"I don't think the tape was what made Tracy change her mind about Randy. I think it was the idea that Janet and I would go to such lengths to show her who she was with. We convinced her there were a lot of men out there who were good lovers, but some of them had jobs and minds as well."

Perhaps the adage "Never go grocery shopping when

you're hungry" is in order here. If we find ourselves feeling especially needy or desperate, it's too easy to choose paths we never would take when we're feeling secure and loved. A girlfriend can give you a little extra TLC when you're with a man who doesn't treat you right. Once you're back on your feet emotionally, you'll be better able to decide if this guy is worth your time and love.

Not only can girlfriends save us from making a tragic mistake by letting go of a negative relationship, they can help us pick out the good men and stay by their sides. Cindy told us that a girlfriend of hers was thinking about marrying a man who was a bit more interested in marriage than was she when "they had a big fight. She called me and after she calmed down a bit, I pointed out all of his good qualities. I said, 'I know you've just been through something here, and you're angry and hurt. But you opened the door for my advice, so here it is. I want to ask, "Do you really want to give him up? Is this man, with all of his great qualities, someone you want to walk away from?"' They're married now, with a beautiful child. And they give me the credit for keeping them together at the start."

When asking a friend for her opinion, it is important to take into account her particular point of view. For instance, if she is newly married or newly divorced, she may be eager, consciously or unconsciously, to have someone share her status. The opinions of even our best friends, who we know want the best for us, are going to be somewhat colored by their experience. We can accept the help they are offering and at the same time be aware of the influences in their lives, so we can interpret the information in a helpful way.

What a Girlfriend Can Do

Sisterhood is powerful.

—ROBIN MORGAN

Book title

Because our girlfriends trust us, we can have a tremendous amount of influence in their lives—and with this trust comes responsibility. Over and over we heard from the women we interviewed that the most important thing they received from their girlfriends was a listening ear. Often, by talking about a situation or expressing feelings, a woman can figure out for herself what is the best next step in a romantic relationship.

First, commit yourself to telling the truth, as you see it, even if it may be something your girlfriend doesn't want to hear. Some women hesitate to speak their minds because it feels like they are poking their heads in where they don't belong. When we spoke with Dianne and her friend Jan, Dianne expressed her reservations about stating her opinion about a friend's boyfriend: "If I was to say, 'Break up with him, he's not good for you, he doesn't want to commit,' you could break up with him, and he could come running back in two weeks and propose. In the meantime, I would have said all these negative things about him. Also, whether it ends up working or not, what you choose to do is not my decision and is not my advice to give you."

Her friend Jan agreed. "I think there's a tendency among people who consider themselves good friends to not say something because you don't want to put yourself in the middle, you don't want to be misunderstood. I think there's this whole 'mind your own business' attitude in society. However, I have recently said to a friend, 'If you ever see me doing something stupid, I hope you will tell me. I might get mad at you in the moment, but I consider you a friend, and that's what I want you to do. Tell me.' Because if I know that they really care about me, then I know that they are saying it only because they don't want to see me do something self-destructive or dumb or be in denial or whatever."

We agree with Jan. But what if you are the friend watching, or you are being asked for advice? What do you do? One suggestion is to give advice or take action in a way that suits the severity of the person's situation and her mental state. As Alicia suggests, "You have to be really careful about how you put it, especially given a person's vulnerability or sensitivity to her own situation. But if you are in an extreme situation, like your friend is going to walk home with this man and you know he is really awful, you physically have to make sure she doesn't walk home with him. So it depends on the situation and your relationship with your friend."

Alicia also suggests giving advice that doesn't include a judgment, by reflecting back to your friend what you see as the facts of the situation and not your opinion of it. Or, if you give an opinion, you can make sure you say that it is just your opinion, while acknowledging that you may not have all of the facts: "Handled right, being honest with a friend only strengthens the friendship. I have talked to friends about situations, and I have said, 'These are the facts, guys. These are what I see as the facts.' I'm not necessarily giving advice, just saying, 'This is the way it is, this is where you came from, this is the way his parents are,' and so forth."

How do we know a friend is asking for advice? Because sometimes we may want someone's opinion but may not know how to ask for it. As Jan says, "Sometimes you are almost testing what you are doing, you are not really sure of yourself, so you are telling your friends about it. Sometimes we test without saying directly, 'What do you think of this?' I might tell a friend about something going on that I might know is not very smart but am testing it out on them."

And what constitutes "asking," anyway? When someone is your close friend, you will learn the ways she seeks advice, other than just asking for it. She may start by saying, 'I really don't know what to do' or 'I'm confused' or 'I'm upset' or 'I don't understand men.' You know when it happens. Be kind, but tell the truth.

Understanding the Differences and Similarities

Marriage involves big compromises all the time.
International level compromises.
You're the U.S.A., he's the U.S.S.R.,
and you're talking nuclear warheads.

—BETTE MIDLER

Parade

Communication

We have to face the fact that either all of us are going to die together or we are going to learn to live together and if we are to live together we have to talk.

—ELEANOR ROOSEVELT

New York Times

All the women's magazines and daytime talk shows stress that, in order for a relationship between a man and a woman to work, we must "communicate." Intellectually, we have all grasped the concept, but many of us do not have much experience at telling another person what we are thinking or feeling in a way that solves a conflict while nurturing the relationship. Or perhaps we have never even really learned the importance of the skill. However, if we are married or living with someone and interacting every day with that person, our need to communicate in a positive way becomes all too clear, as we (sometimes blindly) grope our way to a successful relationship.

Can We Talk?

The biggest mistake is believing there is one right way to listen,
to talk, to have a conversation — or a relationship.

—DEBORAH TANNEN

The Wit and Wisdom of Women

Do men and women communicate differently? One way to answer that question is to observe how we relate to our same-sex friends. As we toured the country talking with men and women about our book, *girlfriends,* many women regaled us with stories of their women friends, often with tears in their eyes, making comments such as, "I don't know what I would have done without her" and "I can tell her anything and know she will support me." Almost every woman we talked to emphasized how much she relied on and valued a girlfriend relationship. But the men? When discussing the emotional bond in friendship, we were frequently met with glazed eyes and a response such as, "Huh?" or "I don't get it."

Men's and women's friendships seem to differ around "doing" a friendship or "discussing" a relationship. Chloe said, "My husband organizes his friendships around activity. In fact, he's almost critical of the way I do my friendships, you know, how we talk and talk and talk. He told me once that he didn't understand why we didn't go out and live our friendships, rather than talk about them all the time. Doing things together is having a friendship to him. Talking isn't doing anything, and is therefore not having a friendship."

Friendships between women, in contrast, are often characterized by discussing every minute detail of every conversation, each interaction, exploring what it all might mean. Beverly told us, "I've realized recently that the men I talk with are not as concerned with the emotional aspects of relating as are my girlfriends. For example, I rarely go through the ritual of 'how are you?' with the man who lives next door to me, the way I would with a girlfriend. He gets right to the point and asks, 'What's that smell in the air?' or 'I noticed you planted a new rose bush.' He's very friendly, don't get me wrong. He just shows his concern in a more direct, action-oriented way."

According to Deborah Tannen, author of *You Just Don't Understand: Women and Men in Conversation*, differing styles of communication can cause conflict in a relationship between a man and a woman. She points out: "The seeds of women's and men's styles are sown in the ways they learn to use language while growing up. In our culture, most people, but especially women, look to their closest relationships as havens in a hostile world. The center of a girl's social life is her best friend. . . . For grown women, too, the essence of friendship is talk, telling each other what they're thinking and feeling, and what happened that day: who was at the bus stop, who called, what they said, how that made them feel. When asked who their best friends are, most women name other women they talk to regularly."[9]

In contrast, men would respond that their wives were their best friends, and then, "after that, many men name other men with whom they do things such as play tennis or baseball (but never just sit and talk) or a chum from high school whom they haven't spoken to in a year."[10] If the men in our lives treat us like they do their male friends, it is easy to see where the frustration may come in. After all, if our girlfriends weren't sharing their experiences and feelings with us, we would know they were upset or angry with us! We, as women, frequently apply the same reasoning to men and therefore feel cut off or excluded.

Occasionally, when we were speaking on women's friendships, men approached us out of curiosity because their wives or girlfriends had close friendships with other women that they did not understand. Some noted that they felt envious of the strength of the bond. We have noticed that some men are starting to adopt a more "female" model of friendship. Pointing out that her husband defies the male stereotype, Veronica told us, "My husband has a couple of friends who are really intentional about communicating with each other. I've heard them talk about how the culture has made it hard for them to relate on an emotional level to each other. They have very few legitimate outlets, such as yelling at a football game or something like that. So I love watching these guys go against the grain. They'll talk on the phone and actually say that they love each other. It's kind of strange hearing it from guys, although I'm comfortable saying the same kinds of things to my girlfriends. But these guys have really worked hard at the whole idea of communicating with and understanding each other, and understanding how the culture has affected them. It's really neat to watch." Although many men still would never dream of saying they loved each other, except perhaps when one of them is on his deathbed, it seems that more men are turning to their friends for help when they need it.

While men may be perplexed or inspired by the way we relate to our girlfriends, one element of our communication style can be a source of consternation for men when they realize we're very likely telling our girlfriends *all* about our romances. Some women we interviewed held to the old school of thought that, once married, it is inappropriate to share marital problems with their friends. The concept of presenting a united front to the world, not "airing dirty laundry," still affects many of us. But most women we interviewed did not see anything wrong, and much that is right, with sharing problems, joys, and private information with friends. Janice told us, "My husband gets a bit unnerved wondering what I've said about him to my girlfriends. I've assured him that I don't sit around and trash him or say anything about him I wouldn't feel comfortable saying to him. After all, I want this marriage to work, and if my friends think my husband is a jerk, they'll be hard-pressed to support it. So when I need an outside perspective, I am careful to present the situation fairly. I don't want my girlfriend to take my side, I want her to take *our* side."

Talking with friends about your relationship, especially a friend who knows and cares about both of you, can frequently help resolve an issue in a relationship. Friends who know us well can allow us to blow off steam, point out a factor to which we may be blind, or help us figure out what really is bothering us. Some women reported that their partners expressed gratitude for the friends of their wives and girlfriends, because they took the pressure off them to talk about feelings! As long as we are using friendships to support the relationship instead of divide it, our friends can help keep the relationship standing in difficult moments. And remind us of why we fell in love with this particular man in the first place.

Compartmentalized Communication

When a man is stressed he will withdraw into the cave of his mind and focus on solving a problem. He generally picks the most urgent problem or the most difficult. He becomes so focused on solving this one problem that he temporarily loses awareness of everything else.

—JOHN GRAY

Men Are from Mars, Women Are from Venus

One of the stereotypes prevalent in our society is that men tend to be linear, "left-brain" thinkers, while women, more prone to rely on the right side of their brains, experience life more intuitively and more wholistically. Not all men fall into this category, being more "big picture" thinkers. However, if your man is one of those linear-type guys, you may benefit from the experience of other women who also love and live with a more linear-thinking male. Mother of two, Laurine explains: "The one thing that I have seen again and again, especially in my children, is the male ability to compartmentalize his experience, with the ability to say to himself, 'I'm going to focus on this now,' to the exclusion of every other concern. My approach is much more contextual. I see things as parts of a whole, all relating to one another. To focus on one part, I take into consideration how all other aspects will be affected.

"In my marriage, I've been amazed at my husband's

ability to be clear on a particular issue, and absolutely incapable of looking at the rest of the world at the same time. I see everything as part of the same context. This is particularly the case when it comes to career and family and balancing them. It's fascinating to me."

Ursula, married for several years, told us that her husband's tendency to compartmentalize became an obstacle when they needed to get a leaky pipe fixed. She said, "He told me he couldn't possibly call the plumber from the office. Why? 'All you have to do is pick up the phone and call.' But, oh, no. He was at work, and the plumbing problem was at home. He felt strongly that, when he was at the office, he needed to stay completely focused on the issues at work and not get sidetracked by domestic problems."

We often heard women make the observation that their left-brain men drew a strict line between work and home. Laurine, a working mother, agreed: "I'm managing the household, taking care of my husband and the children, starting this new business, and he refused to pick up the phone and make a call for me at work. At first I was hurt by his lack of support. But then I reminded myself that he's not a jerk or insensitive. He just can't do it at the office! It's just too hard to handle. Of course, when he got home that night, it was too late, so I had to do it myself."

The ability of some men to compartmentalize can make us feel that they do not care about us or do not share the same feelings we do about our relationships. As Joan, a lawyer in her midthirties, explained, "I could never figure out why, during particularly sensitive parts of our relationship, Jack didn't want to call me during the day. I mean, I call my friends during the day. I certainly want to talk to someone I'm involved with. His response was something like, 'You know, I'm at work now, I'll talk to you when I get home.'"

This difference can be a source of pain for women and a chance for us to draw inaccurate conclusions about how men really feel. Often women express their frustration with statements like: How dare they? Why can't they connect with us just because they are at work? And if we are having trouble in our relationship, why aren't they more miserable (like us)?

These women also reported that, when their husbands did come home, their homes, rather than their wives, were the focus of attention. As Ursula discovered, her husband needed to be as unwavering in his drive for accomplishment at home as he was at work: "He is a doer. He feels that I am overworked and stressed and having a hard time, so when he comes home, he wants to do something so that he can say, 'Look, this was done by me. I helped you.' I'm following him around the house, he's like a Tasmanian devil, running around doing laundry, mopping floors, and I'm saying, 'Please sit down, I want to talk to someone over the age of five.' He's saying, 'No, no, I've got to change the laundry.'"

"He needs something tangible. I have that need, too, but higher on my priority list is that I want to feel like I've connected with him. I literally chase him around the house, saying, 'Put that laundry down!' because I want to talk."

We are not saying that all men compartmentalize their thinking. We heard several sweet examples of men who would stay connected with their women throughout the workday. Josephine's boyfriend, who was self-employed, would stop by frequently during the day to Josephine's house after she lost her job. And Margaret's boyfriend takes time off in the middle of the day to bring her chicken soup if she is sick. Margaret says she is the one who is the compartmental thinker, with her boyfriend calling her every day from work to keep the emotional connection, and she being the one to stay focused on a project for long periods of time. If you are a linear thinker, and your man is not, you may want to share this discussion with him!

Perhaps the secret to successfully loving and living with a linear-thinking person (if you are not) is to begin by appreciating the differences between you and your partner. At times the differences can seem infuriating, but the differences can also bring spice and adventure to a relationship. Talking openly about the variations in your experience can help both parties see things from a new perspective. And making an effort to translate your needs into his language (and vice versa) can prove helpful, such as letting your man know, if he is a task-oriented, linear thinker, that talking to you is a concrete achievement — it prevents you from being carried away in a straitjacket, especially if you are at home with small children all day.

And remember, you can always call a girlfriend and bemoan, "Can't men just listen?"

Can't Men Just Listen?

If love means never having to say you're sorry, then marriage means always having to say everything twice. Husbands, due to an unknown quirk of the universe, never hear you the first time.

— ESTELLE GETTY

What Women Say About Men

A common complaint women expressed to us is that they didn't feel "heard" by the men in their lives. Rather than "just listen" as women fret or fume, cry or complain, partners tend to get a glazed look in their eyes or cut them off, offering ways to resolve the problem. Not wanting a solution, but a listening, empathetic ear, the women feel unloved; perplexed when their best efforts to help are rejected, men express frustration and confusion. Sometimes these men, in exasperation, correlate the expression of emotion with being "unreasonable." Of course, emotions tend to not be based on reason, but on feeling and this makes some men uncomfortable. Many men do not characterize themselves as being emotional and frequently find women's expression of emotion as less than desirable. Why?

Some point to the fact that men have been socialized to ignore emotion, that they so fear it they cannot adjust to others' outbursts of pure feeling. As Rita, an editor in her midtwenties described: "I'm part-Italian, part-Irish, with a little French mixed in there, too, so I fly off the handle a lot. Sometimes it just feels good to scream at the TV. But Don does not understand that. He thinks that whenever I scream when he's in the room, I must be angry at him. It's as if everything revolves around him or that he needs to fix everything. Maybe that comes from his upbringing. His father grew up in Scandinavia, and so there is very much a separation in how Don was brought up as compared to his sisters. He was taught to be the strong, protective male. Maybe that's why he feels if I'm upset he needs to fix something or do something."

If the problem was upbringing in the Old Country, then it's a problem that has spread to our shores, because many men and women raised here and now are experiencing the same dilemma. So many women we interviewed talked about this problem that we have concluded that, whether it's nature or nurture, we women have to come up with ways to get the emotional support we need, without creating a lot of angst for the men in our lives.

The cultural guru on male and female differences, John Gray, offers some advice (isn't that just like a man?) in his book *Men Are from Mars, Women Are from Venus*. He confirms that men often feel that if their wife or girlfriend is upset, it must be their fault. If a man sees his woman in distress, he wants to fix it.[11] And one approach is that men will try to tell their wives and girlfriends all the reasons why they shouldn't be upset, which can frequently trigger additional frustration. Most women would prefer to have their emotions and not have to justify them. As Rita continued, "I would prefer that he'd just let me spout whatever I'm feeling—whether it's happy emotion or sad emotion or you know, just emotion. He doesn't understand—he's absolutely black and white."

Is there no hope? Will we ever get what we need from the men we love? The most helpful, and least resentful, suggestions we discovered came from women who, rather than insisting that men understand them, made the effort to understand how men's minds work.

One such woman is Gloria, who was quite outspoken regarding the differences between the ways men and women communicate. "I resist stereotypes," insists Gloria, a twenty-something graduate student who has been married for four years. "But," she smiles, "I find that with my husband and with other men I need to provide details before I discuss my feelings. With my girlfriends, I can go directly to describing my emotional response in a conversation I had with someone else. But if I try that with my husband, he'll interrupt me and ask things like, 'So where was the conversation?', 'How long did you talk?', and 'You were at lunch?' He gets fascinated by the little details."

Scrunching up her face, she said, "It was awful at first! I'd get my feelings hurt because I didn't think he cared about me. But then I realized that he processed the information differently than my girlfriends do. I've gotten really good at being very succinct when I bring up an emotional experience I want to talk about. I say, 'At work, in the elevator, where I was alone with a man I worked with once last year . . . ' and then I can tell him about how upset or relieved or whatever I was feeling. He really is a very sensitive man and wants to support me emotionally. As long as he gets all the details up front, he is able to do that for me."

While being more understanding of the male perspective does not guarantee that your man will respond in kind, many woman we interviewed told us about the ways their men did go out of their way to better understand and communicate with them. We found that some men don't listen to us because they simply do not know how. Nina, married to Dylan for twenty-five years, told us about the early days in their marriage, when she never felt heard. She said, "We would have these dinner table conversations that would sound something like, 'Well, I've just been thinking about, struggling with, or wondering about this or that.' And he'd respond, 'The Giants just traded so and so.' I'd get upset with him and blurt out, 'Did that have anything to do with what I was saying?'

"We went to a counselor who told Dylan it was part of his growth to listen to me for forty-five minutes a day. He told me that I had to look at how Dylan opened his heart. So my husband actually attempted listening, and I tried to help him. I said to him, 'If you could just say, "That's interesting," instead of going right into the Giants, just that little transition would make a big difference.' So I watched him—first of all, the fact that he went to the counselor, and then that he actually tried to listen, I thought, 'Boy, there's hope.' It truly changed my sense of being adversaries. I used to think I was never going to get through to this guy. Now I will tease him when he'll say something off base to me, because now he ponders things, too."

Assuring the man that he's not to blame for a woman's feelings can also be a key to better communication. Antonia, a mother of two, told us, "I have found that when I am having a tough moment or my husband sees me crying, I have to say clearly that the tears or the emotion is not his fault. Then he can relax and talk to me about what is going on. Otherwise, he gets this look on his face like he wants to run."

Brooke, married for over thirty years, also found that her husband was initially resistant to listening to her talk about her feelings because he secretly assumed he had failed her in some way. She told us, "My husband processes factually and I process emotionally. He didn't understand it when my needs were not being met, because he was thinking factually. He'd say, 'Well, tell me what it is, write it down on a piece of paper,' and I can't do that because it is a feeling.

"A lot of people think that all a woman wants is a rich man, and a lot of men think that, too. A woman wants to be emotionally supported. If women only wanted things that are material, then why do women divorce men who have given them the million-dollar house, the new Mercedes, the membership to the country club? Their emotional needs are not being met. The men say, 'I don't understand it, I gave her everything.' If a man gives her everything but doesn't make her feel cared for, then she wants to walk away. If a woman is having all of her emotional needs met, she will stay.

"It took my husband a lot of years to understand that a woman sometimes just needs to be held. 'Just hold me, I have had a horrible day, things have gone wrong.' At first he didn't understand, and he wanted to pull away from me at the precise time I needed him to come toward me. I don't think a woman should try to avoid the emotional side of her and be like a man. There are times when we are hurt, we don't process it like a man, we need to get it out, we need to be held."

When we asked her to explain how this transition occurred, she replied, "I think he used to feel responsible when I was emotional, but now I think he realizes my moods have nothing to do with him or with his competency. It is just being a woman. I know when he was giving advice to our daughter's husband when they got married, I was really amazed because he said, 'Hang in there during the emotional times and just hold her and make her feel cared for. A woman must feel cared for.'"

We heard story after story about men making a special effort to learn how to give emotional support to the women in their lives. Angela told us how impressed she is with her husband's efforts to listen without trying to fix things for her or to direct her to action as he once did. She told us, "I thanked Scott for letting me talk on and on and then asked him why he's changed. He told me that he'd dropped by the bookstore a while back and took a look at a few books meant to help men and women communicate. That gave him the perspective that this was something a lot of couples deal with, not just some weird emotional problem I was having." She laughed, "I was comforted to know he no longer thought I was emotionally troubled!

"And then Scott told me something else I found interesting. He said that he listened purely because he loved me, but that the only way he could tolerate not giving advice was to say to himself, 'Well, you could fix that by doing such and such.' We started laughing when he told me this, and I really loved him for it. Here he is trying to give me what I need, even though he'd still like to just solve it and be done with it."

Men like Scott are as close to the ideal as might be possible in this world. But we'd be remiss if we didn't point out that, no matter how understanding a man can be, he's still a man. There are times when, to get that I-know-exactly-what-you're-going-through kind of empathy, we need our girlfriends. We don't have to explain what's it like to be a woman to our friends. Fortunately, we don't have to choose between the men we love and our girlfriends. We get to have both.

He Won't Tell Me About His Feelings

Men seemed to truly hate to cry or throw up; both somehow represented losing some part of the control that they believed essential.

—GLORIA NAGY

Marriage

The women we interviewed felt that men in general, and their partners in particular, are better at navigating emotions than the stereotypical "John Wayne" type male. Nevertheless, we have all heard our girlfriends complain (and have probably whined a bit ourselves) about men who lose interest in talking about feelings long before the women feel satisfied. Even those "sensitive" guys often want to deal with feelings as if they are problems to be solved and then move on as quickly as possible. Author

Deborah Tannen postulates that men and women use talking for different purposes: "To him, talk is for information. . . . But to her, talk is for interaction. Telling things is a way to show involvement, and listening is a way to show interest and caring."[12] According to the people Tannen interviewed, many men don't experience their passing thoughts and feelings as important and so rarely share them with anyone else. Tannen found that women in her seminars were helped by realizing that their men were not trying to distance themselves by withholding their feelings from them; rather, men tended to dismiss their feelings as unimportant.

Joy, a thirty-year marriage veteran, told us that she found that self-esteem played a large part in getting her husband to talk. "When we got married, he wasn't a communicator. He communicates beautifully now. Many times when people feel they have nothing to say, it is related to their self-esteem. You can teach people to communicate by being very interested in what they say, asking them questions, looking in their eyes, and telling them that you find them really interesting. They start feeling more worthy and that it is safe to share feelings. But if someone says something, and the other person says, 'That is the stupidest thing I have ever heard,' or 'You know that is not right, how could you say that?' they are going to put a wall up. Words are like fists, words can hit you in the face as hard as a fist. Sometimes they are worse, because the words have to be thought up, and sometimes they hurt more."

Within the stereotypically macho male often beats the heart of a man a bit bewildered about the mysteries of human emotion. A feeling is just a feeling, after all. Once it gets out on the table, frequently it loses a lot of its power. Once we let them know that it's safe to share feelings, men often are more inclined to tell us what's *really* going on with them.

Is There a Mind Reader in the House?

So much to say. And so much not to say! Some things are better left unsaid. But so many unsaid things can become a burden.

—VIRGINIA MAE AXLINE

Dibs: In Search of Self

Time and again women told us about assumptions they made about men, only to find out later their assumptions were way off the mark. One such story was told by Melissa, who wanted to get her marriage off to the right start by including in her menu repertoire some of her mother-in-law's recipes. She tells this story: "Early on in our marriage, I asked John how his mom cooked meatloaf. He said that she used the recipe off the oatmeal box. Needless to say, the recipe was geared to help with oatmeal sales. After making meatloaf this way a couple of times, noticing that John never took seconds—in fact he didn't finish his first helpings—I decided to make it the way my mom had taught me. John went back for seconds; he loved it.

"I said, 'I was beginning to think you really didn't like meatloaf.' John said, 'Well, you asked me how my mom made it, not whether I liked hers or not!' I think it's interesting how our assumptions can affect the outcome of so many things. My mother is a great cook, I loved her food, and I had assumed that that was John's experience, too. I had been way off base; John's mom hated to cook, and it showed. My assumptions and the question that I had asked had set the stage for misunderstanding. Granted, the meatloaf incident was not a potential marital pitfall, but it did provide us with a funny story and a gentle way to learn an important lesson."

Two people bring two very different backgrounds to a relationship, and the smallest assumption can be erroneous. And while we all may compare notes with our girlfriends about "what men want," we can't assume that what our man wants is what our best friend's man wants. Don't be afraid to ask the obvious questions, even when they seem unnecessary. You may be surprised at what you learn.

Conversely, we can't expect men to know what we want if we don't tell them. Most women have been taught from day one to "be nice." So, when it comes to saying how we feel or what we want in a direct way, we can be afraid of sounding mean or rude. Isabel commented that the "biggest challenge for me in my marriage is being true to myself, especially when I know it would hurt his feelings."

Dr. Pat Allen, in her book, *Staying Married . . . And Loving It!*, claims that men and women experience love in different ways, that women experience being loved as being cherished, and men experience love when they feel respected.[13] Because we may experience love differently, men and women may have contrasting expectations from a relationship, which also affects how we communicate with each other. Without realizing it, we may talk to our partners "as if" they needed the same things and make these need known the same way we do.

as the Bible tells us

John Gray, in *Men Are From Mars, Women Are From Venus*, agrees with this perspective. He finds that many women "make the mistake of thinking they don't have to ask for support. Because they intuitively feel the needs of others and give whatever they can, they mistakenly expect men to do the same. . . . She assumes that if her partner loves her, he will offer his support and she won't have to ask. She may even purposefully not ask as a test to see if he really loves her." Gray finds that "this approach with men doesn't work. . . . Men are not instinctively motivated to offer their support; they need to be asked."[14] He believes that men do not want support unless they ask for it and generally consider it insulting to be given advice without having asked for it.

Penny told us that, while she wanted her husband's assistance, she unwittingly kept him from helping her by the way she presented her problem to him. She had gone to work on the other side of town, forgetting an important folder she needed for a presentation she was making that afternoon. Penny told us, "I called Doug, who works at home, to make sure the folder was there, and then we started discussing how I could get it in time.

"Doug offered to meet me halfway with the folder, since he was also working a deadline and didn't feel he could spare the time to drive all the way to my office and back. Without telling him I was nervous about being in that part of town by myself waiting for him, I simply refused his offer and said I'd come home to get it. I could tell I hurt his feelings, so I paused for a moment, then told him that I was afraid of going downtown, possibly getting there before he did, and parking on those streets alone. Once he understood that I wasn't rejecting his attempt to help me but was genuinely fearful about the solution he had offered, his whole demeanor changed. He said he'd call me right back, and he arranged for us to meet at the office of a mutual friend so that I'd have somewhere safe to stay in case I arrived before he did."

Like Penny, we've found that most of the time the men in our lives are eager to contribute solutions, once we've clearly communicated the problems. They seem especially willing to carry out solutions they have suggested. One woman, married for twenty-five years, finds that if you want something done, "you always let the man think it's his idea, whether it's his idea or not. You plant the seeds in him and let him come up with it later, like when I suggested to William that he put his den in the basement. He thought I was out of my mind, but a few months later he said, 'You know, I thought about that, honey, and I think it's a great idea, the sooner the better.'"

When a man loves a woman, he is motivated to make her happy. But he can only do so when she is clear about what she needs and wants. If we want help with a problem and not simply empathy we need to say so. Therefore, ladies, speak up and then watch them do what many of them do best—create solutions. Sounds good to us.

Sex

*Men make love more intensely at twenty,
but make love better, however, at thirty.*

—CATHERINE II OF RUSSIA

What Women Say About Men

Sex is one of the primary reasons men and women are supposed to be together, right? Our biological job is to reproduce our species. Yet we humans have made sex quite complicated. Little else fascinates, repels, attracts, or incites strong opinions or misunderstandings from both men and women as much as the subject of sex does. When to have it, with whom, where, and how often have all become issues, not to mention all of the religious, moral, social, and relationship issues that revolve around this — we must admit — rather odd physical act.

When sex is involved, every other issue in a relationship is affected. To make matters more difficult, men and women seem to have differences of opinion about sex — among other things, what does sexual union mean for a relationship? And, worse, we have been discouraged from talking about the subject for hundreds of years.

It is a wonder any children have been born at all! Nevertheless, we will address here some of the issues that women raised when they talked about one of the most sensitive topics of all.

In Bed

*My mother said it was simple to keep a man, you must be a
maid in the living room, a cook in the kitchen and a whore in
the bedroom. I said I'd hire the other two
and take care of the bedroom bit.*

—JERRY HALL

Untamed Tongues

Perhaps nowhere are differences between men's and women's perceptions more noticeable than in the area of sex and what meaning it has to the two parties.

Hope, a therapist in her midthirties, believes that if she hadn't recognized that her husband of thirteen years was "wired" differently than she, her marriage might not have lasted this long. She said that she believes that women need to be emotionally connected up in order to want to have sex, whereas men need to make a sexual connection in order to get back in touch with their more vulnerable, more feeling sides. She told us, "If I'm thinking that Bart is just a horny animal and all he wants to do is have sex, that doesn't make me want to get close to him. Especially if that's not where I'm at. But if I cross-reference in my mind that he really wants to be emotionally connected to me but he comes at it from a different direction, I can come out of my space and make a sexual connection first. I'm willing to do this because I know it's a surefire bet that if I do, he's going to get all touchy-feely, warm, and emotional. Then a lot of the really good emotional stuff happens after that point."

This does not mean that Hope thinks the woman should do all the adjusting. Bart also respects their differences and has learned how to relate better to his wife. Hope smiles when she says, "He's gotten very good at saying all the right emotional stuff, knowing that it's a surefire way to get laid." Perhaps that's what is meant by the phrase "enlightened self-interest." The important thing is that Hope and Bart have figured out ways to meet both their needs, in spite of their differences.

One woman told us that she was at a shower for a young woman about to be married, and as women offered advice for a good start in marriage, the eighty-something grandmother of the bride-to-be offered: "Always make mad passionate love with your husband when he wants you to." Although this is decidedly pre-feminist movement thinking, there is an element of truth. If sex is as important to him as talking is to you, then perhaps we should try to satisfy both our needs, and as long as sex is loving and nonabusive, it may remove some barriers and open the way to deal with more difficult issues.

When we asked Judy, married for forty years, how her marriage has gotten better, she told us, "I realized that there really is a difference between men and women, especially in the way we relate to sex. I thought when my husband wanted sex, it was self-gratification. But now I see that it's his way of showing love to me. Many men don't know, were never taught by their fathers, to put bubble bath by her bathtub once in a while or buy her some nice lingerie and put it under her pillow. They were not taught those things, so their expression of love is through sex. Many women think they are just pigs, but that's a misunderstanding.

"Having been married all these years, I never said no to my husband. Probably we were married over thirty years before I really truly had a headache." She laughs, "I just felt that it was part of a man, part of his nature, something that a wife should be compassionate about. If he is not being abusive, and you are not being taken advantage of, then what is the point of saying no?"

While Judy's marriage rather closely fits the stereotypical view that men need intercourse and women need cuddling, we found a few women who wanted sex more frequently than their partners. A thirty-something poet named Phyllis told us about a new relationship, "I've finally found someone who needs lovemaking as much as I do! All my life I've been with men where I wanted it more than they. It's a relief to be with Tom."

We talked with many women who indicated that both they and their men have a need for both sexual expression and affection. Olivia, fifty and married for twenty-five years, finds that sex is very important in keeping her and her husband emotionally connected: "The sex drive is not there like it used to be, but it's there, and when I want it, I want it. I have friends, some older and some younger than me, who say they don't have any sex drive anymore. I can't imagine that—sex is just a bond between us, one that we both want. Not necessarily often, but it has to be there. You can drift apart—you do your thing and he does his—but sex really gets you back on the same track." Some women also indicated that needs may shift for all of us, men and women, as we get older. We may become more interested in touching and affection or simple physical contact than in intercourse, or vice versa, as we age.

Whatever the case, finding out what is important to ourselves and to our mates is crucial if we wish to avoid the misinterpretations and conflict that many couples face over the topic of sex. Now is the time to start practicing those communication skills we have read about earlier. And we have to give ourselves some time on this subject, as this may be one of the most difficult topics to discuss with each other. Start slowly; if either or both of you feel embarrassed to talk about something, perhaps you could put your thoughts about what is important for you in notes to each other. (But remember to destroy the notes before your children or mother-in-law finds them!) And, if possible, have some fun. Sex is already informal (most activities we perform naked are) and puts us in a vulnerable spot, so shed some humor on the subject!

How Do You Know You Are Ready?

Sex is never an emergency.

—ELAINE PIERSON

Book title

Rosa told us about her decision to have sex for the first time in her life, with the man who was to become her husband: "We were having our cocktails in his apartment facing the sunset. It was totally romantic, and so impulsively I responded to his overtures.

"Here I was, twenty-two, and I had never really been with anybody. I had done this business of looking people over and thinking no. I was very popular, but I always kept guys at arm's length. Then I decided I needed to know about this, and I tried seducing guys who were terrified. Good old Mitch—I was open to making love that night, and he just never questioned it. I said to him, 'Well, there's always a first time.' He blanched. He was astounded that it was my first time.

"When I got home that night, I stood before the mirror wondering if I looked any different. From then on, I looked at guys differently, able to envision their whole body. The whole thing was fascinating. To think back, to 1962, it was light-years away from today in terms of this kind of exploration and knowledge. We were so ignorant and so naive."

When we asked her how she knew that the time and

the person were right for her, she said, "Because I was ready. This was an experience I wanted to have. I felt very safe with him. He seemed like a very solid, good person, and I trusted him. I trusted him from the beginning."

Some women (and men), because of religious, moral, or social beliefs, do not believe that anyone should have a sexual relationship before marriage. As one sixty-five-year-old actress and mother of five told us, "Sex before marriage takes away the most important bond a man and a woman can possibly share, that once-in-a-lifetime, first-time giving of the very core of who you are! If you've had a previous sexual relationship and have then gone on to find 'Mr. Right,' sex may be wonderful, perhaps even more fulfilling than it was before, but there's always that part of you that will never be the same."

Other women can't imagine not knowing what a sexual relationship would be like with a potential husband until after the marriage. Their reasoning is that the sexual side of their relationship is a crucial part of their long-term union, as well as being revealing of the character of the man.

These are important considerations for every woman, and each of us has to weigh carefully what we want. The key here is that every woman may take all the time she needs to make up her own mind. We talked to many women who felt pressured into having sex with someone they cared for before they were ready in their own hearts and minds. One unfortunate result of sexual liberation is that now, although we are free to have sexual relationships outside of marriage without a lot of societal stigma, there is a lot of pressure the other way—many are considered "prudes" or "frigid" if they don't jump in bed at the earliest opportunity!

One woman told us, "I did not really have a moral problem with sex before marriage, but I recently had a relationship where I got sexually involved faster than I was comfortable with. Ultimately, I felt that hurt the relationship, not because he then thought I was loose, but because it made the relationship too intense right away. I just don't believe there is such a thing as casual sex, at least not for me. Sex intensifies the feelings, then I find I'm expecting more from the other person after that. We never had a relaxed chance to get to know each other.

"I learned my lesson. Now I am with a man who I respect and who I know respects me. When we first started dating, he was sexually interested in me, but I told him that I really was not in any hurry. I let him know that I was not going to explore sexually with him until I knew he was someone I could see being with for the long term. I knew that was not easy for him, but he respected it and he didn't push. That made me feel positively toward him, and we had the opportunity to get to know each other. When we finally did have sex months later, it was lovely—relaxed and loving. I was glad I waited."

If we have questions about the "right time" for us or just need some support in our decision about whether and when to begin a sexual relationship, we may find it helpful to talk to a close, discreet friend. Our friends cannot make our decisions for us, but sometimes it helps just to hear our own voices talking out loud to someone we trust. And our friends can help remind us of past mistakes or values that they know are important to us.

Similarly, if we see a friend who is struggling with a decision about whether to begin a sexual relationship with a man, we can offer our help to her in letting her talk. One woman said, "My friend was hinting that her new boyfriend wanted to go away with her for the weekend and all that that entails. I could tell she was a little anxious about it and seemed to feel a bit unsure about him and the relationship. I knew her pattern: she would get involved too quickly with a man, many times selling herself short and being with a man who didn't deserve her. Soon she would discover that he was not someone she wanted to be with, and then she would feel pressured to make that relationship work (usually at her psychic cost) because she was too invested in the relationship! It was a catch-22 situation.

"I usually try to be more subtle, but finally I blurted out, 'Take your time with this. If he cares about you, he is not going to go anywhere. When you know you are crazy about him, then go for it. But for now, you set the pace, and go by your instincts.' She actually did slow down and, consistent with her gut feeling, eventually decided the guy was not right for her. I was glad to see she didn't have so much invested, so she didn't hang on to the connection longer than she should and could leave without so much trauma to her."

Our close girlfriends can help us make important decisions about when and with whom, so rather than make a rushed decision, give yourself plenty of time to share your concerns (if you wish) and make your choice. After all, what's the rush?

Fears and Fantasies

It doesn't matter what you do in the bedroom as long as you don't do it in the street and frighten the horses.

—MRS. PATRICK CAMPBELL

The Duchess of Jermyn Street

Like many aspects of relationships between men and women, there is no right way to carry on our sexual lives with the men we love, with a couple of exceptions: no one should get hurt, and both parties need to want to participate in whatever is going on, whether that is covering the bed with rose petals, watching X-rated movies, role-playing, or whatever gets both of you excited. But finding out what excites both of you and keeps your sexual life active or satisfying may be difficult, as many men and women are shy about expressing what they like in bed.

Even people who feel they are sexually liberated may

have this problem, since we have been told or, more likely, we have received hints, throughout our lives that sex is not to be talked about or celebrated. So even though a man and a woman may begin their relationship feeling free and open with each other, as they stay together, ingrained teachings from our religion or our parents may start influencing our behavior. If we were raised in a traditional religious home, or if our parents did not have a solid sexual relationship, we may have learned that sex is dirty and that men and women who enjoy or initiate it are loose. Even though many of us know in our heads that is not true, our bodies may still hold the belief. Our fantasies may turn into fears or resistance to sexual contact.

Negative fantasies may also appear. Anxiety and fear about our attractiveness may emerge and make us hold back or feel self-conscious in bed, thereby limiting our mutual enjoyment. Granted, there may be a woman on the planet who has no preconceived notions, fantasies, or secret anxieties about sex . . . but she didn't show up in any of our interviews. The women we talked with acknowledged a variety of expectations, dreams, and insecurities related to their bodies, their sexual performance, and the quality of their relationships.

One woman told us, "It doesn't help feeling constantly compared to *Playboy* centerfolds. Although it may come as a surprise to you, I can't compete with those airbrushed beauties, and so at times I feel insecure about my attractiveness." After five years of marriage, and enjoying sex around three times a week, her husband initiated sex less and less. She said, "Eventually, we stopped having sex altogether. I started doubting myself, wondering what was wrong with me. I decided it was because I'd put on a few pounds and that my thighs were too fat. I didn't ask my husband what was going on. I was too embarrassed and too sure that it was because I was ugly."

She laughs, "Almost as abruptly as he lost interest in sex, he rediscovered it. As we were frolicking in bed one night, I asked him what had happened. He said, 'Oh, I didn't want to worry you, but things were really bad at the office. I nearly lost the business, but we've just landed a new contract and we're back on solid ground!' I realized then that personalizing his behavior, especially in the bedroom, only caused me unnecessary grief."

Sex is a great barometer. As the woman above indicated, a change in sexual interest does mean something, but that something may or may not have anything to do with our relationship. Researchers tell us that stress has a momentous effect on sexual desire. So if one of the parties has lost interest, he or she may simply need a rest! A solution as simple as a weekend away from everyday stresses may be just the ticket.

If any other problems are going on in the relationship, they will probably show up in our sex lives, too. The point is, we don't know what the problem is until we ask. Making up stories to tell ourselves will not help; we have to communicate with our partners to find out what is really going on.

Sex can conjure up not only deep insecurities, but also a variety of fantasies, real or out of this world. New-lywed Katie told us, "I thought having sex with my husband was going to be like it is in the movies—you know, with the waves pounding on the shore, fireworks popping overhead, birds singing, and violins playing. Sometimes it is. But a lot of the time it's just nice." She smiled as she said, "My husband would probably be of-fended by that word—*nice*—but that's how it is for me. Comfortable, right, solid."

Some fantasies may help us maintain sexual interest and variety over a long-term relationship. Other fanta-sies, such as what sex is supposed to be like or stories we tell ourselves about our attractiveness or our partner's interest in us, may need to be examined. If something is bothering us, we may need to talk to our men to find out what the real issue is. While it is impossible to not have expectations about sex, we need to be able to distinguish what is truly important to us. Although Katie's husband may not wish to think of sex with him as being "nice," it is satisfying to Katie! And while we may wish we looked like a swimsuit model, our men, if they value us as whole people, will not be expecting that standard.

Who Can I Talk to About This?

We rarely talk of sex the way men do, in terms of I've had this one, I've had that one. There's a friend I've known for nineteen years and all I've known of her private life is what I've heard from others.

—JEANNE MOREAU

The Quotable Woman

For many people, sex is a taboo subject. Some women cannot even talk about it with their husbands in a detailed way. How do we get comfortable enough with this subject to learn about it or improve our sexual relationship with our man? Nina, fifty-five, recalls how difficult it was to deal with the practical issues of sexuality when she was in her early twenties: "Back then you never talked about sex. I needed to buy a diaphragm but didn't know quite how to go about it. One friend of mine was sexually experienced, and she knew a doctor I could go to. It was one of my arty friends, not one of my sorority sisters or anybody I grew up with. It's weird to look back and think how in some ways things are hugely different, and in other ways they're not."

Thirty years later, information about birth control, pregnancy, and communicable disease is much more widely available. If you have questions about what is normal or what is gratifying, don't second-guess yourself. Plenty of material is available in the bookstore. But if you need to check out something specific and want to talk about it, just find someone safe. For some people that is a doctor, therapist, or health professional. For Margaret, a West Coast writer, it is one of her closest friends: "When I think about the advice my girlfriends and I give one another, a lot of it is about sex. I've gotten to the point with my girlfriends—and this has taken years to do—to talk openly, point by point, detail by detail, about sexual activity: 'Have you tried this? How did you like it?' It creates a wonderful closeness, and it's become part of my feminist commitment, to be open with my girlfriends about our sexual selves. I mean, why should we leave this part out?

"One of my best girlfriends and I took a weekend trip to the Sierras last summer. It was a sort of pajama party. We were both beginning new relationships that at the time we were excited about. We were talking about sex nonstop the whole weekend.

"We hadn't talked about it very much before, but over that weekend we really opened up. We were just comparing notes. For me the motivating question was, 'Am I normal? Am I like everyone else, is everyone else like me?' It was a reality check, and it was very reassuring.

"At one point I told my girlfriend, 'Sometimes it's like their bodies are so different from ours. I know what to do with ours, but what do I do next with theirs?' She looked at me and said, 'Well, when I'm making love, and feel like that, do you know what I do? I just ask him,

"What would you like now?" I thought, "Well of course, that's exactly what I would want my boyfriend to ask me! Why wouldn't I do exactly the same thing?"

However, for many women, the topic of sex is still taboo. Many expressed that they had friends with whom they could talk about sex but that with many other friends the discussion would be uncomfortable.

Perhaps this is partly because women may feel disloyal about talking about intimate details with someone who isn't their mate. As we discussed before, men may feel a sense of betrayal if their wives and girlfriends share information about their sexual relationship with someone else. We feel that if our conversations are with someone who is absolutely trustworthy, and we are being respectful and discreet, then maybe we can learn something about men that we didn't know before and can gain help if there is a problem. Then we are not betraying our men but are trying to understand the complexities of our own bodies and our relationships.

What Makes a Good Lover?

What you think is the heart may well be another organ.

—JEANETTE WINTERSON

The Wit and Wisdom of Women

What makes a good lover? We asked women and found that sexual technique was not very high on the list. What was mentioned most often was a man's ability to be emotionally present, to be aware of the woman's needs and not interested simply in fulfilling his own. The word that came up over and over was *empathy*.

Stacy says, "I have one girlfriend who is starting out on the dating scene again, and she asked me what I thought made a good lover. My response was to look for an empathetic person, someone who has the ability to observe, to be in touch with what you're feeling. That's what makes me a good lover to somebody else and what makes him a good lover to me—the ability to get inside another person's skin and experience their experiences. Anybody who has that ability is fun to be in bed with— and everywhere else with! My girlfriend said 'Oh!' and thought back through the relationships she had before and realized that no man she had been with had had that quality. It was a new concept to her."

Jeff, a computer analyst in San Francisco, created a romantic experience when he planned his and Reva's first-anniversary celebration together. Reva, a designer, related to us: "He made me a candlelight dinner on the night before our anniversary. When we finished eating, he gave me this little gift certificate he had done up on his computer that said, 'A night for two in honor of our anniversary' at a hotel. While I thought it would be fun, I have to admit that I was a bit disappointed in his budget-type hotel choice.

"The next day we went to the city and spent the whole day wandering around Golden Gate Park and the Japanese Tea Gardens. When it was time to go to the hotel, we drove and drove, and finally pulled into the Fairmont Hotel, one of the finest hotels in San Francisco. I thought, 'Oh, my god.' I was so surprised I couldn't even collect my thoughts enough to get out of the car. He was very pleased at my reaction and pulled out another certificate that he had made up that said we were going to the Fairmont. He had totally tricked me. So we spent the night at the Fairmont. It was just so wonderful. That place is so beautiful and very romantic."

Since sexual enjoyment and romance are many times so closely linked for women, we encourage any man who might be skimming this book for helpful hints to follow Jeff's example or that of Sean, Nora's husband. Nora told us that when it comes to being romantic, Sean's thoughtful actions were not necessarily sexual: "He is a very, very romantic man. When the children were young, he would call me up and say, 'I want you to wear this. I have hired a baby-sitter,' and so forth. He didn't leave any of those arrangements for me to make, he did that. When the girls were a little older, I went away to camp with them, and when we got home, he had bought all new sheets for the bed and had left me a little love note, and that sort of thing. He doesn't buy me big stuff — so many men think they are supposed to buy big stuff — but instead he continually brings home little stuff that means 'I love you.' Women think that romance is about a weekend. That's not it at all; romance is when they are thinking about you all the time."

A common denominator among all of the things that women found romantic was the knowledge that their men were taking initiative, without the women's input, to do something positive for the relationship. As one woman summed it up, "It's romantic when you know they are thinking about you when you're not there. For instance, I like hearing about things he's said to other people about me." We all love to know we are being thought of in a loving way. The price tag, if any, doesn't matter at all. For instance, some of the things woman found romantic were homemade cards, poems, fixing something in the woman's house without being asked, and mowing the lawn. One woman found it extremely romantic that her fiancé, unbeknownst to her, signed her up for a subscription to *Modern Bride*.

If we are lucky, the men we are with already know how to be romantic. And therefore how to be good lovers. But some may need some help. Don't give up on your man if he is one of these! A lot of men may feel pressure because they believe that they have to make a grand gesture or they fear doing the wrong thing. So they may just need a little gentle instruction. We can get the ball rolling by showing them how pleasing it is to be thought of when the other person is not around, as well as how easy it is. Sneaking love notes into his briefcase, suitcase, or gym bag or surprising him with his favorite meal can help grease the romance wheel. If we need some ideas, we can ask our friends how they show their men that they care about them. Our friends, if they are also on good terms with our boyfriends or husbands, can also do their part by providing some helpful hints as to what we would like.

Besides providing examples to our men, we can also encourage more romantic behavior by being appreciative of whatever romantic things they do now. Even the smallest gesture deserves some notice and appreciation. And it may lead them to delight us again in some way in the future. If we are happy and enthusiastic when our man washes our car for us or brings us flowers, he will remember that. Keep in mind the Golden Rule, because it applies to romance, too: If we want our partners to think about us when we are not around, to do something for us that they think we would like, and to appreciate what we do for them, we need to start doing the same.

Friends and Lovers

I have always detested the belief that sex is the chief bond between man and woman. Friendship is far more human.

—AGNES SMEDLEY

Battle Hymn of China

Gone are the days where the workplace was a male arena and home was the domain of the female. As men and women both have lives in the home and outside world, we're all working with, and possibly making friends with, members of the opposite sex. These friendships can place a lot of strain on dating relationships and marriages. One twenty-four-year-old told us, "When we were first dating, Rick had this woman friend in college who he was really close friends with and who I felt really threatened by. They had known each other longer than I had known him, and so whenever they would hang out together, I always freaked out, constantly asking him, 'How do you really feel about her?'

"He didn't understand how I could be upset about it since, in his mind, she was just a friend. Even when I would tell him that his lack of understanding hurt my feelings, he had the hardest time shifting from his point of view to see things from my perspective. And even now, five years later, it still is a challenge for him. One of the things we argue about the most is that he has a hard time putting himself in other people's shoes."

Asked whether they have come up with a way to deal with this, she responded that time and many discussions were the keys to helping him understand how others feel: "He's gotten better. After many arguments about this, he at least can say, 'I can understand and acknowledge that you might feel this way, but I just don't understand it for myself.' He's come a long way from, 'Well, if I don't feel that way, how could I understand it if you do?'"

So even when an outside friendship is nothing to worry about, according to our partners, there may be conflicts, and one option is to talk about them. Another option is to take steps to develop a friendship with the other person—whether this is a friendship or something more will become clear very quickly. If he is comfortable with our doing that, we can be pretty sure that nothing more than a friendship is going on here.

Conversely, if he is uncomfortable with our befriending his friend, it does not necessarily mean that he is a having an affair with her. She may be someone that he has relationship discussions with, in which case he will probably be afraid that it is only a matter of time before she discloses what he has said to her about the relationship. The most obvious course, and the easiest one, is to tell him that getting to know this woman better is important. We can assure him that we are not trying to invade the friendship. We would establish a relationship with his male friends, wouldn't we? So we should do the same with friends who are women.

The understandable fear is that a friendship with another woman is just a courtship disguised as an innocent friendship. The situation is more complicated when our man is friends with a woman whom we know to be attracted to him sexually. One woman, twenty-six, found that she could not make her boyfriend of five years understand that his friendship with another woman made her feel jealous and angry. As she told us, "They met at a garage sale that was at our apartment. Since then she has professed her fascination with and crush on Don. He says that they've 'had it out'; that she knows that Don and I have a very strong relationship and he has no feelings for her, et cetera, et cetera. But I am somehow overwhelmed with anger, jealousy, extreme emotion, every time he goes and has coffee with her. She sends him cards all the time.

"Up until a few months ago he couldn't quite understand how I felt. For his birthday she invited Don to go to dinner at a restaurant at which the man that she's currently seeing is a waiter. Don came home from that and said, 'You know, it was a little awkward. It was sort of weird. I kept thinking about what her boyfriend was thinking while I was sitting there with her having dinner.' And I said, 'Oh, you thought he might feel awkward?' And it was just like this amazing watershed to him. 'Oh.' He finally put himself in my situation and realized, yeah, it might be awkward. Or yeah, of course there's nothing going on, but the partner can just feel bad. Even if there's

176

not a rational or logical reason for a person to feel a certain way, the person simply *feels*."

Okay, so now we come to a different problem—someone who is trying to interfere with a romantic relationship. We think you have a right to get involved, even if she or he is your mate's friend. In this situation, even if the man really is not interested, a woman has a right to be uncomfortable. There's also a problem if her discomfort doesn't seem to bother him. At worst, he is trying to make her jealous; at best, he is being naive and enjoying the attention (who doesn't love to be adored?). Ultimatums—"I'm leaving you unless you stop meeting that woman."—don't work unless we are willing to act on them. So the best course of action is to calmly tell him that this behavior is disrespectful and to set some guidelines around what is acceptable. We may also decide to reevaluate how much we want to be with someone who does not respect our feelings.

Now, what about former boyfriends who are now friends? (Whew, life can be complicated for those of us who have dated for most of our lives.) Some couples have managed to salvage a lovely and supportive friendship out of a less-than-successful romantic relationship. To use an old phrase, they've made "a silk purse out of a sow's ear."

One forty-something writer found that these "mixed relationships" have their own appeal: "I like doing both friendships and sexual relationships. The best of all possible worlds is that if I have a little romance with some-body and then both of us decide mutually that it's not what we want, we can become friends after that. It broad-ens my horizons to see what the world looks like through the eyes of somebody who has had some significantly different experiences than I have and who's been accul-turated to take on drastically different roles than I have."

Some women do not feel that way; they agree with Harry in *When Harry Met Sally* that men and women can-not be friends. Other women feel that you cannot go back to a friendship after a sexual relationship, regardless of the degree of intimacy. We think it is probably true that a friendship between a man and a woman, especially if they have been lovers, may have different characteris-tics than a friendship between two women. So it is up to us whether we want to be friends with a former lover. If he treated his lover badly, without respect, then he is probably not going to make a good friend, either. But if he was honorable, and the relationship was a caring one, then there may be a friendship in the making. If we are not sure, our friends' feelings about an ex may be a guide. A close girlfriend can give us a perspective on whether a former boyfriend is "friendworthy," whether he would be loyal, truthful, and supportive—whether in short, he would exhibit the qualities we look for in our girlfriends.

But most people find that it is at best awkward and often upsetting to consider each other friends until both have become involved with other people. Our personal experience is that an important romantic relationship is not really over until the next one begins.

And then there is the new person to consider. How comfortable will he be with the old boyfriend still in the picture? One woman uses the "naked rule"—if someone has seen you naked, then your new boyfriend or husband has the right to rule that person out of your social life (that goes for his old girlfriends as well). A black-and-white rule can be a place to start, with appropriate exceptions made after discussion and agreement. One exemption would be exspouses with whom a partner shares in the raising of children. Other exceptions may be people who were ex's in the distant past; with hope, everyone has moved on after a few years.

What Happens When the Children Come?

Now the thing about having a baby—and I can't be the first person to have noticed this—is that thereafter you have *it.*

—JEAN KERR

Please Don't Eat the Daisies

How to prepare for children? Is there any way to prepare for an earthquake that is a 8.5 on the Richter scale? We cannot think of many other circumstances in which your relationship can be changed so quickly.

Women talked about the first obvious change: less sex. Ursula, who has three small children, expounded: "When my husband found out that our friend Linda was pregnant, his first thought was not 'Oh, I'm happy that they're having the baby that they've really wanted.' His first thought was, 'So that means that Richard got laid last month, and I probably didn't.' My response to that is, 'Excuse me, I've had three kids crawling all over me eighteen hours a day for a year and a half, I'm sorry I'm not really into having sex! I would rather be sleeping than having sex, let's just be straight about it.'"

This change extends to other aspects of the relationship. As she continued, "I do not nurture him anymore. Now I'm much more likely to say, 'You're a big boy, take care of yourself.' It's not just sex, it's making him a cup of coffee, giving him a backrub, whatever. If it's nurturing, I simply don't have the strength at this time in our marriage to give that to him. I did before, and I hope I will later, but not now."

Ursula's friend Joan, who has her first child, a newborn, agrees: "What is interesting to me as a new mom is that my husband is really worried about whether I like him. He is constantly asking me. I think it's because he doesn't get the kind of nurturing that he used to get. I don't think for a minute about whether he likes me, because I'm too busy wondering if my nine-week-old likes me. That is also probably a change in our sex life, too. I don't really worry about whether he is getting enough sex. At this point I'm too focused on whether I'm getting enough sleep."

You also lose that connection time, however and whenever you smooth out the kinks in the relationship that arise in the normal course of life. As Gina, a mother of three noted, "It's just that the time for working on the relationship, such as Sunday morning in bed reading the paper, is not there, so you really have to rely on the past and just try to stay solid. I think that what happens to me a lot is that I don't want to ruin the little time we have together by bringing up issues that I have, so I stuff them. Then they blow up. It's because we used to be able to air everything because we would spend so much time together and we had the room; now I just feel like, he works so hard, I work so hard, we've got the kids, we found these two hours to go out with a sitter, there's no way I'm going to bring up that he left a plate of food out. But you know what? I'm annoyed about it, and at some point it comes out. So that's been hard for us, taking care of the little odds and ends."

Asked if she had found any way to deal with that problem, Gina said, "I think it is really important, even if it's a five-minute call at work, to just chitchat here and there and try to catch up with each other. Not that you have to sit down and have a meaningful conversation, but at some point in the day it helps just to check in, or maybe you just touch each other in a warm way or show each other that you have thought about each other. Try not to let the day go without making some kind of contact, not that it has to be beautiful or meaningful, but some sort of connection."

A chat every day probably is not as satisfying as the sex that the two of you used to share, but it may be the best you can do in an exhausting time. "Do the best you can" seems to be the watchword when the chaos of children is added to the already busy lives of two people.

While the very real facts of sleep deprivation and chore expansion can have deleterious effects on any couple, the effects of the baby can bring out sides of the two people not before known and can bind them together in ways that may be surprising. Laurine described it this way: "I remember when I gave birth to our son, our first baby. My husband, who does not wax poetic, ever, was waxing poetic about how we had finally achieved what we were here on the earth to do. This was a whole side of him I had never seen or heard. . . . Well, there I was still groggy with the effect of the drugs, thinking 'I wish I was here for this experience. I really want to hear what he says.' But through my fog, what I recall was that in his mind, we are truly here to couple, to bear children and be a family, and that is the paramount role that we as humans have to play."

Some women said they never knew that for their husbands, having and raising children was a significant motivator in choosing them as wives. Laurine continued to learn about her husband after their first child was born:

for him, having children was "the source of all happiness and completeness. What my husband was looking for in a woman was one who would help be that partner in raising children but not necessarily a partner in fun. Fun was kind of a bonus — 'oh, gosh, we can have fun, too' — but truly being the partner in the family was most important. Very — I don't want to say — fifties, because our relationship is not sexist in that way, but a very traditional framework, which is interesting to me. The more men that I have become closer with, the more I'm realizing that having a family really seems to be a motivator for them."

Laurine's friend Gina smiled when she recalled their first baby: "My husband said to me, 'I knew you'd make good babies because of the way your body was shaped.' I told him, 'I never knew that you had thought about that.' Of course what he was saying is, 'You've got those big old hips,' but I never knew he had thought about it in that way. I thought I was the one who was more interested in a family. And that surprised me."

Of course, some men are clear about their desire for children. As Ursula said, "My husband was always right out there, wanting kids from the beginning." She laughed. "He was talking about the second one when we were at the hospital with our first."

Our girlfriends can play a vital role in our having children, such as sharing their practical wisdom on diaper changing, when to call the doctor, or talking to us on the phone in the middle of the day just so we can hear an adult voice. Special girlfriends may even volunteer (or be persuaded through bribes of some sort) to watch your children so that you and your husband can have some time to yourselves. We doubt that any mother can give what her children need unless she has been nurtured herself, so we encourage you to call on your girlfriends to give a little extra to you, especially when your children are young.

Expecting or Just High Expectations?

We were raised with the idea that we had limitless chances and we got very shocked to learn that wasn't the case.

—LINDA RONSTADT

Knight-Ridder Newspapers

The decision to have a child together is a momentous, exciting one. Expectations are high, and once the decision is made, everyone is eager to get the show on the road, and find the positive pregnancy test. But many people find themselves disappointed after a period of time that the desired result has not been reached. Now you face fertility tests to determine if the two of you are capable of conceiving a child. Talk about scary—not only are you trying to find out if you can conceive a child, which may be an important goal for your marriage, but both of you are facing the expectations our society has about what makes a "real man" or a "true woman."

One hears all too many jokes about men who "fire blanks." Unfortunately, men are made to feel less of a man if they have a health problem of "weak" or "insufficient" sperm. If a man cannot impregnate a woman, so the old thinking goes, he is less of a man. What a burden! Perhaps because of the dread of finding this out, many men, in the situation of not being able to conceive with their wives, assume they are not the problem. Gloria told us about two couples she knew, both trying to get pregnant, both facing the fact that neither wife was conceiving. She told us, "These two couples don't know each other, and yet they are handling the prospect of infertility similarly—the woman is getting tested first. The husbands are resisting going to the doctor and want their wives to get checked out before they go through any tests. Maybe it's a macho thing or fearing that they are inadequate in some way. I just think it's interesting that the women are willing to go through the process first, less anxious about what it says about them as women, than are their husbands."

Infertility is a human affliction, and the chance that a man or a woman will suffer from it is not insignificant. According to the *San Francisco Chronicle*, "about fifteen percent of American couples have trouble conceiving."[15] What is unfortunate is that we as a society and, consequently, we as individuals frequently assign other meanings to something that is simply a health problem. And each individual will react differently to the problem. A woman may not understand why her husband is so upset that his sperm count is low. A man may not understand why a woman is so defensive about not being able to conceive. Expect that people will react differently to the same circumstances and for different reasons. All you can do as a mate is to encourage your husband or wife to get medical attention to rule out any illness, and then be as understanding and accepting of the other's feelings as possible, not trying to talk them out of feeling that way.

Also know that there are other ways to be "potent" in this world. There are technological ways to deal with potency and infertility, although they may be painful, emotional trying, and expensive as well. Alternatively, if the problem is conceiving a child, there are thousands of children out there who need love *now*. If you and your mate are having difficulty, and you really feel that you have a lot to offer as parents, you may want to consider adoption. One woman, a successful writer who has been with the man of her dreams for three years, told us she was not ready for motherhood: "If we have children I think it will be through adoption or another method. I'm not ready and I'm forty-two. When I was a young girl I thought I would probably be someone who adopts later in life. Some odd child will come to us, I feel, that really needs someone. He or she will be eight years old and we will be great parents in that regard. Also, I feel like my creative expressions are my children in a lot of ways. There has been a lot of fulfillment for me there. I don't know that I am ready to alter that."

Finally, we know many individuals and couples who have never had children and yet who have "mothered" and "fathered" many people in their lives. We all probably have someone in our lives to whom we have looked up to and have gone to for advice, men and women who are childless but who may have been able to help us with problems about which we could not turn to a parent or to our peers. Sometimes young people simply need a perspective from someone who has had a different experience than that of their parents.

In *It Takes a Village*, Hillary Rodham Clinton encourages us as a nation to pull together to bring up our country's collective children. As women, most of us have probably already helped with the raising of a child, either a younger sibling or, as adults, the children of our friends. Both of the authors are "aunties" to many of their girl-friends' children. Perhaps if you are childless and are going to stay that way, you are destined to be one of these "community parents," one who helps our friends when needed and who contributes to many lives, not just those of your own children.

Can He Be Trusted?

How desperately we wish to maintain our trust in those we love!
In the face of everything, we try to find reasons to trust.
Because losing faith is worse than falling out of love.

—SONIA JOHNSON

From Housewife to Heretic

While we might pride ourselves on being modern, informed women who have risen above sexist stereotypes, most of us fall prey to assuming "the worst" about men when we feel insecure or frightened. Certainly entrusting your heart and body to a man can be scary, and it's important to know if the man you've chosen is, in fact, trustworthy.

How can we know if the man we love is trustworthy? Author A. Justin Sterling in his book, *What Really Works with Men*, advises women to "listen carefully to men's actions because men are constantly communicating with you on that channel. Through their actions, they communicate their true thoughts, feelings, fears and expectations. What you see is what you get."[16]

Even when men demonstrate an ability to be trustworthy, we might have trouble putting our emotional weight down on what we see. The biggest challenge for Yvonne is to get to know her husband, Manny, "as a person. When I get frightened, I say to him, 'Oh, you're just like all those other men. You're going to be irresponsible. You won't stay faithful to our marriage vows.' But when I look at who he really is, the man I've consistently seen him to be, I realize that I'm being unfair to him. I tend to group all men together as being interested only in themselves. Not all men fall into the stereotypes. There are a lot of men who are growing beyond the adolescent male who makes all of his decisions from his pants. My husband is one of those men."

Corinna, a writer and artist, says that she has "been paying a lot of attention over the past few years to reverse sexism. I have a lot of men in my life that are wonderful and that are humanists, feminists, very tuned into women's issues. They are the ones pointing out to me, 'Hey, I'm not like that stereotype, I don't say things like that.' I was so angry with men for so long that I just found example after example of how they were 'bad' and all their ways were 'bad.' I finally had to start looking at how I was 'bad.'" Corinna makes an excellent point. Both genders are capable of betrayal and both can prove trust-worthy.

When trust is broken in a relationship, specifically through infidelity, it can feel like the whole world has been turned upside down. As Nora Ephron writes in *Heartburn*, "The infidelity itself is small potatoes compared to the low level brain damage that results when a whole chunk of your life turns out to have been completely different from what you thought it was. It becomes impossible to look back on anything that's happened . . .

without wondering what was really going on."[17]

If we are in a monogamous relationship, we *hate* the thought of our man having a romantic or sexual relationship with another woman. How can you avoid an affair? One woman had this to say: "By staying on the same track, not going your separate ways."

One woman we spoke to felt that an affair usually signals a bad rift in the relationship. "If one of the partners went to the length of actually having sex with someone else, it means that the original relationship may have some pretty serious problems. In the kind of relationship I'm looking for, you'd stay up-to-date with the other person enough so that you would talk about the fact that you were attracted to someone else. You would explore inside yourself and perhaps even with your partner, asking, 'What does this attraction say about what I'm looking for?' 'What does it say about what I'm not getting here?' 'Is it possible to get that with you?' So, a lot of those steps of communication and heart-to-heart conversation would take place before the step is taken of actually getting involved with someone."

This is good advice for prevention. But what about if you have been cheated on? You know the sense of breathlessness and dizziness you feel upon finding out, as if someone just delivered a blow to your stomach, followed by feelings of rage — "How could he do this to me? to us?" — interspersed with overwhelming sadness — "It is over, how can we ever go back?" — and insecurity —

"What is wrong with me? Did I drive him away?" And if someone in the relationship has been sleeping around, there is the additional upsetting knowledge that you are now subject to the risk of a sexually transmitted disease.

Take care of yourself by getting tested for any physical maladies. Then decide what you have to do to take care of yourself emotionally. Can you live with this breach of trust? Ask yourself honestly if there is any good that can come from this experience.

If an affair happens, the relationship probably won't ever be the same. But a crisis such as an affair can also provide an opportunity for deepening the relationship. Although it will take a long time to build up trust in the other person, an affair can bring a lot of seemingly unrelated problems to light. As Christine explained, "If an affair actually happened, obviously there would be a serious jolt to the trust level, and then it would become a problem to work through—finding out where the hurt was, what was missing, what the person was looking for. Of course, it is anybody's guess whether the two people are going to choose to be that honest with each other."

If they can be that honest with each other, maybe good things will result. Issues that have been simmering under the surface of a seemingly happy marriage will come immediately to the surface. To apply the Nietzsche quote to relationships: "What doesn't kill us will make us stronger."

Asked whether a marriage or monogamous relationship can survive an affair, one woman, married twenty-five years, had this to say: "I think it can recover, but I don't think it ever can be the same. There will always be a little separation there. If it's a one-time fling, I think that it can survive it. I suspect, although my sister never said so, that her husband, whom I really like, had an affair, and they separated for over a year. She said he'll never hurt her like that again. But their marriage has survived and it is very good—they're very close, their marriage is wonderful and they have four wonderful children. He's grown up, I think he was in his early twenties when it happened. It's been about twenty-five years ago. So I think it can survive, but I think it takes a lot of work."

When we spoke with a group of thirty-something women, most of whom are married, as to whether they thought their marriages could survive an affair, they also agreed that it depended on the characteristics of the affair and the intensity of the violation of trust. Beth, married ten years, told us, "It depends on the type of infidelity. If I was to go out and have a one-night stand and just get my 'ya-yas,' I think our marriage would survive. If Griffin was to go out and get his ya-yas, which is inconceivable to me, because I don't think it's in his nature—I'm much more the one who would do that—I think our marriage would survive. But getting intimate? Sex is one thing, but the intimacy issue—that's a whole different thing."

Her friend April agreed that there were different degrees of betrayal: "If your husband is in love with someone else, there's so much more of a general sense of betrayal. I mean, you can have sex and it can be meaningless, but to have your husband be in love with someone else, genuinely caring about someone else, would be like taking something that belonged solely to you and giving it to someone else."

Beth added, "For example, if he was behaving in ways that he wouldn't behave with me, I would feel like, 'Hey, that's what I deserve.' That would be tough. But a one-night stand, shoot. I'll be surprised if I don't have a one-night stand in the next sixty years. I'll be surprised if he doesn't. How can you not? It belies anthropology, but god forbid, either one of us has anything beyond that."

All the women of that particular group of friends agreed that it was not so much the sexual act with another woman that was such a betrayal but the fact that there was the plan to betray and the amount of dishonesty that a long-term affair required. As April described, "I think there are ebbs and flows in every relationship, and sometimes a one-night stand happens because all of the details are right. I think it could happen to both parties at different times, but most of the time all of the details aren't right. If all of a sudden all the circumstances were right, and one of us succumbed, then it would be, 'Oh my god, what did I do?' and the person would never repeat it again. For me to have a long-term affair means

I am choosing to do it. That's what I think a relationship couldn't take."

Cheryl agreed, "For me it just comes down to the dishonesty. How can you have a long-term affair with somebody else without lying to your spouse again and again and again and again? The fact that the sex and intimacy were going on with someone else would be an incredible betrayal, but the fact that my husband looked in my face and lied to me again and again and again might ultimately be the most painful."

Joan, married for five years, added, "I think people say that infidelity means something is wrong with the relationship, and I think that that is much more true of a relationship that involves any sort of emotional attachment than it is of a one-night stand. A one-night stand may or may not mean there is a problem in the relationship." When we asked if then she could forgive her husband for a one-night stand, she just smiled and said, "Not as far as he knows."

Women who have gotten involved with married men suffer as well, often in retrospect. We talked to one woman who was involved with a married man when she was very young: "At the time, I just thought having an affair made sense because I didn't want someone who would make too many demands on me. I wanted to have other lovers, too. So here was someone who was exciting. I didn't want to break up their marriage. I was very clear about that. I had no awareness of how harmful this could be. Maybe because now I feel ashamed, I feel remorse, I feel very sad. It was wrong."

When asked how she deals with that experience now, many years later, she replied, "I think with a lot of self-forgiveness and acceptance of who I was then and realizing I'm not that person now. I would not ever make a choice like that again. I made a terrible mistake. The experience is something that is part of me, and I live with it. I no longer feel that I'm a terrible person."

Asked how she would react if a young woman said she was thinking about having an affair with a married man, she laughed and replied, "Young women have asked me that, and I am pretty ruthless. I say, 'What the hell are you doing?' Some have been very disturbed and have said to me, 'I happen to know that you had a relationship with a married man, so who are you to now say that?'

"I respond with, 'That's exactly why I can say it.' I ask them, 'What are you doing and why? Describe to me why you think that this is a good decision.' Almost always they will say, 'I know it's not right' or 'I know it's no good, but I love him so much.' My response to that is, 'I don't know if that's love. I don't know if you are being self-loving.' If they are asking for my advice, I have the right to say, 'I don't agree with what you are doing. You have your right to have an affair with a married man, there's no question about that. But you have come to me and told me this story, so I need to say to you, 'I believe it is wrong; I believe you are harming yourself and the other person, and I believe it's all very bad.'"

If one of our friends comes to us with news that she is having an affair with a married man or with a man outside of her own marriage, we may wish to ask her the same questions: Why is she doing it? Why is it a good idea to her? Not only is it harmful to the marriage and to the third party involved in the affair, there is the old adage of "Be careful of what you wish for." Even if you think this is the love of your life, the unfortunate realization of every woman involved in an affair is if that man has an affair once, then he is capable of doing it again.

And if a girlfriend comes to us with the upsetting knowledge that her husband is the one having an affair, we can support her by listening and offering our help in any way we can. Bernie, whose first marriage ended when she learned of her husband's infidelity, told us about the surprising but helpful long-term advice that she received from her friend Wanda: "She said three things to me. One, that indulging in spite would only diminish my recovery; two, that fear of the future was the most difficult to deal with; and three, that the future held whatever wonders I would allow it to. It was not quite the 'hang the jerk' speech I'd hoped for."

Since then, Bernie has embarked on a fascinating career and a second marriage, which has lasted for twelve years. "Wanda is still my best counsel. Over the years since my divorce, I've shared with many people in my circumstances and given them Wanda's advice. The fastest way to becoming whole again is forgiveness, for ourselves and the offender." She can say this truthfully because she lives it daily.

Could He Be Gay?

Should I consider [gay men] misogynists for their aversion? Or should I, as I do, love them because they're my dear friends and understand me better than a thousand straight men?

—CYNTHIA HEIMEL

Get Your Tongue Out of My Mouth, I'm Kissing You Good-bye!

Sometimes a woman may start to feel that there is something fundamentally wrong in her relationship with a boyfriend or husband—noticing indications that he is basically more interested in men than women. And as society becomes more accepting of homosexuality, more men and women are leaving their heterosexual relationships and openly acknowledging they are gay. Finding out your husband or boyfriend is gay can feel very similar to finding out he has had an affair—only the feelings are more complicated as the object of his desire is not another woman, but another man.

Annie told us how her eight-year marriage ended after her husband told her he was seeing his best friend, a man who had spent a great deal of time at their home. She said, "It took my breath away, realizing that he had been sleeping with this guy who I thought was our friend, not his lover. For a week I was in a stupor, and then I came to my senses and moved out. Even though I was in a lot of pain, it was also a relief. I could start telling my friends the truth about our marriage.

"Looking back, there were indications that something was wrong. We were good friends, but there wasn't much of a sexual charge between us. He even told me a couple of weeks before the wedding that he struggled with gay feelings, but he was in therapy and assured me that he would never act on those feelings. But on the honeymoon I knew it was a mistake. He didn't desire me the way a straight man would — and instead of owning it, he blamed me. He told me all these things were wrong with my body. By the time the marriage ended, I'd lost all sense of myself as a woman."

Since sex is such a private issue, often women like Annie feel unable to talk to their girlfriends about what is troubling them. She told us, "My friends could tell something was wrong, so I pulled back from them. I'd only see them in short intervals so that I could fake being happily married. My husband told me not to talk about his problem, not to betray him. So I was silent. That was the hardest part — losing contact with my girlfriends. But once he told me about the affair, I felt free to tell the truth. That has been very healing for me."

A woman in Annie's situation may have a variety of responses. She may feel confused as to her responsibility for the situation—was it her fault? Was she not a good enough mate? She may even wonder, if she takes the "correct steps" after she finds out, can she make him come back to her and forget other men? She may feel shame over the situation and think that she was not enough of a woman to keep her man. And even though rationally she may know better, she will feel rejected—who wouldn't? He is not only rejecting you, he is rejecting the very nature of you as a woman.

The truth is—and this is the most difficult and also the most liberating aspect of this situation—that the female mate of a gay man, or the male mate of a gay woman, has nothing to do with his or her homosexuality. If a man is gay, then we believe (although many will disagree with us) that he was gay before he met his wife or girlfriend and he will be gay for the rest of his life. Her actions and reactions, her appearance, and her attitude have nothing to do with it.

He may believe (and there are many who agree with him), that he can change his behavior, that he can force himself, through enough prayer, therapy, or other work on himself, to change into a heterosexual. Mel White, a Christian who was a speech- and ghostwriter for such evangelists as Jerry Falwell, Pat Robertson, and Billy Graham, talks about his struggle with his homosexuality in his book *Stranger at the Gate: To Be Gay and Christian in America*. In light of his knowledge that he was homosexual, he agonized over his multiple roles as a father, husband, and an important voice in the Christian world, and he suffered from the knowledge of what he was putting his family through. Undoubtedly his wife and children suffered, too. It is hard to imagine what other therapies he could have taken up to deny his homosexuality, yet he eventually decided to accept and share with his family and the world that he was gay.[18]

Whether or not a person can change his or her sexual orientation, if you are a straight woman and you are involved with a gay man, you can know a couple of things: First and again, his gayness has nothing to do with you, nor is there anything you can do to increase his heterosexual feelings. Second, you need to decide what is best *for you* to do to deal with it. If your husband, for instance, tells you he is gay and has decided to live openly as a gay man, then you need to protect yourself — physically and emotionally. Physically, if he is having sex outside of your relationship, get yourself checked for communicable diseases, and if you do decide to continue having sex with him, protect yourself.

Then make sure you take care of yourself emotionally. We think it would be extremely difficult to continue to be with a man who has acknowledged his homosexuality, although some women choose to do so, especially if he (or she) is of the belief that he can change his orientation. In that case, however, you have to live every day with what seems to be the ultimate rejection — knowing that your husband does not prefer the very essence of who you are as a woman. If either of the authors' friends were in this situation, we would say, "Get out!" However, we know that such a decision has to made by the woman going through that experience. We do advise staying aware of the long-term costs to your mental health.

Money

*When there was enough money for their needs, the ties between
them had been strong, but once the money was lacking,
what a strain was put on their love!*

—GABRIELLE ROY

Tin Flute

Money issues can raise a lot of dust in a relationship.
From the different attitudes that each party brings to
the table about how money should be allocated and the
process by which it should be spent or saved to different
beliefs regarding what constitutes financial security and
different expectations about who is, or is supposed to
be, bringing in the dough, opportunities abound for misunderstandings, hurt feelings, and disagreements.

Many ways now exist to support a household, and
no longer can many households expect one person—in
the past, usually the man—to financially support the
home. (Of course, there have always been two-income
families, only now they are more socially acceptable.)
There is no one way to handle money, and each couple
will have to work with each other in figuring out how

their assets will be allocated, what is important to each of them in a material sense, and what each of their duties are in supporting the household.

Financial Confidence

Lina had no backup. Every middle-aged single woman that she knew carried the weight of this terror within them.

—GLORIA NAGY

Marriage

The topic of money can trigger anxiety and fear for both genders, but we believe that, in general, this fear means something different for women than it does for men. One thirty-year old woman we spoke with said that she experienced money issues differently than the man in her life. "I was in a secure job for several years, while my boyfriend was working out of his home as a marketing consultant. I was starting to hate what I did every day — I was a foreclosure officer at a bank — and although I was making a good salary and had great benefits, I wanted to go back to school and get my credential so I could teach. I kept putting off quitting, and yet was complaining on a regular basis about my job.

"My boyfriend didn't get it. He could not understand why I didn't just leave. As a consultant, he didn't have a steady income, but he didn't seem to sweat it, either. He always believed the money would come, and it always seemed to when he needed it.

"I, on the other hand, had a very deep fear of leaving my job. I came to think of it as my 'bag lady' complex — if I contemplated quitting my job, if I had to dip into my savings, then I pictured myself on the street, picking my dinner out of garbage cans.

"I finally went to a career counselor who said that she had a lot of female clients who felt the same way I did—that basically they felt there was only 'one shot' at making money in life, and that a woman's survival instinct told her not to give up a steady income. Perhaps it is because we women don't have the money making history of men, or we may have watched women of previous generations with no careers suffer through a divorce and be left high and dry. Whatever the reason, I saw a lot of difference between how I look at financial security and how my boyfriend did. After I started being conscious of why I felt that way, we were able to talk about it, and he could encourage me to take the risk, which I eventually did."

Hillary and her mate, Phil, handle their money in different ways: "Phil and I are in gender-specific investment groups. Although the clubs' goals and bylaws are quite alike, that is where the similarities cease.

"Gathering after golf, Phil's club meeting lasts about an hour. In the informal atmosphere, stocks are bought and sold in a lively manner as motions are debated vigorously. Bylaws are rarely referred to and occasionally conveniently overlooked. Lively banter and quick decision making are the norm. All leave in good spirits, most often laughing.

"In my club the women arrive from their different

jobs. Meetings are run by parliamentary procedure with our 'bibles,' copies of the bylaws, at the elbows. Decision making is a long and painful process, as we invest our souls, taking ownership and nurturing with pride our individual, chosen stocks. For some there is never enough information to make that informed selection. Meetings go on for hours, and most go home with headaches.

"Where the men find laughter and expedience, we women find work and responsibility. One never knows when Chairman Greenspan may call us women for our advice!"

As we see more and more women in financial roles such as stockbroker, business owner, banker, and lawyer, we see them handling money and making financial decisions with confidence and ease. These women have little problem managing their money. So it does seem to be a question of practice. Like Hillary, if we do not have a lot of confidence in our own financial life, we may want to form an investment club with our close women friends. As anyone with a good girlfriend or two knows, we have more strength in numbers. Perhaps as women gain confidence in ourselves as money makers and managers, we'll be able to lighten up and enjoy this process a bit more — like we see many men doing now.

Who's the Breadwinner?

Need of money, dear.

—DOROTHY PARKER

Writers at Work, when asked what was the source of most of her work

Both men and women have lots of expectations about what their lives will be like in marriage. Sometimes these expectations coincide, sometimes they do not. We've observed that a lot of men have very strict expectations of themselves in relationship to their wives and families. One area in which many men can really be tough on themselves revolves around their perceived responsibility to bring home the bacon.

This expectation can show itself when the couple is first dating, as Joyce explained. "When Ray and I were dating, we were both totally poor college students in southern Wisconsin. He drove a junker that you could hear coming five blocks away. I'd be in the dorm at night, and you could hear the car coming down the road. The other girls in the dorm would say, 'Joyce, your date's here!'

"I didn't find out until later, but during this time he lost one of his two contact lenses, and he's blind without contacts. But he went ahead with just one contact for six months because he couldn't afford to buy a second contact. But he continued to take me on dates to Chicago and take me out for pizza. This wasn't extravagant spending, but he always did nice things for me and there was always money for us to go out. I didn't find out until a year later that he'd been going around with one contact for six months. But he said he wanted to take good care of me, and part of that was not letting me know that he was eating popcorn for dinner because that was all he could afford.

"This was very problematic once we got married. He was of the mentality that it was up to the man to keep all financial worries to himself, even though they were now worries that included the two of us. I'd find out something was really stressing him out, and I'd get really upset! It took him a while to be able to share the experience of the two of us worrying together, without him feeling less of a provider."

Similarly, Mira, now married twenty years to her stockbroker husband, Zach, talked about her surprise at the amount of time her husband spent at work. She told us, "When you're dating, of course, all the attention is on each other, and you focus all of your activities around that person. When we got married, his attention shifted, so that was somewhat difficult to wrestle with—how to negotiate the time. Back then, we weren't very good at communicating, so I just let it go and figured that was what he did.

"I don't think it made me feel unloved, but I did assume that he had lost some interest in me. I also felt scared, because he was so driven about work, always this element of push-push-push and never time for re-laxation. There was never a sense of 'here we are and life's okay.' In fact, a tone of desperation underlined his work. I think it is a fairly common pressure for men. I look at my sister's relationship with her husband, and I see the same things now. He has his own business, which had been his recreation and his life up until the past five years, until she finally said, 'We're your family, and if you don't have time for us now, you're not going to have the kids anymore.' Then he started to make changes. That's been similar for Zach, too. Once his business started being more predictable, he started to ease off."

In our society, the more access to financial security one has, often the more secure that person feels in the world. In traditional marriages, men have been desig-nated to provide financial security for the family, and generations of women felt the uncertainty of having no direct access to earning power. Times have changed, and more and more women expect to work and to pay their own way through life. We consequently enjoy much more freedom, independence, and opportunities than past gen-erations. But new problems have arisen as well, and with these new expectations come new challenges.

As more and more women are proving themselves successful in the workplace, it's becoming more common for the woman to have a larger income than the man in her life. According to *Working Mother* magazine, twenty-two percent of women in two-income households bring in more money than their mates.[19] Kristen, a highly accomplished corporate executive with a shrewd business sense, attributes the discrepancy in income as a major contributor to the ending of her marriage. She told us that she was attracted to her creative husband because "he was a free spirit. In the beginning, when things were going well, it was a good match. At the start, he felt, 'Wow, this is great!' However, my husband became too dependent upon me financially, and after a number of years the only thing he felt he could do was to rebel against that and leave.

"I was completely devoted to his art and excited about investing in his business, his creative life, his genius. But he never got it off the ground. It ended up with me supporting him, being the major breadwinner simply because I was earning so much more than he was. It's difficult to keep things even-steven. It didn't matter to me on some level who was paying more. But it seems hard for men, even those who may be perceived as the more 'sensitive' type. I think I discounted that. I suspect that he felt like a kept man, beholden to me.

"From my perspective, I was contributing to our marriage, although eventually I felt disrespected, like the cow who continuously gives milk. I started collecting resentments. In some ways I felt he appreciated what I was doing for him, and at the same time I had trouble dealing with how he was spending 'my' money. It was hard reminding myself that, once brought into the marriage, it was no longer mine but ours, and his."

Not only can it be stressful to individual men and women when the man is not the primary breadwinner, sometimes pressure is put on couples from friends and family members if the woman takes the financial lead. Veronica told us about a time in her marriage in which she was the main wage earner. "We managed a shelter in exchange for an apartment and a small stipend. It was important to us that he be there to manage things that happened during the day, which turned out to be a half- or three-quarter-time job. The money that came in was whatever I earned.

"We were happy with the arrangement, but we got a lot of comments from friends and family members. Some of them looked at my husband as if he were defective or something, like he had some personality quirk for not going out and getting another job. People would say, 'Well, Neil, you've got to look for a job sometime. What are you going to do when you have kids?' I think he felt bad at times, but I'd say, 'Don't worry about that. What do they know? Look at all the problems they're having in their lives. We don't have those problems.'

"But there was still tension, especially from my side of the family. My family is blue collar, where the men are 'real men.' I think that was the hardest thing for us. It would have been different if we'd had people around us who would support us figuring out what was best for us. But they all felt there was a problem with this arrangement, and the problem was Neil. They felt I was working too hard and that he should go to work so I could sit around the house. They felt that it's okay for a woman not to work outside the home if she's married, but it's not okay for a man to do the same."

But not all couples have found the traditional model a workable lifestyle, choosing instead to live with the stresses that come when the woman brings in more money than the man. Lilly told us, "No matter which one of us is making more money, there is a certain amount of tension. Whoever has the most money has the most power, so it's difficult to maintain a marriage of equals when there's always some imbalance.

"Our relationship has shifted back and forth over the years. When we were dating, Kenny paid for everything. We had a very traditional courtship. But once we were married, it became clear to us both that I was the more ambitious one. I pushed ahead and finished my doctorate. Even though we're both therapists, I've had the larger practice. The only time Kenny brought in more money than I was during a short period at the end of my pregnancy, and the first three months after the birth of our twins. I was physically exhausted and getting the hang of being a mother of two rambunctious boys. But once I got on my feet, I started seeing patients again. Now that the children are nearly two, I'm once again the primary wage earner."

This issue comes up later on in some marriages. We

asked Judy, a successful motivational speaker now married for forty years, what happened when she started making more money than her husband. She found that while she didn't start working full-time until later in the relationship, her treatment and attitude toward her husband and the respect they had for each other was the ultimate factor in keeping them together.

Judy feels that both parties need to feel powerful in the marriage, and that ~~this~~ is achieved by both parties showing respect for the other. She adds that whoever is making more money has be more aware of not treading on the other's toes: "The person who has the money has the power. A woman can easily destroy a man's self-esteem, a man's ego, by completely gobbling him up. So you can't usurp your husband's power. If you are making more money, and the one with the money has the control, you have to be very careful to balance out the power; you have to sometimes go to him and ask him, 'What do you think about this?' Even though you may not agree, you take his advice sometimes.

"For example, there were times when I wanted to buy refrigerator A, and he had decided on refrigerator B. You don't stand there and always demand your way. What the heck? Or I sometimes would deliberately ask for advice when I didn't need it. 'What do you think about this?' Then I'd let him have his input and then say, 'You are absolutely right.'"

She smiles confidentially, "I still do that. And when

he is right, or maybe I didn't agree with him in the beginning of a situation and then he turns out to be right, I make a point of saying so, instead of just avoiding it."

When we wondered if this was just game playing, Judy described it further: "It is building each other's self-esteem. Similarly, I think that men also need to come to their wives and not treat them like idiots. They need to ask, 'What do you think about this?' Respect each other's judgment and where they are coming from. There is nothing more appealing than someone asking your opinion. If you do not have total respect for that person, what is the point? Total and complete respect is the bottom line."

We agree. Theoretically it doesn't matter who is making the money. But many men, especially those raised in earlier generations, feel that they are not doing their part if they are making less money then their wives. A woman's sensitivity to that, at no cost to her, will go a long way to dealing with that insecurity. For example, after a particularly difficult period in their marriage, Judy let her husband know how she felt about him, loud and clear: "We were in the car one day, and he said to me, 'You deserve a man who could buy you a Rolls Royce; that is the kind of woman you are.' And I said, 'Look, here is something you have to understand. You know that I make enough money now that if I really wanted to, I could put a down payment on my own Rolls Royce. I can make my house payments now. I don't need you, I *choose* you. You are the man I want, not the man I have to have for car payments, <u>house payments</u>. I am not helpless, I have finances, I am in a good position, I *choose* you.' When he realized that no matter what, I chose him, it brought us full circle."

Respect for each other's professional goals, sharing decisions regardless of who is bringing in most of the cash, and having support from those around you for the lifestyle that you and your man have chosen for yourselves are all important factors in helping women find our way in the money game. If we see a friend struggling with these issues, whether she is someone who is entirely dependent on her husband's income or someone who brings in more than her share of the household income, we may want to offer our emotional support. Many people feel self-conscious bringing up money issues, and our girlfriend may appreciate knowing that she can talk about some of those issues with us. Even if she does not wish to talk about it, she may like merely to hear that we understand that some issues may be thorny. Sharing assets can make us all feel vulnerable, and just knowing that a friend is empathetic to our situation can provide salve to our psyches.

What Happens When the Working Mom Stays Home?

It seems to me that since I've had children, I've grown richer and deeper. They may have slowed down my writing for a while, but when I did write, I had more of a self to speak from.

—ANNE TYLER

The Writer on Her Work, vol. 1

We talked to several women who had successful careers and who decided, at least for a while, to stay home with their children. As one mother of three said, "My husband wants to fix what happened in his family. His mom was a working mom. I think he considers it a mistake. He's always told me I can do what I want and I believe he would support me, but I know his first choice is for me to be at home. We made the decision together, but without a doubt I have paid the greater price in staying home. I believe staying home is the right choice for our family and I wouldn't change my mind, but it's been very hard for me."

Her friend Joan, who is a first-time mother of a nine-week-old son, added, "I think it is true that men look for someone who they think will create the kind of family environment that they want to be in and that they want their children to be in. In fact, it's been a real issue in my relationship what is going to happen with me working, because my husband has such a strong feeling that he wants his children to be raised by me, almost like he picked me to be the mother of his children, which was not something I realized at the time.

"He is very up-front about how he wants our children to spend as much time as possible with me. It's not 'I want someone like you to raise our kids,' it's 'I want you because you are the person I trust the most to raise these children in the way, and in the environment, that I want.' It's because it was an environment that he wanted, and I think he wants the same kind of environment for his kids. I don't think he wants to replicate his childhood. He wants to replicate for his kids the kind of environment that he has with me."

When we talked to Laurine, a mother of two, she said, "I think all men would like their wives to stay home with the children; my husband would love that, and he has never, ever said it!"

We need to point out that, although many people assume that if one person is going to stay home with the children it will be the woman, there are couples who decide that the woman will continue to work outside the home and the man will stay home with the kids. We know of one couple living in a small town in the Midwest, who chose this "nontraditional" course. He is a consultant with an office at home, and for their child's first few years, he was the primary parent. Then, over the years, they took turns being the primary parent. Both parents have benefited from their time of closeness with the child.

We predict that we will see more of this circumstance, as men and women feel more free to chose who would be the better-suited person to stay home. Some women already know they are *not* the one.

April, who is single, said although she recognizes the benefits of staying home with children as they grow up, she doesn't think she could do it: "I don't think I could come to terms with staying home all day with children. My mom stayed home with me and my siblings until I was fourteen, and I loved it, but when I picture that for myself, I don't think I could do it. I can just imagine myself waiting every day to sit down with my husband after he comes home to have some adult conversation. I picture myself in tears, 'Let me talk to an adult, or I'm going to have a nervous breakdown.'"

Her friend Ursula, a mother of three who is a stay-at-home mom, laughed, "I really had to come to grips with it. For the first couple years I struggled a lot with the decision to stay home but now I really feel like it was best for my children and my family. I'm much more philosophical about it now and am comfortable with my decision because I see it in a greater perspective. My oldest child is going to kindergarten next year and it seems like just yesterday that I started this process with her. You can't go back later and do it differently. It really was the right thing for me to do."

Joan summed it up: "No one has pulled any punches with me. Nobody really wants me to go back to work except my boss!" All of these women shared the same experience: their husbands wanted them to stay at home with the kids, and while they thought it was a good idea in principle, it was difficult for them, as women who are confident and competent in the outside world, to lose that identity to "wife and mother." Any woman who chooses to change her identity in this way will face similar challenges. Not only are you starting over at a new "job" that you know nothing about (but which you have a nagging feeling that you are supposed to know about if you are any kind of a mother at all), but you have lost your income, your independence, and your work-oriented identity. And you will be spending your days trying to communicate with someone who is not going to have an adult conversation with you! Don't let anyone tell you this is going to be easy!

When you are making the choice to go back to work or not, try to let your husband know what is going on for you emotionally and some of the pressures that you are feeling. Try to tell him if possible, *before* you reach your emotional limit and just want to scream. He may not get it, or he may get it only partially. This is one of those times when girlfriends really come in handy.

To ease the stress, we've found that many women rely on their girlfriends, both those who are working but who are available to listen and provide emotional support, and also those who are at home with their young children. If we stay at home, our girlfriends can provide some conversation as well as remind us that we do have abilities beyond changing diapers and picking up toys. Similarly, if we go back to work, our friends can be an enormous help. Many women told us how their women friends helped them maintain their sanity when raising small children—how friends would take care of each other's children when one of them had something important to do, how they listened to each other and compared notes, how they helped reassure each other that they were being "good enough" mothers.

Yours, Mine, and Ours

We are made loveless by our possessions.

—ELIZABETH OF THURINGIA

The New Quotable Woman

The thought of joining banking accounts can make some women stop cold, whether or not they are married. One woman told us, "I think I would have less of a problem giving up my last name than I would giving up my bank account." For her, and for many women, one of the scariest things about getting married is sharing her assets with someone else.

After two failed marriages, Adelle has set new ground rules for any future romance. She told us, "In both of my marriages, I made significantly more money than my husbands. If I marry again, I would have to be with someone who makes more money than I do. I've never had that, and I think it would be great.

"Even if they didn't make more than I, I'd expect them to have their own finances. I can't imagine, at this point, commingling my money again. I can't imagine being in a relationship where it wasn't more financially equitable. They have their own money. I have my own money. We share in common expenses. There are parts of that I'd hate, but if it worked, that would be a change for me."

While separating bank accounts may be the solution for Adelle, Heather has decided to proceed in the opposite direction with her live-in boyfriend, Wally. She told us that combining their finances is "something we've talked about for a long time. I think for me it has a lot to do with watching my parents' relationship. My parents have separate accounts and they very carefully split up who pays for what. I didn't like growing up in that, and I now feel that it's not a healthy way to have a relationship.

"I feel like sharing money is a way of saying we're really in this together. The way we manage our money is an emotional thing for me, on one hand, because it represents our commitment to each other. We're looking at long-term savings and long-term goals. Do we want to buy a house together at some point? Maybe we should get a money market account together. Talking about money has brought up all kinds of issues about our future, our dreams, and our commitment to each other. It's been really great for us on an emotional level.

"On the other hand, money management is also very logical. We are making financial decisions in a very thoughtful way. We both have our checkbooks computerized, so we were able to print out our expenses and look at them and realize that, even though he tends to spend more money than I do, we're both really living within our means. It's not carved in stone, either. If it's not working in a few months, we can always figure out something else."

Which brings us to one of the most important aspects of money in a relationship—talking. Like sex, money can be a difficult topic to discuss. Many times issues about money come up early in the relationship, especially now when women are more likely to pick up the check than in times past. Racquel told us, "When David and I first started dating, we never mentioned money. Without discussing how either of us felt about it, we split the check when we went out to dinner. As we spent more time together, we were doing more things that involved money.

"I didn't want to voice my opinions because I thought maybe he wouldn't like what I thought about money. I hoarded a lot of feelings about income, which would then all come out in sarcasm and begrudging behavior, like reluctantly handing over my share of the check when we would eat out.

"We recently had a breakthrough and decided to hold monthly money meetings. We just had one. It was unbelievably relieving for me. I said all the things that I was mad about, which, to my surprise, only took about ten minutes. Having them all bottled up had made the whole issue more charged for me than needed.

"I said, 'I don't want to pay for things on our behalf without a plan for how your share is going to be repaid.' I don't like floating, nebulous things that aren't written down and aren't clear. I feel unsafe, it makes me nervous. I like financial arrangements to be current, up-to-date, cleared up along the way.

"He was great about it, realizing that I was telling him how I felt, not blaming him. I was saying, 'Here's what I need, and I want you to help me meet that goal.' He hadn't realized that I was feeling unsafe. I had been keeping these feelings inside 'for the sake of the relationship,' and it wasn't even necessary. I feel so much better about him and our relationship in general now."

So often our fears are worse than the reality. Talking about an issue may reveal that there is no problem at all! Further, when we can talk about our vulnerability or concerns about money (or anything) with our men, we not only name the problem and determine how much of a problem it really is, we perhaps begin the resolution of a spoken or unspoken conflict. Layer upon layer, as we unpeel our hearts and minds to each other, our knowledge and understanding of each other grows, and our long-term connection deepens.

Spending Styles

I make money using my brains and lose money listening to my heart. But in the long run my books balance pretty well.

—KATE SEREDY

The Singing Tree

A corollary to having confidence in one's earning power is being able to spend money easily and to choose freely where to spend it. We often hear the stereotype that husbands have to continually watch out for their wives' irresponsible spending habits. However, we spoke with several women who described themselves as being more concerned than their partners about how much money was flowing out of their household.

One woman, twenty-eight, found that she has to say no to her long-term boyfriend regarding visits to the local music store or the motorcycle dealership. Similarly, a twenty-four-year-old woman told us, "Money management has been a big issue in our lives recently because our styles are so different. Ned is very impulsive and spends a lot of money. He makes a lot of money, so he can afford to do it. I, on the other hand, have a harder time letting go of money. I'm kind of a miser and always worry about it, even though I try not to. He's helped me loosen up a little about it, which I think is good."

Frequently money tension arises over our expectations of how money is supposed to be earned, spent, and saved, even when we are not aware of those expectations. And we all learn those expectations from our experiences growing up in our own families. For instance, Katie told us, "I'm the only child of two working parents, so there was always enough money for the things we needed and often for things we wanted as well. Not that my family threw money around, but I have never seen my mother compare prices of toilet paper or clip coupons. It just never happened. So when I married Gerry, we had quite a jolt when we started shopping together.

"His relatives are the quintessential hunt-the-best-deal shoppers. No effort is too great to find an item at a cheaper price. Gerry would drive me nuts driving all over town to save a few dollars. And he would be aghast at what he called my cavalier attitude toward money. He'd ask me, 'How can you flush hard-earned money down the toilet?' and I'd ask, 'How can you waste our Saturday over a few pennies?' Those first few years of our marriage were quite an adjustment for both of us. Even now, there's tension from time to time, even though we're more accepting of each other's styles."

The important thing is to be aware of what each other's expectations are and to work out a way to live with them. Once Gerry and Katie understood each other's process and came up with a middle ground (for instance, comparison shopping on items over a certain price), they could reach some peace with each other. Again, talk, talk, talk, negotiate, negotiate, negotiate. No one gets total autonomy in a relationship when financial resources are shared. That means one person doesn't get to buy whatever he or she wants, just like it means that one person doesn't get the veto power on all purchases.

Because we learn so much about money and how to spend it or not to spend it, as the case may be, from our families, we may want to check in with third parties, such as our friends, about what is reasonable. If we spend all afternoon shopping for the cheapest price on tapered candles, is that reasonable? Is that a good use of time? Our girlfriends are familiar about our attitudes toward money, and if we are having money issues with our mates, we may want to check in with our girlfriends to get some feedback about our own attitudes and money beliefs.

Power

If men can run the world, why can't they stop wearing neckties?
How intelligent is it to start the day
by tying a little noose around your neck?

—LINDA ELLERBEE

Untamed Tongues

Some might say that all of this talk about money, or sex, is really about the subject of power. Many people use both money and sex as instruments of power to control others. And isn't power the underlying issue in any argument or negotiation with our spouse or boyfriend? Regardless of how amicable the discussion, we may really be asking, Who is going to have their way? Whose opinion or belief is the correct one?

We may believe, when we are first in love with someone, that we want the same things, that we will not have conflict because the welfare of the other is always foremost in our minds. However, it usually doesn't work out this way. Gradually, we all start wanting our own way again, and we discover that "our way" is frequently not the same as "his way," and vice versa. A long-lasting relationship requires the ability to share power, knowing when to hold our ground, when and how to graciously retreat, and how to find a solution that will satisfy both parties.

Compromise and negotiation: these are not skills we are born with. We don't send eighteen-year-olds to negotiate peace treaties, do we? We send those with experience, with patience, with the knowledge to recognize how far he or she can push or retreat in a situation. So it is with love. With practice, we can learn to do this really well.

When to Call the Decorating Referee

Marrying a man is like buying something you've been
admiring for a long time in a shop window. You may love it
when you get home, but it doesn't always go with
everything else in the house.

—JEAN KERR

What Women Say About Men

You have probably gotten the idea by now that a relationship means there are going to be changes in your life
that you do not like or compromises you weren't expecting to make. One of the hot spots when two people decide
to share physical space is how that space is going to *look*.

We may not realize how important our physical surroundings or particular objects are to us until we are
actually faced with what to do with his Aunt Mary's hid-
eous wardrobe (complete with gargoyles) or our lovely
but obviously feminine white lace duvet cover. He may
look wounded when you point out you'd like a different
piece of furniture than the milk carton crates which he
currently uses in his apartment to hold all of his albums —
a piece of furniture that may, heaven forbid, be specifically designed to hold albums and look attractive all
at the same time. Not only are you going to have to let
him know that there are some characteristics of his decor
that you might not find appealing, he may not agree that
it is worth spending money on a new piece of furniture

to appease your taste.

If you are partnered with a man who says, "Doesn't matter to me. Decorate however you'd like," then you're home free, so long as he is not disturbed by the cost and the disruption of decorating. But you may find that your man has powerful feelings about decorating your place together, as Cecilia shared with us: "I had a strong feeling that I wanted us to make this home. I wanted it to be a place that I was really happy and comfortable in and that reflected me—not to the exclusion of him, of course, but it was my first time making a real home for myself. I'd had the typical studio apartment up till then.

"What I neglected to realize when I married him was that he, too, had very strong feelings about the decor. I knew our tastes were different, but I just didn't think he was going to impose his on me. He had this huge collection of wildlife prints that I called the 'Wet Dog Carrying Dead Duck' prints. Frankly, they were very good, if you liked that style of art. I happen to hate it, with a passion. He wanted it on every wall. He wanted what I describe as the 'Men's Club Library' decor—dark woods, lots of antiques, oriental carpets, dark-covered chairs with ottomans, and stuffed pheasants, to the point of being gothic. I was horrified.

"I set off on my merry little way thinking I'm going to have slip-covered sofas with canvas fabric, high-tech lighting, and bleached floors. Well, I don't think so! We had no discussion about it, we both just went into it blindly."

When we asked her how they extracted themselves from the impasse, she replied, "We hired a decorator to make sense of the mess. She earned every penny! For instance, I wanted pale, almost-white sofa covers, and he wanted to keep the covers that were on the sofa, which were orange, blue, and gold, complemented by gold velvet pillows. He couldn't see why we needed new covers at all. But our designer was brilliant and came up with a scheme that we were both able to live with. I was very happy with the result in most of the rooms. For instance, in the living room, she took a lot of the ethnic stuff that I like so much and pulled some really bold colors together. We ended up with red sofa covers. Bold colors supposedly appeal to men, so that was my compromise. It was fine for the most part."

Bringing in a third party (a decorator, a therapist, a girlfriend, a referee) can be very helpful in negotiating a compromise, especially at the beginning of a relationship when the couple is still figuring out *how* to compromise. If we watched our parents struggle over family decisions and did not learn how to give and take, we may find it difficult to learn how to negotiate. Further, even if we did have excellent models of compromise when we were growing up, we may have lived on our own for a considerable time as adults and have gotten used to making our decisions without considering anyone else's point of view.

There is nothing shameful about needing to learn ne

skills, so getting help from the outside—whether over what color your couch is going to be or repairing a serious rift in a relationship resulting from arguing over the color of the couch—is a perfectly appropriate solution. A girlfriend who has some fashion sense and the ability to communicate to both you and your partner can be just the buffer zone for compromise and color coordination.

Ugh . . . Housework

I've been married to one Marxist and one Fascist, and neither one would take the garbage out.

—LEE GRANT

Untamed Tongues

We found that men and women rarely have the same idea about housework—what housework is necessary, when it is accomplished, and how often it is done. As trivial as it seems in theory, inanimate objects like piles of mail, dirty socks, and used coffee cups can create a great deal of animated hostility and tension between two people. Joan, married for several years and a new mother, told us: "If you made a list of the big issues that happen in relationships, there's sex, there's money, there's time, and there's sorting out basic household duties. I wish we had evolved more in this society, or at least in my marriage, so that there was no longer an assumption that the

default person responsible for housework was me. But there is definitely that assumption in our relationship, even when we are both working."

Many women found that their men would not take care of the domestic scene. Tanya tells us about a test she ran on her husband: "With Grant, there could be garbage from upstairs all the way down in the kitchen, and he won't see it or pick it up. In fact, I specifically left on the dining room floor a pair of socks that had fallen out of the laundry basket. He has to go through the dining room every day, and he never picked those socks up. After three weeks, I picked them up myself. He never even saw them."

Melanie echoed this experience when she told us about arguments she and her husband have had over picking up after himself. "I fight the urge to pick up after him, but usually I just can't stand it. Or someone will be coming over for dinner and I am too well trained by my mother to leave shoes or mail sitting around. We have had several battles over this topic, with me getting mad and him just agreeing that he is messy and that he will try harder, but then nothing really changes. Part of the time I just feel petty; I can't believe I am making such a big deal about some messiness.

"Petty or not, I have to face the fact that I like things neater than he does. I am willing to do more to keep it clean because I know it matters to me more that the house not be a mess, but I still feel it is unfair to have to do almost everything. Finally, we agreed to hire someone to come in every couple of weeks to do the major cleaning, but we still have to deal with the everyday mess. I have figured out that what makes me feel anxious is the sense of clutter, every surface covered with mail or dishes.

"So we're now talking about small changes that may not result in it being as spotless as I would like, but that would clear away the daily buildup. We're going to put a couple of baskets next to the door in which mail will go into when we walk in from work at night, we are going to take ten minutes to clean up the kitchen after dinner, and we're going to put hooks on the inside of his closet door so he can hang clothes up easily. I think we'll get it eventually, but it isn't worth losing the relationship because I can't stand having his socks on the floor!"

Psychotherapist Harriet Lerner, in her classic book about couples' long-term patterns, *The Dance of Anger,* addressed the issue of housekeeping as it related to Lisa and Rich, who had had "countless housework battles."[20] Dr. Lerner emphasizes that we only can control our own behavior. In her example, Lisa, who was unhappy about the way that she was doing more than her share of the housework, finally decided to take a different approach and figured out what was most important to her. "She made a list of tasks that she would continue to do (for example, a clean living room and kitchen were extremely important to her, so she would not let things pile up here) and a list of those that she would no longer do. For these, she hoped that Rich would fill in, but if not, they would just live without their being done. Then she shared her plan with Rich and put it into force.

"Lisa stood behind her position as Rich tested her out for two months by becoming more of a slob than usual. . . . She found other ways, however to save her time and energy." Lisa cut down on the amount she did when Rich entertained his business associates or friends and cooked simpler meals for herself and their children several nights a week, leaving Rich to his own devices on those nights.

So Lisa had to decide what she had power to change and had to make up her mind to make those changes, not as a tactical device to manipulate Rich's behavior, but as a way to help herself with her problem of being overworked. As Dr. Lerner notes, "Lisa made these changes out of a sense of responsibility for herself — not as a move against Rich. If she had gone 'on strike,' or this was no more than a plot to shape Rich up or to get back at him, the probable outcome for this couple might well have been an escalation of their difficulties." Rich did indeed start initiating housework duties, but Lisa then had to resist the temptation to criticize his efforts and tell him how to do it.

While many couples conform to the stereotype of the woman doing more of the housework and the man being the messy one, other women find that their men are almost dictatorial about what has to be done around the house and according to what standards. Laurine told us about her ten-year marriage: "My husband is the one who walks around tidying up, exhibiting the classic stereotype of a woman who drives you crazy. As he cleans up, he gripes at me, 'You did not take out the garbage,' or whatever. He is the totally angry wife, and my response is 'I'm sorry, I'm sorry.' I have never in the ten years of our marriage asked him to do something around the house, ever. I could ask him about other things—there are a whole host of things I want him to do—but household chores? He just does them. Not only does he do them, but he's telling me, 'We have to clean the kitchen today.' I'm a slob. He cares about it and I don't."

One woman, a writer who has been married to her husband for almost thirty years, said her husband's rules drove her crazy: "I wrote them down one time when I was mad at him. 'Do the dishes after dinner'; 'Don't leave anything in the sink'; 'The mail goes in the cubbyhole, it doesn't sit on the desk'; 'The newspapers go in the drawer, they cannot sit on the breakfast room table.'

Asked how she reconciled herself to those rules, she answered, "I think at some level I pulled him into my life so that he could teach me about order. In fact, his sense of order appeals to me. But creating order just isn't in my nature. I still haven't gotten used to it, but my sense of humor and sense of cooperation get me through."

So here the tables are turned—the man is the fastidious one and the woman just doesn't care as much.

Perhaps some of us look at this situation with envy, but we may also realize that it would be hard to perpetually not measure up to our spouse's standard of household care or, even worse, to be expected to conform to someone else's idea of cleanliness. Whatever your perspective, it is clear we have two choices. We can accept things the way they are and try to live with them, probably feeling resentful all the while, or we can try to learn what our and our partner's perspectives are and settle on who is going to accomplish the household chores most important to each of us. Or we may agree to spend some money to hire a third party to do some of the work. What we cannot do is change anyone's behavior but our own. We may want to ask our friends to remind us of this fact when they start hearing a chronic complaint from us about our man.

Lessons from the Laundry

Sometimes I really believe that men are put on this earth for the sole purpose of driving women crazy. Not in any great big premeditated evil way, just inch by inch, infuriating habit by habit.

—GLORIA NAGY

Marriage

Ever try to do something nice for the man you love and your efforts were overlooked or, worse yet, misinterpreted? This dilemma can go both ways, as we found out when we asked women if their partners had tried to do something thoughtful for them that had backfired. We were amazed at how many stories we got involving laundry.

Joyce told us, "When Ray and I were in graduate school, we'd reached a point in our marriage where we were at each other's throats, just hating each other. So to try to bridge the gap, Ray decided to do something nice for me—to surprise me by doing the laundry. Unfortunately, he was working nights at a shipping company shoving boxes onto a conveyer belt after he had marked them with a large blue pencil. The lead in the pencil was almost as soft as crayon. One of these huge pencils was left in his pocket and thrown into the wash. Plus, he put a pair of jeans in with some of my delicate, white, lacy tops. When they came out of the dryer, every piece of clothing had indelible blue smeared all over it. It was . . . really sad.

"I knew in my rational mind that he was trying so hard to do something nice, while every fiber of my being was yelling, 'You blew it! You ruined my best blouses! How could you do this, you idiot?' I didn't say that to him. I tried to be nice, but he knew. Even now, twelve years later, he's paranoid about the laundry. He's scared to death to even put underwear in the machine. In fact, after he puts clothes in, he'll ask me to come and push the button!"

Ronni told us a similar story of good intentions gone awry. Her husband, Hal, put some things in the dryer "that he shouldn't have. Now, if he does the laundry and I'm not around for him to consult with, I'll come home and find most of the items hung up on hangers all over the house. He'd rather have everything sopping wet than run the risk of shrinking anything else! Poor guy. He means well. But he just doesn't grasp the concept that you don't put rayon in the dryer. He figures if it can go in the washing machine, then why can't it go in the dryer?"

Lest we make all men out to be "laundry losers," we want to include a story we heard from Yvonne, the mother of two grown boys, one of whom recently married. She told us, "My son does all the laundry and won't let his wife touch it, she's messed it up so many times. But then, he's been doing his own laundry since he was a teenager.

"Back then, I got upset at the amount of money both

my sons wanted to spend on designer clothing. I just couldn't rationalize paying more for a label. So my husband and I decided to give both boys clothing allowances to pick out their own clothes. If they chose to use up all the money on brand names, then they had fewer other things to wear. Because of this, they became very conscious of keeping their clothes nice and would get mad at me if I goofed up on something. So they ended up doing their own laundry, which worked for me. I didn't have to worry about how they spent their money *or* do the laundry!"

Apparently, laundry prowess is not genetically based. What seems critical is that at least one person in the couple grasps the importance of sorting lights from darks, knowing when to dry and when to hang, and, by all means, always emptying out the pockets. Additionally, if there is a piece of laundry that is delicate or especially important to either of you, we suggest that the person to whom it means most take responsibility for cleaning it!

They Don't Call It the Remote Control for Nothing

*If a man watches three football games in a row,
he should be declared legally dead.*

—ERMA BOMBECK

What Women Say About Men

One area in which battle for control is frequently experienced or, even more frequently, relinquished, is on the sofa in front of the television. In the battle of the remote control, the winner determines the evening's entertainment. One woman, thirty-four, recalls growing up and watching her father take charge: "Every night after supper, my father would switch on the television, and we would all watch like zombies until we fell asleep. He always had control of the remote, and he would flip, flip, flip the channels. I think it drove my mother crazy, but she never really said anything. She would read the paper and go do other things."

Have circumstances changed much, years later? Even in the homes of younger generations, where both the man and woman are wage earners and may have a more equal relationship than couples of yesteryear, many men continue to exercise power over the remote control—and they are still watching sports! One twenty-six-year-old woman described the worst thing about living with a man as "watching sports, twenty-four hours a day. It's so automatic that he has taken the remote control with him to the bathroom!

"I hate it admit it because it is so cliché, but sports are of no interest to me at all. And it's hard because of the fact that he doesn't ask. In some ways it's my own fault because I let him take over the remote. Then I don't have to deal with feeling guilty for turning on something he doesn't want to see. So he just runs with that freedom. There's a reason it is called the remote control.

"Since I'm complaining, let me add that he's also a channel surfer. He cannot stand ads. I'm a passive watcher and would just prefer to put it on a channel with something I'm watching and leave it there until whatever I'm watching is over. He *actively* watches TV and needs to watch three shows at once."

Her twenty-four-year-old girlfriend has the same experience at her house: "We watch every single football game. Tom likes golf now, too, and he also likes watching the Yankees, especially if they're in the playoffs or the World Series. I don't mind the football because I like it, but sometimes, I think, if it's two teams I'm not interested in, who could care?

"Another difference between us is if there's nothing on I'm interested in, I turn the TV off. He always wants it on, and it drives me nuts. Background noise gives me a headache. If I'm putzing around in the kitchen and we're both outside of the living room and the TV's on, I ask, 'Why is it on? Just turn the thing off.' But he just likes having it on, even if he's not really watching it.

"And he always wants it on in the evening. Like last night I asked him, 'Why don't we just sit and read this evening? It would be nice not to have it on.' His reply? 'I really want it on.'"

We are not saying that this an exclusively male phenomenon. We do know women who are rabid channel surfers (one of the authors in particular) and who enjoy watching sports on television. Remote control and sports on television—perhaps these sound like trivial matters. But if one of you in the relationship is someone who likes quiet, if the television causes conflict, or if you feel that your relationship is lacking intimacy, you may want to take a serious look at the television. Because of TV's mind-numbing capacity and the opportunity that watching TV provides to tune out everything else, some psychotherapists treat television as similar to a drug to which one may become addicted.

Harville Hendrix, author of *Getting the Love You Want*, counsels troubled couples and requires as one of his ground rules that both people agree not to leave the relationship for a certain period while they try to work out their problems. He emphasizes that there are many exits that don't look like divorce or separation, such as the small exits people use to avoid the problems in the relationship. One of these exits is television: "It is harder for many couples to close the dozens of small exits in their relationships than it is for them to close the catastrophic exits; in other words, it may be harder for them to cut down on TV viewing for three months than to agree to give up the option of divorce."[21]

One woman told us this story: "I have watched these friends of mine continually follow the same procedure. I will be at their house, and we will all be standing in the kitchen, and she will start making comments about how her husband has no time for his family, he is always working, and so forth. All of a sudden I can see his eyes glaze over. Then within a few minutes he will have left the kitchen and gone into the living room and flipped on the television, not reachable for the rest of the evening."

Watching television is not in itself a bad thing, but when it substitutes for conversation between two people or serves as an escape from facing reality in a situation, it may mask other problems. If you notice that you or your mate are locked in to TV on a regular basis, perhaps that is a signal, so to speak, to turn the TV off and spend some quality time together. Even if there are no big problems in the relationship, we may be guilty of using the TV as protection. For instance, one woman, who couldn't figure out why her boyfriend did not like putting the commercials on mute, finally discovered that he kept them on full volume because he thought she would use the silence to initiate a conversation about their relationship! He didn't hesitate to mute the commercials after she explained to him that she just didn't like the noise and that it wasn't a scheme on her part to ambush him with a "talk." They instead scheduled "grudge" sessions on a regular basis, so that each party knew ahead of time when bothersome stuff would be brought up, and no one was surprised with it at some other time.

So if our men like to have on the TV and it drives us crazy, we may want to create some safe time so that the TV watcher will know that he can relax and do other things without having to process an issue. Just make sure, like the couple above, that you give yourself an opportunity to clear the air between you. Then, when he is ready to watch three football games in a row, you have an excellent opportunity to catch up with your girlfriends without suffering rancor.

Drawing the Line

What's with you men? Would hair stop growing on your chest if you asked directions somewhere?

—ERMA BOMBECK

When You Look Like Your Passport Photo, It's Time to Go Home

Some men express love more by action than by words—actions that can confuse us women from time to time. Sometimes the best intentions go wrong when "taking care of" feels more like "taking control." As Ronni, a graduate student, said, "I think that men feel like taking care of us is caring for us. But today's woman feels like it's patronizing and degrading. Sometimes I feel like saying, 'Hey, don't you think I have enough wherewithal to take care of myself?'"

One of the most common arenas for the control-or-caring confusion to occur revolves around the fine art of car maintenance. Yvonne noticed that both her husband and her married son made sure "the wives" drove the more reliable car so "we won't break down. I think both my husband and my son have the image that they are taking good care of their spouses."

Tamara, one of the authors, had a similar experience as she was growing up: "In my family, my father always was the deal maker when it came to negotiating for car purchases. He loved to buy and sell cars and was great at negotiating. He would wear down any unfortunate sales person who had to deal with him. Even now that I am older, two thousand miles away, and established in my own career, I always wait to buy a car until he is visiting me. He is so good at it, and we always have a great time checking out various models and test-driving them. So even though I am giving him some control over the process, I trust him and know that not only will I get the best deal, we will have had a positive experience as well.

"It's a lesson that I have tried to apply in my romantic relationships. When I am with someone I trust, I let him help me without micromanaging every detail. In the past, I may have resisted letting someone help me, even if he really wanted to do so. I would work so hard to prove that I could take care of myself that sometimes asking for or accepting help seemed like an admission of weakness."

As women and men learn to share power, whereby each person has his or her say and each knows that his or her thoughts and actions count, we may find there are pockets of retained control by both parties. We women can be just as controlling (or caring?) as we accuse men of being. We may find that we refuse to share control of a realm we consider our own, such as gardening or managing the household finances. Conversely, many women we spoke with didn't understand when their husbands weren't open to their suggestions, even when the women felt their ideas would be helpful. This complaint showed itself through the much-cited complaint from women that their men will not stop and ask for directions!

Ronni told us how good intentions turned into a battleground: "Hal tried to surprise me by taking me to a restaurant we'd never been to before. I was thrilled, until we started driving around and around. Eventually I said, 'So, where is it?' He said, 'Oh, it's right around here,' like he really knew where he was going. I realized that we were lost. Something that drives me crazy about my husband is that he won't ask for directions. He would rather drive for five hours, just driving around trying to find it, than stop at a gas station and ask for help. So after driving and driving, I asked, 'So, did we miss it?'

He said, 'I don't think so, let's just drive a little farther.' We ended up having this big fight because we were lost and I wanted to ask for directions and he insisted we weren't lost and he wouldn't stop. This was not how either of us had anticipated spending the evening together."

Perhaps when we see our men refusing to share control in a situation, it is because they believe they will be seen as incompetent if they accept help from someone else. Some of the women we interviewed say they approach a problem thinking, "How do we deal with this situation? Here are my ideas, what are yours?" On the other hand, men will often recoil from a woman's words of advice as if they were a criticism. Many of our girlfriends have wondered why the men in their lives feel threatened by these women's simple attempts at teamwork.

These are ways that some men keep their sense of personal power — running their own projects and not taking advice unless they ask for it. It can be irritating, but on the small things no harm is usually done — unless, of course, he is driving you to the hospital to give birth and won't stop to ask directions to the hospital! Retaining power in these areas is not taking substantial power away from someone else in the relationship, and in any healthy relationship, one person will likely retain more power in some areas, such as finances, housekeeping, and so forth, while relinquishing more power in other areas. Additionally, the person who has more power in one area may shift in that area as time goes on. When someone is retaining all the power or when attempts to retain power turn into aggression we need to take a serious look at the relationship.

Some women find that men in their lives become critical of them in order to have all the power in the relationship — putting women down to build themselves up. We heard several stories about women who left their husbands because they were verbally abusive. One woman married for forty years, reflected on patterns in her and her daughter's marriages: "I knew what I would stand for and what I wouldn't stand for. If I had wound up with a man who was abusive, it wouldn't have lasted. Abuse mostly comes from the mouth; people are abusive with what they say as much as anything.

"The importance of maintaining self-esteem and not being abused was passed on to my daughter. Her first husband was being abusive with his mouth and didn't even know it. He was ripping out her self-esteem in all kinds of ways, so she walked away with two little girls and said, 'I would rather scrub toilets than put up with this.' He would try to control her by putting her down. He thought that if he brought her down, he would be able to keep her under control. But because she had been brought up in a healthy household, she knew what healthy was and what it should be. She kept trying to show him how you are supposed to treat somebody; she didn't speak up, she just kept trying to show him. He would attack verbally, and she would put a stone in the wall, and pretty soon the wall was so high, so wide, so thick, that it was irreparable."

If control like this turns into physical violence, we believe there is no option but to leave. One woman we talked to used the one-hit rule: "When I was in college, I dated a boy who I thought was very attractive. Soon, however, I started sensing he was enormously insecure, although he tried to hide it by acting cocky. We went out for several months, and I finally figured out that this guy was kind of abusive and then clingy at the same time. I decided to break up with him, but when I did, he would beg and beg me to give him another chance, and I would stay with him, because I was confused about my own feelings and didn't have the gumption to tell him to get lost.

"Finally I was at a party with him and we got into a fight. He was drunk and insisting I stay with him at the party when I just wanted to go home. It escalated, and I started yelling at him to leave me alone. That is when he slapped me to shut me up. Evidently he thought I was hysterical and needed to be calmed down. Well, that was it! I had seen my parents argue but they never hit each other, and finally the big red light flipped on. I got out of there fast, and there were no more negotiations—I could see that he would only get worse and more violent, no matter how much he begged me to forgive him. It seemed to me that even if I was confused about my feelings for him, the physical blow prevented me from continuing that relationship; it was like a thick black line of 'no return' had been crossed. Although it was painful, it was a good lesson. Now I look for those signs of extreme insecurity—the cockiness, the macho attitude. When I see them, I stay far away."

If we want healthy relationships, girlfriends, we better have our backbones in good working order. As one happily married woman told us, "A woman must know what she believes in, what she will stand for and what she will not stand for. You make those rules very early on. I found that men will almost always go in the direction of the standards that the woman has set up. If a woman has set up very high standards—I'm not talking about finances, but about lifestyle—a man will gravitate toward that. It depends upon the woman. I have found that the woman sets the whole moral tone of the relationship."

And once we decide what kind of relationship we want and where we will make no compromises, we can enlist our girlfriends' help in seeing our relationship clearly. Sometimes it helps us to talk out loud about what is important to us, what kind of behavior is a pattern that has to stop, and when we need to look at our own issues in a relationship. Our girlfriends can help us sort out when to let unimportant issues go, when to draw the line, and when to walk away.

Fighting Fairly

Never go to bed mad. Stay up and fight.

—PHYLLIS DILLER

Phyllis Diller's Housekeeping Hints

Although abuse of any kind is not acceptable in a relationship, conflict is inevitable, and resolution is a necessity for an enjoyable, long-term romance to survive. Many people resort to futile arguments where nothing gets resolved or even to abuse because they do not know how to fight productively. Creating rules to fight by has been an important endeavor of many women we interviewed. Especially important seems to be the idea of fighting fairly so that understanding, not wounding, can result.

Gloria told us that she and her husband, Henry, are both committed to having a marriage that is different from the marriages of their parents. "I never seemed that much like my mom, or my dad either for that matter, when I was single. But when I got married, this stuff just came out. I acted just like my mother or just like my father. I can be like either of my parents. And Henry can be like either of his parents, too. Sometimes it feels like six people are in the room!

"For us, hitting below the belt in the middle of a fight is telling the other person, 'You're acting just like your mother' or 'You sound just like your dad.' Sometimes we just start laughing, because I'll say, 'You're being your father and I'm being me' or 'I'm my mother and my father, so who are you?' And then, to get a little psychological here, there's our adult selves and our childlike selves. It can get very crowded! But our challenge is to break these ingrained patterns and create something of our own, uniquely ours."

Another woman who has been married for twenty-five years has another favorite rule of engagement for her marriage: "Don't slam-dunk your partner. I think a lot of people do that—live together and talk just terrible about each other to other people. Even though I may be upset with my husband, everyone knows I love him. I admire women who you know are burning on the inside but who wait to take care of it at home. I admire women who handle their husbands in a classy way."

In addition to avoiding slam-dunking our partners, we can choose carefully how we say things. One rule that both of us have found productive is using "I" statements instead of "you" statements when expressing a concern. This allows our partner to know how we are feeling without attacking him. For instance, if we feel that our husband is spending too much time at work, instead of saying to him, "You don't care about me any-more, all you do is work," we can say, "I feel like I want some more attention from you, and it feels like you have more interest in work than in me." This gets the point of what we are feeling across and allows him some room to respond without having to become defensive.

We have also learned to avoid general, absolute statements where the words *always, never, all,* and so forth are used. For instance, we suggest trying to avoid the "you never help me around the house" type of declaration. For one thing, such statements are rarely true in the extreme, and for another, they just make the other person angry and defensive. In such a situation, we may say (remembering the "I" rule as well): "I feel like I am doing more of the housework, and I need some help from you." How we say something is as important as what we say.

Finally, to borrow some sports analogies, we sometimes need a time-out from each other, and maybe even a referee. If you feel like you have gone in a negative spiral struggling with the same issues over and over, a little time and space from each other can help each of you calm down and think clearly. It can be as short as a weekend apart, or you may find you want a more extended break. Don't panic about letting the other person go; just do it in an emotionally safe way. Make sure that you have some rules about your time-out — that neither of you are going to start a relationship with someone else, that you will speak at such and such a time, and that neither one of you is going to disappear and not be reachable by the other. And a referee — a therapist, counselor, or clergyperson who we trust — can help us when we are not able to get out of the mess ourselves. Sometimes our conflicts are so deeply ingrained in ourselves that we need a third party to look at it from a fresh perspective and help us sort it out. Seeking help is nothing to be ashamed of; there have been referees in every game involving two people throughout history!

The Power Struggle of Opposites

Men and women, women and men. It will never work.

—ERICA JONG

What Women Say About Men

Many of us are attracted to those who seem to have opposite qualities from us. Quiet, introverted people are frequently seen paired up with outgoing extroverts; people who are comfortable with their bodies may be connected to those who live in their heads; friendly, warm people end up with cool and aloof people. Why do opposites attract? We talked to Nina, a psychotherapist, about her own twenty-five-year marriage, and she observed, "We did enjoy doing things together — I remember, however, our way of doing things together was different. It was the 'being' versus the 'doing' dilemma. I just moved slower than he did. He was a real doer. Our sense of rhythm was different, with me wanting to just sit and daydream in front of a sunset, and when we did, I always felt him saying, 'Okay, I'm ready to move on, what's next?' or 'Let's get moving.' I had this sense of always being pulled along. So, after many years of marriage, I traveled by myself for a few months. By the time I returned, I had some understanding of needing to look at and respect my own rhythm in our marriage, my own decision-making process, all these different things, because he was such a forceful personality. Interestingly, one of the things that I liked about him was that he was always so definite. Of course, in the tough times, that turned into being, 'He's an opinionated jerk.'

"As a therapist, I see this issue of opposites as a very interesting one. We're attracted to those very qualities that are unlike us because they're really telling us something about parts of ourselves that we haven't developed yet. We're seeing them out there and wanting to bring them into our lives, when in fact our work to become whole isn't about bringing in this person to do it for us but about really recognizing that it's a part of ourselves that we need to develop. I saw his definiteness as a way for me to get more structure and order, a sense of real clarity, because he was so clear. Then it turned it into a wall that I was bumping against, and that I resented."

Nina has described a process that Harville Hendrix, in his thoughtful and readable book *Getting the Love You Want: A Guide for Couples*, describes as happening to hundreds of couples whom he has counseled. His theory is that generally we become attracted to people who most closely match the positive and negative characteristics of our primary caretakers as we were growing up—parents, older siblings, relatives, nannies, and so forth. While this process is mostly unconscious—we don't know that we are doing it—he theorizes that we actually more closely look for the negative characteristics in order to have a chance to heal any psychic wounds we sustained as small children or to reclaim a part of ourselves that we have suppressed. His theory is that we continually seek out people with whom we can recreate, and then heal, our childhood injuries.[22] For instance, a woman who was raised with an emotionally or physically distant father may choose a man who is unavailable to her—who won't talk to her, or who takes long business trips. He, on the other hand, may have had an invasive parent and may have problems as an adult letting someone else be close to him and may describe his wife as emotionally clinging and too dependent.

Upon first meeting we have a physical response; we feel whole, fulfilled, satisfied, "in love." But as time goes on, we realize that the characteristics of the person that we picked have the capacity to hurt us again, and hurt us profoundly, opening reserves of pain that were initiated at a very early age.

If we look at Dr. Hendrix's theory, it may seem that love is not so wonderful, that "falling in love" is a dysfunctional act that will only end in a painful reenactment of childhood. According to him, that is the bad news. The good news is that, if we are both willing to grow and change in the relationship, then the very person who can harm you like no one else can also help you like no one else. Using our earlier example, if the "clinging" wife and "distant" husband can heal her abandonment issues and his intimacy issues, she can heal the pain that has been plaguing her all her life.

This is what happened with Nina and Dylan. His ability to have definite opinions about most things was something that drew Nina to him, perhaps was a part of herself she had yet to develop. Yet once she started bumping up against it, his characteristic became a problem for her instead of an attraction. She started resenting what she saw as his inability to be openminded or flexible.

"One weekend my friend, who was working in an art gallery, brought up some artists to Dylan's and my country house — an art gallery director, a poet, and someone else. I was just fascinated by these people, and I just wanted to hang out with them. Yet I could feel Dylan bristling. I knew that he thought these people were jerks and he was annoyed that we weren't getting our chores done. That kind of conflict continued — that was one of the big things that I had to bump up against.

"Another time a great photographer was in a nearby city, and some friends there invited me to come have tea with her. It would have meant driving fifty miles to the city and driving back, just to have tea with some famous person. Dylan's response was, 'What would you want to do that for? You could get in an accident on the freeway,' which at the time was all it took to stop me. My fear level of acting alone was high — here I was this person who ran all over Europe, had adventures galore, and what happened to her? I was so terrified that I could not get in a car and go to the city to have tea because I was afraid I would be in an accident and my husband could say, 'I told you so.' That was where my head was at. That was probably a very interesting thing to look at in this whole business of being individual and being partners. How do you keep some of that zest of the individual in a partnership?

"Then a few years later we had some friends — a guy I met who was very dashing and playful, and he had this poetess girlfriend who was quite dramatic. They invited us over for dinner one night, and we got there and she hadn't started cooking yet. So we ate at midnight. The next invitation we got, Dylan, who learns from the past — which can really limit you if you say 'it's going to be like this *now* because that's how it was *then*' — said, 'I am not going to those people's house, I am not eating at midnight, blah blah blah.' I remember saying, 'Well, I'm going to go.' I didn't go on time, I got there about an hour late. I remember driving down a narrow country road at night, alone, thinking, 'I could get killed on this road.' I was terrified, as if the universe was going to send me some huge test. Here I was, actually defying authority. I got down to their house, and they'd had dinner waiting for an hour. That was one of the times when I started gathering my own information and making my own decisions. As I did that more and more, I was risking displeasure from Dylan, but I was starting to gather strength.

"But, part of me was also casting about for some-place to put my energy. By this time we had moved to our country place and were working, working the land, always working. I decided to take this yoga class, so I gave myself one day, and I called it 'Princess Day,' and it was my day to wear my nicer blue jeans and go off and do something frivolous. I met such resentment from him, that I wasn't working as hard as he was. I really had to fight for not doing it his way."

While this struggle for power and for autonomy is painful and difficult, Nina has found that she and Dylan have brought out new characteristics in each other. "I've gotten to the point now where I'm not sure who's who. I think we both really take the other's projection and we both have both parts. Because he can be a social butter-fly, which is usually my role. He tells me about himself in college, where he was the one that planned all the par-ties and kept everything going. But now because I tend to do it, he takes the other position. Then we will switch; I find part of me wants to really be alone and explore things that need aloneness to explore, and he wants a playmate. This balancing act is just constant." It took years, but Nina said that ultimately she has found bal-ance between her marriage and outside interests.

So the good news is, that according to the experts — those who have either studied couple relationships or who have lived them — if we are struggling with our relationship and doing things that feel like we are being stretched to the limits, we are growing! Granted, continual growth can be tiring, and we may pray, "Not so much growth, please!" But Nina feels that we are molded and formed in the heat of this conflict and struggle: "I had to grow up in relationship. I don't think we've gotten it yet that marriage isn't about fulfilling romance. My mother-in-law, when we got engaged, said to me, 'Marriage kills romance,' very matter-of-factly. I thought, "Oh?" But it is true. What is really going on is this tempering process, this growing process.

"Then, when two people feel whole and they're not grabbing on to each other for either the romantic melodrama or for filling in the holes of our own selves, then you end up with a whole that is bigger than the parts. What do you call it—synergy? It truly enhances your life to have this other person there.

"I think what we're all faced with, men and women alike, is acknowledging that we're basically acting out externally this process of coming to balance internally. Once we're in balance internally, it's not by need but by choice that we get into relationships. Relationship is the great teacher."

Are You Still Trying to Change Him?

*The only time a woman really succeeds in changing a man
is when he's a baby.*

—NATALIE WOOD

Was It Good for You, Too?

Because so many women are practiced at taking care of others, we may fall into the habit of knowing what is good for the men in our lives and acting accordingly. Not only does this assume that our men cannot take care of themselves, but also it provides us with the tempting opportunity to patronize them, treating them like children who are not responsible for themselves. Besides being a misuse of personal power, this may backfire by in fact tempting them to act like children and depend on us to take responsibility. Certainly seems like a bad cycle to start.

Kit, now married for sixteen years, had the good sense to avoid beginning this cycle. "A very silly incident occurred fairly early on in our marriage and has taken on a 'marriage lore' status. It was the Decaf Event. We had invited our friends Dennis and Lucy over for dinner. Lucy and I were in the kitchen about to make some coffee, as Dale had said he wanted some. I told Lucy that I didn't understand why Dale would want coffee, because I knew that it would keep him wired, he's very caffeine sensitive. She suggested that I go ahead and make decaf—he'd never know the difference. I was not sure that I approved of this plan.

"First of all, if I made decaf and passed it off as coffee, he would continue to be unaware of the fact that coffee kept him awake (he would think 'I drank it last night and I went right to sleep'), and, second, I didn't think I could pull off the deception. We made decaf anyway. As soon as we entered the living room, Dale asked, 'So, is that real coffee?' I immediately confessed that it was decaf. Lucy was horrified, my betrayal of our plan was so swift."

Kit realized that what might have been passed off as an innocent "white" lie would have set her marriage off balance, with her deceiving her husband supposedly for his own good. Whether Dale ever found out about the coffee, he would have been affected by the unspoken message that his wife did not respect him enough to allow him to make his own decisions and his own mistakes. Kit was wise to treat her husband with respect right from the start.

But many of us have not made such wise choices in our relationships and instead have tried to change the men in our lives. Those of us who have made that attempt know how frustrating it can be to bend another person to our expectations. A man who disdains household duties when he is single is going to disdain them when he is married. A man who plays around with other women while dating one woman, ostensibly exclusively, will play around with other women after he marries. A man who has no time to pursue his girlfriend's interests with her when they are dating will not have any time for them after he is married either. Our desire for our mate to change is not going to bring about that effect. All we have control over in life is our own actions. For women who are considering spending the rest of their lives with a particular man, we repeat the wise words of the women we interviewed: "What you see is what you get."

This is not to say we are powerless over the situation, nor are we powerless over ourselves. Some of the best advice we received from women in our interviews was, if you want to change somebody, change yourself! Our change in actions and attitudes will ripple through the relationship, sometimes with positive results. For example, Jean tried and tried but couldn't get her boyfriend to show up at anything on time. She told us, "One time he was supposed to pick me up at a certain time when we were going to drive to another town twenty miles away. He didn't show up, and so I just left and went without him. He finally showed up, found I was not there, and called me to say that he was there now and to apologize for being late. I said, 'Well, that's too bad.' And he said 'You're kidding, right? You're coming back to pick me up?' I said, 'No, I'm not coming back for you. Next time don't be late.' And that was the last time he was ever late."

One sixty-year-old woman told us her action-packed husband of thirty-three years has mellowed over the years, but only after she made some choices of her own: "When we dated and for the first twenty years of our marriage, he was only interested in his own activities, usually involving hunting or fishing. Practically every weekend he would be off at 3 A.M. to hunt some poor animal, depending on the season. We didn't do much as a family, unless I went with him to sit in a duckblind or something equally exciting. Although I was not happy and frequently let him know how unhappy I was about it, I was raised to not necessarily do things without my husband, and so life pretty much stayed the same.

"However, I finally had enough, and after our kids were old enough to take care of themselves, I decided to do some things I enjoy, whether or not he came with me. After I started traveling a bit and going to more cultural events, he started tagging along. Now he actually enjoys them, and we do many events together."

One theme we heard over and over was how futile it is to nag men to change. Sometimes going your own way makes a difference, and sometimes being especially supportive and nurturing can have an impact. For example, Melanie told us, 'I used to get embarrassed by the way my husband would show off in public, loudly insisting that he pick up the tab for everyone at the table. Our friends, not feeling like they could respond in kind, invited us out less and less. I didn't know quite how to handle it, because I didn't want to hurt my husband's feelings.

"Instead of criticizing him, I started telling him how

wonderful a provider I thought he was and how much I appreciated all he did for me. I told him he had nothing to prove to me and that I chose him over every man on the planet. It didn't put an end to his grandstanding, but he mellowed out considerably, so that he now allows each couple to pay their own way at dinner. And oddly enough, the more I told him how much I respected him, the more I actually did. What started out as a bit of manipulation turned into a real enhancement of our love for each other."

Not only is it things that we do and say that foster positive growth in our spouses; the challenges and experiences of life can also chip away at those sharp corners. We have all seen men who were wild and unaccountable in their youth turn out to be loyal, steady "family men" in their older years. When we asked Nora, married for forty years, whether people can change, she said, "They can grow up. The basic fundamental person is there, but attitudes can change, yes—especially, I believe, through counseling. I know my niece's first husband, whom she divorced because he was verbally abusive, now sees the total error of his ways. He sees what he did." Nora's niece's actions had an effect on him, and although their marriage is over, he may treat their children, and any women in his future, differently.

When we change, we force a change in our relationships, as the balance between the two people is disturbed and needs to reestablish itself. We have probably all seen a situation where two people start out their relationship sharing an addiction such as alcohol, food, or smoking. If one decides to stop his or her habit, the other person may react in various ways: he or she may act out in worse ways to try to get the other person back into their familiar and comfortable pattern, he or she may become angry with the change, or he or she may try to make the change, too. While we cannot bring about the actual changes in our mates, we can initiate the process of change through our own actions and attitudes.

Most of us need some help in recognizing what we can and cannot control in our relationships. We may want to turn to our trusted women friends to help us sort out what of our own actions and attitudes we can change to address a problem. Sometimes we think we have a lot more control then we actually do, and we need our friends to tell us that it is not our responsibility or within our power to fix everyone; we can only work on ourselves. And if a change is occurring in the relationship but not quickly enough for our tastes, we can call our friends to express our frustration without criticizing our mates. We may want to set some ground rules with our friends so they know what their "job" is. For instance, we may want to tell our friends, "Joe and I are going through this struggle right now, and although he is starting to respond, I just need to vent!" Then our friends know that all they need to do is listen and empathize, not judge or fix the problem.

Girlfriend Guidelines

*Well, what is a relationship? It's about two people having
tremendous weaknesses and vulnerabilities, like we all do,
and one person being able to strengthen the other
in their areas of vulnerability. And vice versa.
You need each other. You bolster each other.*

—JANE FONDA

Los Angeles Weekly

Expect to Be Surprised

Sometimes I wonder if men and women really suit each other.
Perhaps they should live next door and just visit now and then.

—KATHERINE HEPBURN

Untamed Tongues

If you are starting a relationship, get ready to consider someone else's opinion! As a single person, you were able to make decisions by yourself, but once you are coupled, there are few decisions that can be made without taking someone else into consideration. As one woman who had been married ten years said, "I think that one of the downsides of having a relationship is all the compromises you have to make. As an individual, you make the choices and act on them without having to make those compromises."

Deciding to move in together generally signals a step forward in the relationship. When we live with each other, we get the privilege of seeing each other at our best and worst at a significantly closer range than when we were dating. The little things we found so adorable when we were gazing at each other through muted candlelight, can become sources of abrasive irritation when glaring at each other through a steamed-up bathroom door. When we share the same space, we must address a lot of issues that we could avoid or ignore if we lived in separate places.

We asked women how marriage differed from what

they had expected, and we got a variety of answers, many of which brought a smile to our faces. Sylvia, a psychologist who waited until she was thirty to marry, told us, "Even though I knew theoretically that married people live together, I found myself surprised that he didn't leave for his own place at the end of the day. I'd look at my watch and think, 'Why doesn't he go home?' And then I'd realize, he was home!"

Sharing space, especially when one is used to living alone and calling all the shots, can reveal expectations and attitudes that were previously invisible to us. Victoria, a woman who recently married, confessed, "I keep forgetting I'm a part of a couple. I'll talk to my friends on the phone, and they'll say, 'Hey, you want to go out to eat with me tonight?' and I'll say, 'Sure!' and we'll make plans. After we hang up I'll realize, 'Hey, wait, my husband thinks I'm eating with him tonight. Maybe I should include him or see if he even wants to go out.' That has been the biggest change for me, and something I just didn't expect."

Caren told us she hadn't expected how hard it would be to share a bedroom. "I've shared apartments with girlfriends for years, so I thought it would be a simple adjustment to move in with Jerry. But when I was sharing an apartment, I always had my own room. When I needed privacy, I simply went to my room and shut the door. My girlfriends respected my space, and besides, they had their own rooms to go to. But once Jerry and I moved in together, my room was his room. When I went to my room for privacy, I'd look up and there he was—in the same room! Even though I love sharing 'our' room with Jerry, and all that goes along with that, a part of me still misses having my own room, a space that is mine alone."

Sharing space, both emotional and physical, seems to be the source of a great deal of conflict and, therefore, compromise. If our communication skills are not developed when we move in together, we had better start working on them immediately, if not sooner! The first step is talking to each other about what is important to each of us and coming up with ways to satisfy as many of those needs as possible. For instance, it is not unreasonable for Caren to want some privacy once in a while. Instead of getting to the point where she feels resentful against Jerry for lack of alone time, she might broach the subject now. She may even find out that he would like some private time as well, or she may find that her need for privacy makes him feel excluded. The two will be able to resolve their differences only if they start talking about it and trying to find a solution that works for both of them. When a situation needs compromise, the best way to begin is to start talking about it.

This goes for our other relationships as well. A change in our relationships with the men in our lives will ripple out to our relationships with our friends. Once we are sharing space with a man, we may also need to communicate with our friends about how to maintain the friendship. For instance, we may want to reassure our friends that we are still available to them even though we have become more bonded to the man in our lives. Some women may feel inhibited or resentful if they sense they are being replaced by the men in our lives. We may want to set up a regular time to get together with a friend every week or month so that we stay connected. Not only do we and our friends continue to need one another's support and the fun that we share, we also need the special perspective that close women friends provide. Our girlfriends are probably the ones who know most about our relationship with our chosen men, so we can continue to rely on them to give us insight about how to proceed in romance.

We may also want to set up some guidelines with our friends about what they do and *don't* want to hear about with respect to our relationship with a boyfriend or husband. One woman told us, "There's a fine line between talking about men and not violating their privacy. Sometimes with friends I've had to put my hands up and say, 'I don't want to know that, that's really personal and private.' Although it is very tempting to say, 'Let me tell you what he did,' and include every detail, there's a way to share a story about a man without revealing incredibly personal things that he would never want someone else to know. When you hear those things, all of a sudden you are in a triangle of the most essential kind, and you find yourself sitting at dinner with this poor man, thinking, 'Oh, I know what you do late at night.' It can be horrifying."

We agree. There is a fine line between sharing with our women friends and respecting our man's privacy. We may want to express our feelings to a girlfriend about an event in the relationship, but we do need to protect the details of our mate's private life (unless he is hurting us physically, of course). For instance, talking about his particular anatomical arrangements or a specific sexual practice is not such a good idea, although we may wish to talk about our own experience of our bodies with our friends. A little of the Golden Rule can come in handy here: What would we feel comfortable with when he is talking to his friends about us?

Maintain Your Sense of Self

What you have become is the price you paid to get what you used to want.

—MIGNON MCLAUGHLIN

The Neurotic's Notebook

After the first flush of a romantic relationship, men and women realize that the world out there has been eagerly waiting for them to rejoin it. The realities of jobs, families, and other friends reassert their importance. Now is the time when a couple struggles with what couplehood means. How much is the individual a part of the couple, and how much is he or she alone, separated from the mate and pursuing other interests?

When we talked to Mira, who is married to a stockbroker and found herself disturbed early in their marriage by her husband's focus on his work, she told us that there was a shift in the other direction as they grew older: "The interesting thing is that for me, and maybe for many women who had children early without establishing a career, was that the relationship later shifted between Zach and me. When the children were old enough, I pursued my dreams whole-hog. My attention was all devoted to my career and my interests and my schooling. Then Zach, poor thing, and I had to deal with why I was uninterested in him, and why wasn't all my attention on him? It was strange to wrestle with those issues from the other side.

"I still don't think the issue has been resolved. I think we both recognized what was happening and learned that just because I had interests other than Zach in my life, it didn't mean I wasn't committed to my family and marriage—that it's just part of growing up for both of us. I think we're a lot better off now in terms of accepting the marriage as it is now—two independent people, instead of two people who are enmeshed in some way who have to fight to get free or just stay enmeshed."

Even when Mira had not yet branched out on her own, she said that she maintained her individuality "by maintaining my own relationships with the few women friends that I have. Then school became a big part of being my own person, and my writing. I guess it's identifying the things that are uniquely me and keeping a hand in those things. That's the biggest part of staying my own person. I don't know that I ever made Zach feel comfortable with my branching out."

As many women of her generation experienced, fifty-five-year-old Esther, a writer, gave up some personal plans in order to get married. She talks about her courtship with Brad: "We continued to have a growing relationship, and I still had a ticket to go to Europe. I just wanted to go fool around, broaden my experiences. In his inimitable way he said, 'I don't like your reasons for going on this trip to Europe. I can't tell you not to go, but there's no guarantee I'll be around when you get back.'

"I was just going to go off on an adventure, maybe for three months, something like that. He told me, essentially, that I couldn't be secure in knowing I could come back to what I'd left. I just agonized over the 'bird in the hand,' and I decided not to go. It really was the two parts of my nature. I was seeking adventure, but I was intensely practical, too. The practical part of me was saying, 'Wait a minute. This is lunacy. This relationship is solid, what are you fooling around with this for?' So I made the practical decision, and then the adventure in me was on hold for years."

Asked what effect that had on her relationship,

Esther replied, "Well, I've probably had one foot out the door for twenty-seven years. When I look back at myself then I think, 'I had no sense of self. I had no sense of confidence in my own worth.' When I think back now, if I had gone, then he would have been the one who would have had to sit with the idea of 'How important is this person to me?' Maybe he would have gone and found somebody else, but I would have, too. But I didn't trust that at the time."

Every relationship requires compromise. However, if you find yourself, or if your husband finds himself, giving up a deep personal desire for the sake of the relationship, get ready. That desire will probably emerge in some form in the future; it is not going to disappear.

Another woman we talked to recognized that she needed to make some changes in her own life for her own physical and mental health, but that it was frightening to think about the effect on her relationship: "I need to take better care of myself, I need to take more time off, I need to do a lot of things for myself that people (including my family) will look at as selfish, but it's just going to have to be. Part of the risk in doing this, and part of the way I was raised, is that any kind of thing that you do as an individual puts the relationship at risk, because you are all of a sudden creating a space around yourself, and if that person isn't bonded to you, he can just drift off."

When we asked Esther to describe how to deal with

the uncertainty that comes up around individual change and its effects on a marriage, she bluntly stated, "You're scared a lot. The fear level or the anxiety level during every one of these new personal movements is incredible. You don't know. You're getting into the unknown territory, constantly."

When we as individuals change, we can expect a response from our partners. Humans are very committed to keeping things the same, so even if there is a change for the better, likely your partner will set up resistance to test you. Nina, a therapist, says she gives her clients a systems lecture about change and homeostasis: "There's always a test, 'Do you really mean this?' When it comes to new behavior the other person or the system knows exactly how to hook you back in. So you'll always be tested to see if you're really going to shake things up or if the system can get back to comfort level. As I got firmer in changes I'd made in my life and would actually trust my own judgment and stand my ground, the gap between my husband and me would get too great, and then he would have to choose to come along or not, which is always a source of fear for me. But, every time, my husband came along. It was kicking and screaming, but there he was again. He always shifted enough so that it was always workable again."

We see a lot of women whose expectations of a relationship (and we are not excluding ourselves here) are so high that they are not willing to be in the relationship unless their autonomy or some other expectation is wholly respected. Both of us have been in places in our lives where we were so focused on our careers or writing books or going to school that we didn't have the time or energy to devote to a committed relationship.

However, the women we spoke to who had been in long-term relationships seemed willing to make some compromises; they can and want to make the time and place in their lives for that union. One woman said, "What you sacrifice by staying alone is that sense of community and being part of something that is bigger than you." And Mira described why she sticks with the relationship even though there is a lot of tension and compromise: "I like having a companion and friend who is always available. I can go home and know he is there, and I can have a conversation with him. If we started taking tango lessons, I don't have to look for a partner, right? I think a lot of it, too, is that there is so much history that the marriage and the relationship becomes a separate entity, it would be almost like I was destroying another entity in leaving that relationship. We have so much history, and so much we've worked through. To leave that behind would leave a tremendous void."

So it becomes a balancing act. When two people come together as in a marriage or other long-term relationship, there's the man, the woman, and the relationship; all three deserve care and support. If either of the people or the relationship is neglected, that entity will be lost.

One woman shared this analogy with us: "I heard some-one say the other day that we all juggle balls in our lives—what you have to do is decide which are the rub-ber ones that are going to bounce back. 'I can let that promotion go, I can let that night at the movies go, I can let that vacation go—because it will come back. I have a chance to do that again. But this one is a crystal, not a rubber, ball, and if I let it go too many times, it's not going to bounce back, it's going to smash. So there's no way you get to have everything."

Learn to Trust the Process

One advantage of marriage, it seems to me, is that when you fall out of love with him, or he falls out of love with you, it keeps you together until you maybe fall in again.

—JUDITH VIORST

Redbook

In every long-term romance, there is a time when the honeymoon is over. This rarely occurs on the day the happy couple returns from the airport, and it can occur years into the relationship. If you are anything like us, you have been indoctrinated into the ways of romance by hundreds of movies and television shows that tell us what romance is, how men should act, and how our love relationships should be in every respect. Guess what?

No relationship will ever match that picture, and if it does, it won't maintain that standard for long.

Joyce thought her marriage to Ray was nearly perfect until they moved away from the familiar surroundings of the Midwest to California to go to graduate school. She told us, "There were several years when it all hit the fan. I can remember one point in particular where we looked at each other and said, 'I don't like being with you. I'd rather be by myself than be with you.' Saying it out loud made it so real. But then, because we'd made a commitment to each other, we both said, 'Well, somehow this has got to work. And we'll find a way.'" As a consequence, they both went into therapy and made the changes necessary to enjoy the positive relationship they have today.

Few relationships can survive on love alone. Ronni told us that she didn't think her marriage would have survived without outside supports. She said, "My husband had been in therapy for three years before I met him. And in many ways, we entered into our marriage with a lot of resources, a lot of support, a lot of therapy, and a lot of life experiences. As I see marriages fail around me, I'm glad we have these resources. It's a struggle staying married. It's wonderful, but not easy. Hal and I often ask each other how we would have made it without this help. I don't think we would have made it through the first year."

That first year, with all the changes and adjustments, can be very challenging. Veronica told us that her first year of marriage was "the most difficult. At one point we thought about forgetting the whole thing, just divorcing and going our separate ways. I remember one time calling my father and hearing him tell me, 'Well, just remember the first year is the best one and then after that it's all downhill.' And I thought, 'This is going to get even worse from here?'

"There was one thing that kept me hanging on. The man who performed our wedding ceremony gave us the illustration that marriage is like two streams coming together. At first there's a lot of turbulence as the two streams collide, but further downstream it's much quieter and smoother going. I can remember clinging to this image, hoping that if we just held on through this rough period, things would smooth out. Having that image in mind helped me learn to grow together with my husband. And I'm glad I stayed."

As one woman photographer, now married for twenty-six years, noted, "Reality hits like a thud at some point along the way. I guess that point for me was when I realized we didn't have the romance every day. It was a shock to me. He'd rather read the paper than be seduced. Or, he has his daily schedule, and that is going to take precedence in places. I'm not going to be the center of his attention. I went back to graduate school in art, and I started wanting to develop relationships there and get into that whole thing. But I was married, and I was expected to come home and fix dinner, so I couldn't hang out with my school friends and discuss our classes. My husband came first. I ended up in this struggle."

Because many women have more economic freedom today, many relationships may fall apart at this point of disillusionment, especially if there are no children. Without economic or family constraints, it becomes easier to leave, and when a couple is in a difficult struggle, it may seem there is no point in staying. However, as difficult as it may be, this juncture provides an opportunity to look at who this other person really is and who you really are. The fantasy is no longer the lens through which you see everything.

This is where the rubber meets the road. Not only are you going to have to figure out what his thought and emotional processes are, but after you learn to trust those processes, you will have to hear his conclusions about an issue and include those conclusions in your decision together. This is very tough, and it will not happen overnight. Just be patient while both of you learn this new skill. We suspect everyone who has been in a relationship wakes up one morning and says, "Who is this person lying next to me? I don't know this person." That is the time to sit up and start facing the challenges. Good can come of sticking with the process, we can all grown and mature as adults as a result. As one woman said, "Marriage can be really wonderful, and it can be really awful, but it is always very hard! Yet my husband and I wouldn't have it any other way."

Recognize That No One Is Going to Fulfill All Your Needs

Paradoxically though it may sound: whenever one tries too desperately to be physically close to some beloved person, whenever one throws all one has into one's longing for that person, one is really giving him short change. For one has no reserves left then for a true encounter.

—ETTY HILLESUM

The Wit and Wisdom of Women

It is perfectly natural to need human connection, and yet many people are made to feel that they are being too demanding if they look for it in their marriage. As one woman told us who just left a marriage of fifteen years: "The message that I got in my marriage was that my needs were out of line and childish and that in order to be an adult one had to be self-sufficient. I've come to recognize how much bullshit that is. I've come to value the fact that I need people, and I've come to value the fact that they need me. This need to be 'independent' creates a lot of neurotic doubt in ourselves because we second-guess ourselves so much: 'Why am I so needy?' Because that's the natural human state! We're pathologizing something that is normal. It is normal to need other people. We are social creatures."

What may take the pressure off our primary relationship is being able to spread those needs around to a variety of people. In our society the family is the basic economic and social unit, and many people expect that they and their spouses must not go outside the family in order to do the activities they like or create valuable bonds with others. Therefore, if one person cannot fulfill a need of the other in the couple, a lot of frustration results. Women told us that the women they admired among their friends were those who could accept what was missing from their relationships and find it elsewhere.

Christine told us, "My friend has a relationship that's from time to time difficult. I've admired how she can let things go like water off a duck's back in a way that I can't. She reaches a point where she gets frustrated with her partner, and then she says, 'This person isn't going to change, and I have chosen someone who is difficult to live with in this regard.' So she takes responsibility for her own choice. And then, when he gets obnoxious, she basically blows him off. It's a saving grace to the relationship, and most of the time it looks to me like she does it without compromising herself. She's saying, very clearly, 'I need this particular thing, and it's not available here, so I'll get it somewhere else or I'll do it myself. I'll take care of my needs, but I'm not going to keep pestering him to do it, because he's not at that point. I love him anyway; he does these other things for me.' So she can accept him without either getting resentful or falling into a victim stance, which is pretty valuable and pretty rare. I think it's a real sign of emotional maturity, and I respect her a lot for that. She's spent so many years working on herself and becoming aware of herself, and that's what it really takes; that's the foundation of making any relationship work. Both people have to be really committed to becoming aware within themselves."

She continued, "We wouldn't be so disappointed in our parents and we wouldn't be so disappointed in our mates if all these needs that we all have for intimacy, for deep sharing, were spread around a larger base of people. I see that as a really big factor in the stresses on primary relationships in our society. We don't know how to do community in our society."

Another woman, Laura, told us this story: "I have a good friend who is very clear about who a guy is or isn't, and she acts on it without a lot of sentimentality. Not necessarily without pain, but without getting tied up in knots. She can say to herself, 'This is the situation, I can't change it, and I have to decide if I can live with it or not.' For instance, she realized that her husband was going to travel during the week with his work and that he was not going to be there for her a lot of the time. She had to decide if she could live with that, because it wasn't going to change. Yet she knew she didn't want to sit at home by herself every night during the week. So she went out and created a whole 'weekday' life for herself. While she made trade-offs that I don't think I would have wanted to make, she was very clear about what he was and was not going to do for her.

"I really admire that — when people have enough clarity to call it what it is and accept it and be happy about it or else say, 'I'm never going to be happy' and leave. The times I've hated myself most in bad relationships was when I was just complaining and whining about it. When I see my friends say, 'Hey, this is what it is and I can't live with it,' I really admire that. They don't allow so many veils to come down that make it look pretty and soft and very attractive, and they're not feeling so afraid of the truth, whatever it may be. That's something I need to learn to do better."

Many women told us that they rely on their girlfriends to supply them with some of the emotional support they need or to share activities they enjoy. While a man and woman may adore and share and support each other in a marriage, sometimes we need to talk about our experiences with another who loves us deeply but in a slightly different way. Men and women both benefit from having many loving, supportive relationships, and we gain insight and knowledge from many perspectives. Connections with our friends can do much to support our romantic relationships as well as improve the quality of our lives.

What a Girlfriend Can Do

I can trust my friends. . . . These people force me to examine myself, encourage me to grow.

—CHER

The Wit and Wisdom of Women

Girlfriends are essential to understanding men. By comparing notes, we can come a little closer to improving our skills in dealing with the opposite sex. Not only do our girlfriends provide a sounding board to talk out our problems or concerns, but because they know us so well, they can help us to see goals and standards that they know to be important to us but that we may not have put into words. As Christine told us, "I was talking with my girlfriend of ten years about the new relationship I'm in, and she said, 'For as long as I've known you, you've been wanting three things in a relationship: someone who'll give you the space to develop in ways you want to develop, someone you don't have to take care of—in the sense of doing all the relationship work—and someone who'll stay emotionally connected.' I started crying—first because I hadn't ever put it so clearly myself, and then because I realized my relationship checks out in all three areas! I was so grateful to her for knowing me so well."

Girlfriends can also provide a safe haven when we need some breathing room in a difficult time. Most women said that their girlfriends were supportive of their healthy relationships and were there to urge them on when times got tough.

However, our women friends are also right there to defend our honor. If they think we are being hurt in some way, many friends will go to great lengths to help. Girlfriends can be proactive, too, not just helpful listeners. One sixty-five-year-old nurse tells this story: "Many years ago my friend suspected her husband of having a girlfriend. One night she called to ask if I would go with her while she tried to follow him. I'll do just about anything for a friend, and of course I told her I'd help!

"After making sure my husband would be available to keep an ear open to the sleeping children, I quickly threw on some dark clothing and drove to her home. She had obviously never watched any spy movies, because she was prepared to drive her own car and she wore pastel pants and sweatshirt! I soon set her straight, and we set off in my 'suburban housewife' station wagon to his office.

"He had called her, just before she had phoned me, to say he would be working late, so we thought we just might reach his office parking lot before he left. I drove very carefully, and when we reached the parking lot I turned the car lights off and coasted in until we located his car. Fortunately we were able to find a parking space that was partially obscured by some low-hanging tree limbs, and we started our surveillance.

"We didn't even have a chance to get comfortable when her husband came out of the office, got into his car, and drove away. You know how when you're in a great rush and everything goes wrong? Well, the keys dropped out of the ignition switch just as I was trying to start the car, and when I found them the 'perp' (that's police talk) was driving out of the lot.

"It was late enough to have the streets pretty much to ourselves, but that meant we had to stay way back to avoid being noticed, and for the first two or three blocks we followed the wrong car! Anyway, we were able to spot the right one soon after running our first red light. We followed him until he pulled over in front of a large apartment building and parked. Eureka! He certainly wasn't working at the office!

"We waited until he was well inside the complex before going into the building and searching the mailboxes for tenant names. My theory was that my friend might recognize the name of someone she knew or at least had heard of but didn't know well enough to know an address. There were no names on those mailboxes, however.

"Back in the car, we prepared to wait all night if necessary. First, we parked under another tree, but we didn't have enough light to read or do anything while we took turns watching for the culprit, so we moved to just under a streetlight a few spaces behind his car. She rested first, but she talked the whole shift while I tried to read a newspaper. However, the night was cool, so it wasn't more than an hour before we were both freezing. She wanted to get out of the car and do calisthenics to get warm, so, right then and there, I told her she was not cut out for this type of work and I could have done better by myself. She got back in the car, and we sang until the windshield was so clouded up we couldn't see the front door of the apartment building.

"After about three hours, well after 2 A.M., out he came, and, sure enough, there was a woman with him. She was just as old as he was, wasn't a bit pretty as far as we could tell, and we couldn't see her body since she was wrapped in a frumpy looking bathrobe. My friend decided right then that if this woman was his idea of a love interest, she'd let him have her! We drove back home, giggling all the way.

"She got the divorce, the kids, and the house, and he got a woman with an apartment, and no income. The other woman got a divorced man with two kids, alimony payments, and continuing child support. I had so much fun I kept asking other women friends if they were absolutely sure their husbands were faithful, and if not, could I 'tail' him?"

Not only can girlfriends help us get to the truth of the matter, they can give us a kick in the pants as well when we are messing up a relationship. One woman we spoke with, Blake, a restaurant owner who was getting engrossed in the success of her business, started noticing that her husband, Kent, was becoming more and more distant from her. When she questioned him about it, he said that yes, he was having difficulty connecting to her, but he really didn't know why. Blake thought Kent might be jealous of her success, but he insisted that that was not it, and he seemed as confused and troubled as she was about the growing distance between them. They did a lot of work trying to sort out various things in the relationship, until Blake's friend Janine finally sat her down and said, "Look, I love both of you, and you are both messing up. I like this guy, and I don't want you to lose him! You are working too hard and haven't put enough time into your connection with Kent. Your success allows you to hire some help at the business, so do it and get your priorities straight! There's always going to be work to do, but you could lose this marriage if you don't shift your focus."

Janine then went to Kent, with whom she had become friends through her friendship with Blake, and asked him if he would like to talk with her. He did. Janine let him know that she thought Blake and Kent were good for each other but that he was going to have to step up to the plate and let Blake know his negative feelings when he had them. In Janine's opinion, he was also going to have to take some steps to put more fun and shared activities into the relationship. When we last spoke with Blake, she said, "It seems to be working better. I am getting some help at work and have more time for Kent. Kent is trying to help me break the patterns that we both had of not saying when something was bothering us. Now we're trying to deal with it right away. We are not out of the woods yet, but having Janine, who we both love and trust to want the best for us, tell us her view as an 'inside outsider' really helped us clarify the problem. I am very grateful for her honesty."

Saying Goodbye

Every arrival foretells a leave-taking: every birth a death. Yet each death and departure comes to us as a surprise, a sorrow never anticipated. Life is a long series of farewells; only the circumstances should surprise us.

—JESSAMYN WEST
The Life I Really Lived

Deciding to Leave

*All sorrows can be borne if you put them into a story
or tell a story about them.*

—ISAK DINESEN

Women and Fiction 2

Romantic songs surround us with the promise of undying love that lasts through eternity. The intensity of a romantic bond can, at times, overshadow the reality that in this life all things, good or otherwise, eventually come to an end. Some relationships end voluntarily through the choice of one or both people involved. Other endings are outside everyone's control, if one spouse outlives the other.

Regardless of how a relationship ends, the loss of a love confronts us with the task of making sense of it all: What was this liaison all about? Was my investment in this relationship well placed? Is love worth the inevitable pain of loss? What will I do now that he's gone? What does life mean for me now?

Meaning making is something women can do well together, telling our stories of love and loss to one another, over and over, until the tales finally do make sense. Our girlfriends are invaluable, if not irreplaceable, in our grappling with the undeniable need to make meaning out of our lives. With their help we can survive the losses that threaten to leave us bereft, confused, and doubting that anything can be put together again in a recognizable pattern. We share snippets of experiences, mixing and matching them, until the fabric of our lives fits together harmoniously like a glorious quilt. Girlfriends help each other make sense out of the nonsensical, turn mistakes into wisdom, and create hope in a world where nothing lasts forever.

Struggles and Separations

I have had enough.

—GOLDA MEIR

Upon resigning

No relationship is perfect, and at times the best solution is to take a break. Some separations serve the purpose of salvaging the relationship by giving both parties the opportunity to think things through and realize that they both truly want to work things out. Yvonne told us that after twenty-four years of marriage, she separated from her husband because "I wasn't pleased with the way things were going, but I still didn't want the marriage to end. I felt I had to make the statement, 'You're not listening to me!' There were a number of things I had tried talking to my husband about. He would seem to hear me, but nothing changed. I got so frustrated that one day I just packed my bags and went to stay with friends.

"I asked various friends from our church community to sit with us different nights so they could hear us bicker and try to work things through. They would tell us their impressions regarding what was going on. Having other people hear what I was up against helped a lot. My husband couldn't just dismiss me as a nagging wife, because our friends let him know they felt I had reason to be dissatisfied.

"Even though my intention was to get back together

301

again, there were times I almost gave up hope. But I never took off my wedding ring. My husband later told me that he found encouragement during the separation when he noticed I kept my ring on the whole time. It was worth the risk of separating. We were back together in three weeks, and we just came back from celebrating our twenty-fifth wedding anniversary."

While some separations can mark the end of one era in a relationship, making way for a new and better way of relating, other separations are the beginning of the end. Indeed, some marriages must end—relationships in which women are physically and sexually abused for example. We believe that one slap, one punch to the stomach, or one violent sexual encounter is one too many and provides grounds for walking out and never looking back.

But many women find it difficult to leave these relationships, even when they are abused repeatedly. Such is the story we heard from Shelley, whose religious beliefs kept her in her first marriage longer than was safe for her physically, emotionally, and certainly spiritually. She told us, "I was eighteen when I got married. I was so young and felt obligated to follow the teachings of my church. Even though he started hitting me soon after we were married, I felt I couldn't leave the marriage or I'd be out of the church. I actually separated a couple of times when I was scared for my life, but he'd promise me it'd never happen again and I'd go back. I lived in continual fear of his next blowup.

"Day-to-day life was a nightmare. My husband was very, very jealous and possessive. The only things I did on my own were go bowling and serve as secretary of the ladies' organization at church. If he thought one of these meetings should have been over at 9 P.M., and I was fifteen minutes late, he'd drive to the church to find me. I think he thought I was Miss America or something, the way he imagined everybody wanting me. I sure wasn't on the prowl. He was just very insecure and would explode into a complete rage.

"One morning, when I was only twenty, I woke up and simply knew that I wasn't going to take it anymore. I'd given it five or six chances, and each time the assaults got worse. Satisfied that I'd done everything that I could, I felt strong enough to face the fact that in the church's eyes, it didn't matter how abusive he was. I was the one breaking the law, because I was the one who was leaving. On that particular morning, none of that mattered. I came to terms with it, and I didn't care what they thought. I knew I was right. I called my mom and told her I was leaving and was going to file for divorce. She said, 'I think you made a wise decision.' Then I knew I would get through this. Not that I needed her approval, but I knew that she would back me, she'd support me through this. I had to make some really serious decisions at a young age."

Fortunately, most of us will never have to leave a marriage in order to protect ourselves from this kind of abuse. But there are other reasons women decide to end their marriages. Since every relationship has problems, whether you have been together a month or forty years, how do you know when to say, "It's time to leave"? When we asked this question of women who had divorced, we heard answers as individual as was each woman telling her story.

None of the women took the decision to divorce lightly and came to that course of action, usually, after years of trying to make the relationship work. Such was Stacy's story, who devoted several years to trying to fix the marriage. When she turned thirty-five, she reevaluated her life and saw no hope of salvaging a lifeless marriage. She told us, "We worked hard on our marriage, going to counseling for seven years. Almost from the day we were married, I knew the marriage was in deep trouble. I hadn't gotten the nurturing and sustenance that I needed from my parents and other adults, and I chose someone who wanted to stay a safe emotional distance away—like a caretaker or a parent instead of a partner.

"As long as I stayed content with the distance, the marriage continued. But eventually I wanted more. I had been growing for years in my career and my creative life. I'd worked hard to find ways of expressing myself creatively. I'd learned, for instance, to turn down work offers that weren't rooted in my own passion, my own creative energy. After following my own instincts and my own passions in my career, it was just a matter of time before my commitment to myself and my own creative passion caught up with me sexually.

"It became clear that I had married somebody who I wasn't passionate about, and the marriage had to end. In order for me to be a fully creative person, I had to be expressing my own passion sexually as well as in work. In a way, leaving the marriage was like what most women experience when they leave home for the first time. I was finally an adult woman, only my first husband had filled in where my father and mother should have been."

Stacy was looking at the person she was becoming, liking what she was seeing, and knew the relationship had to end. Joan, however, who is happy in her second marriage, decided to divorce her first husband when she realized that she didn't like her own development. "I was becoming a meek, nervous person. I didn't like that about myself."

Honesty, especially with yourself, takes a lot of courage. According to Ursula, knowing what is happening to your own personality and feelings "takes such incredible wisdom and self-knowledge. I think it is one of the hardest things, because you get into a relationship and the two of you make your own world with your own rules and your own definitions. If you are so incredibly intimate with one person, they are that mirror to you, and the mirror that they give you for yourself becomes who you are. To have the wisdom to realize that the mirror is warped takes an incredible amount of strength."

Sometimes marriages end because both parties are dissatisfied, neither person feeling like the relationship is a match. After a fifteen-year marriage, Dotty and her husband called it quits when it became apparent that they both needed very different things from the relationship. Dotty told us, "I need someone who wants to create a sense of connectedness, who makes me feel like I'm part of something greater than myself. I want a partner with whom I can go on adventures or go to the movies or run errands or go for a walk. It's a feeling of being as comfortable as I am on my own, a family quality, you know—just being a part of something in the tribal sense."

The man who Dotty chose as her husband "was so concerned about his autonomy and not getting stuck in a relationship that he would sacrifice the relationship in order to prove his individuality. Conversely, I was constantly trying to sacrifice myself in order to be in the relationship. It was a perpetual nightmare. Once I remember him coming home announcing, 'I'm going to visit my friend in Maine for Christmas. You can come if you want to.' I said, 'Wait a minute—shouldn't it be, 'I'd like to go to visit my friend at Christmas. What would you like to do? Can we do that together?' Instead, he made the decision and I could either come or not.

"It was so important for him to make his own decisions and stand on his own two feet, be independent. I thought that there was something wrong with me because I was constantly feeling rejected. But the truth of it was, he was acting for the sake of his individuality, which was really important to him. Now I can look back and see that what he needed I couldn't give to him. Likewise, I needed something from him, and he just did not have it to give to me."

Some people realize the end is near when they are faced with a life decision that forces them to reflect on the quality of their marriage. For instance, some women who may have been relatively contented with their marriages develop serious concerns about their partners when considering the prospect of starting a family.

Selena, a thirty-five-year-old attorney, told us, "When I faced the possibility of having a child with the man I was first married to, I thought, 'I can't do this. I cannot have a child with this person. He just isn't the man I want for the father of my children."

Gina, the mother of two, described how her thinking changed as she grew older. She said, "I think when you get married younger, you don't really think about 'Is he going to be a good father?' It might go through your head, but it's not the basis of your decision to marry. Then as you age, your priorities change. You think, first, 'Is he going to be a good husband?' and then the clock is ticking so you ask, 'Is he going to be a good father?' Maybe your expectations are higher, because as you age you want more for yourself. It becomes clearer what you want in your life. Then women ask, 'Could I have a child with this man? Would he be good father material? If not, the relationship can end."

Another life-changing decision may arise when one or the other of the couple is faced with a move associated with a career change or family needs. One woman found that a move across country prompted her decision to leave her marriage. She told us, "We were living in North Carolina, and my husband got a job offer in Denver. Even though I like Denver, the thought of moving caused me to reexamine how I felt about the relationship as a whole. I asked myself, 'Is this relationship worth all the change I'll have to face?' and I looked at all I'd be giving up for the marriage. When it came right down to it, I couldn't move. If the relationship had been a nourishing one, and a true partnership, that would have made it worthwhile to leave, even moving to a place I didn't like, because my work is mobile. But it became a question of whether the relationship with my husband was worth moving for, and the answer was no."

Some decisions are years in the making; others take an instant, as Cindy described when her husband gave her an ultimatum: "We had been unhappy together for years. He took a job in Buenos Aires and, without discussing it with me, assumed—no, demanded—that I give up my administrative job with a hospital and go with him. I did take a leave of absence for a month but told him I intended to return to Miami. When he dropped me off at the airport, he dramatically announced, 'If you get on that plane, the marriage is over.' I looked at him for a moment and then simply said, 'Okay.' I picked up my luggage and walked straight onto the plane."

Most of the women we interviewed whose marriages ended in divorce told us how valuable their girlfriends were during the entire process. One woman said, "My girlfriend was there from beginning to end—when I told her we were having serious problems in the marriage, when I needed someone to help me sort through my options, when I finally made the decision to leave. Whether it was a listening ear or a night of watching videos and eating too much chocolate, she was there for me."

As difficult as deciding to end a relationship may be, it is simply the first step in the process. Once the decision is made, the next step is to put that decision into motion, motion that usually disrupts every aspect of life and nearly all of our relationships.

Breaking Apart

Being divorced is like being hit by a Mack truck—if you survive you start looking very carefully to the right and left.

—JEAN KERR

Mary, Mary

More than a song lyric, breaking up is certainly hard to do. Even a decision that is right for you is not without massive amounts of pain and disruption. During the breaking-up process, everything is different. All of a sudden your present life and your visions for the future are disrupted. Now you are not part of a couple, you are alone. Additionally, if one is over thirty-five, the societal expectation that older women are less desirable can add to the stress of the situation. (Avoid anyone who quotes the "statistic" that the chances of marriage after that age are less than being killed by terrorists; in our experience, it simply isn't true.) During this turbulent time, we may start telling ourselves some horrible things about ourselves and about men.

In addition to having your emotional world in shambles, your material one may be disrupted, too. All the day-to-day details must be revamped, as Dotty describes: "When Sidney and I split up, not only did I have to continue taking care of all the things I had while in the marriage, I suddenly had to take care of everything he had done as well. I guess I shouldn't have been, I'll admit, but I was actually surprised when faced with doing all this myself—like paying all the bills, calling the repairman, doing all the recycling, taking out all the garbage. It takes a lot of time, and it had been nice having someone share the mundane things."

Another loss can come from an area we most need during a turbulent transition—your friends, especially your girlfriends. Chances are your social life was linked to your husband and that at least some of your friends will feel compelled to pick sides. Cindy told us about how she approached one of her girlfriends who not only socialized but also worked with Ben, her soon-to-be exhusband. "I said to her, 'If this is uncomfortable for you, please tell me.' She said, 'No, I like Ben, but you are my friend.' We got it right out in the open, and we've been friends ever since."

When asked if she lost any girlfriends during her divorce, Cindy nodded and told us about a girlfriend who tried to keep friendships going with both Cindy and Ben. "I'd talk about what I was going through, thinking my comments were confidential, only to find out that Ben was hearing about what I was saying. To make matters more awkward, she let Ben stay in the studio apartment in her house while he was looking for another place to stay. She'd complain to me about Ben's habits as a houseguest. One time she even told me that her roommate thought Ben was coming onto her. That was the last straw. I decided this was too convoluted for me. If she couldn't chose between us, then I'd make the decision for her. I let Ben keep his friendship with her, and I moved on."

Many times, women carry a load of guilt about the relationship — either over the mere fact that they got involved with the guy in the first place or that they ignored the warning signs and kept trying to keep the relationship going longer than they should have. On the sidelines, we can reassure a girlfriend that her desire for a partner in life, and her putting forth effort to make a relationship work are not things to be ashamed of but rather to be admired. Encourage her to learn what she can for the next round and then let the old relationship go without guilt or self-degradation.

During all major life transitions, not just divorce, we need our women friends' support and wisdom and offerings of ice cream. But we advise that you choose your girlfriends carefully, especially during the ending of a marriage, so that the support you receive is sincere and the wisdom is grounded in genuine love, not a heart of divided loyalty.

Deciding What's Yours and Mine

I am a marvelous housekeeper.
Every time I leave a man I keep his house.

—ZSA ZSA GABOR

Untamed Tongues

Once the decision to part has been made, couples are faced with the problem of dividing up their material belongings as well as figuring out child custody and support arrangements if minor children are involved. While amicable divorces do occur, which can certainly ease the pain of the process, many divorces start out amicably and deteriorate or else begin with both parties outraged and thirsty for blood. Unfortunately, we have probably all heard of or experienced divorces that involve lying, accusations, and less than honorable behavior when it came to dividing up the material goods.

Clare, a forty-five-year-old interior decorator, told us this story: "My husband didn't want the divorce, yet we just couldn't make it work. The situation between us was getting worse and worse, and I had to leave. He resented me for making that decision, and that resentment really came out when it came to dividing up our property. I learned that any item I wanted, he became attached to in the divorce, even if he hadn't cared about it during the marriage. I found myself sneaking things out of the house when he wasn't there so that we wouldn't fight about them. He didn't notice that the items were gone; he only noticed the things that I talked about — when I said I would like to have a particular print or dish or piece of furniture. I didn't think that process would ever end."

Not only is there emotional upset over the items that represent the couple's relationship together, but frequently women, especially those without financial independence, have to witness their fear of suddenly having nothing they can call their own actually materialize. One woman whose husband had control over the marital assets for the entire period of their twenty-year married life encountered many unpleasant surprises when they split up: "Although, thank goodness, our children were grown and we didn't have that as a battleground, I found that I knew very little about where the assets of the marriage were. Property that I thought we had didn't seem to be where I remembered it, and I had a difficult time figuring out what our assets really were as a couple. He went out of his way to keep that information from me. It was extremely upsetting to know that the man that I had put my trust in all those years was trying to hurt me in this way. I thought we had a deal, I would raise the children and make his home a pleasant one where he did not have major responsibilities, and he would supply the income. But now he doesn't want me to have anything in the divorce. I feel like I am seeing someone that I have never known before."

Perhaps it is the knowledge that there is no hope left for the relationship that leads people to abandon all caution in their dealings with each other. For whatever reason, we frequently hear that the property settlement process is the time when the gloves come off and all the ugly feelings are acted out. Fear, anger, resentment, a sense that this may be the last chance to exact revenge or to carve out some financial support—all of it emerges. Combined with the scary experience of having to fight it out in a public forum, a court where you may feel that you are being judged, these proceedings can be horrible. Anyone who has had the good fortune not to experience a property division just has to watch the movie *War of the Roses* to get a not-so-inflated view of what can happen when people start using their possessions as weapons against each other.

Along with the financial challenges you may be facing during a divorce, if you have children, you face another level of responsibility. For those with children, divorce marks the beginning of a new era in which one takes on the label of 'single parent.' Pauline told us that she was unprepared for the challenge of raising her children alone. "I underestimated how much time he spent with the children. I couldn't ask him anymore to look after the kids if I needed to run to the store or stay a bit longer at work. Now that I have my new life organized, it's not so difficult. I have several places where the kids can stay if an emergency comes up. But at the beginning, it was a madhouse."

And that's not to mention the emotional response children have to their parents' divorce. Crystal told us, "My middle daughter still has not accepted the divorce, even though I'm remarried and my exhusband is planning to marry soon. I don't want to tell her bad things about her father, and so she doesn't realize the inside workings of our marriage or why it had to end. All she sees is that I was the one who moved out, so I must be the 'bad guy' here. She still has not accepted my new husband and won't speak to him, even though she lives here part of the time."

But there are positive aspects to the change as well. Crystal went on to tell us, "Even though my daughter has been angry with me, she has relied on her church youth group and school for extra support. She has a lot of friends, and even at her age her girlfriends are helping her make this adjustment."

Glowing with pride, Crystal said, "It hasn't been easy on any of us, but now that her father and I have moved on to much happier relationships, she's finally getting the benefits of parents who have more to give her than we did when we were still married to each other. She's actually doing better than she's willing to admit, since she is graduating this year from high school as valedictorian. I'm very proud of her!"

Some children make smooth adjustments to their parents' divorce. But we know now, after years of experience and research, that children do suffer when the parents split up. This is usually another drain on the parents during an already difficult and demanding time. Surviving these times can only be done one day at a time and with a lot of help from our friends. If we have one or two friends we can rely on, tell our horrors to (without the stories being reproduced as fodder for the local gossip mill), and to remind us that the world is not a horrible place and that the property division process will eventually end, we can get through the divorce. Our women friends can also help us sort out what is important to us in the property settlement and maintain our dignity by clarifying whether we are arguing about a matter of principle or a matter of spite ("Do you really want that Barca lounger, or do you just want him *not* to have it?"). And even when our dignity is lost and we have lost our temper or made a fool of ourselves, our friends can remind us that we are only human and that they still love us and are going to support us through the turbulence.

While painful and frequently protracted, the property settlement process will end. Women told us that the process is undoubtedly damaging. One women we spoke with put it this way: "This is awful right now. I'm still reeling from the fact that it is *me* going through this experience. I feel betrayed, sad, and angry, and I just never thought I would have to get a divorce and fight my husband for my fair share. Yet," she went on, "part of me feels like this is for the best, and that when this is over, I can get my life started again."

'Till Death Do Us Part

You never realize death until you realize love.

—KATHERINE BUTLER HATHAWAY

The Journals and Letters of the Little Locksmith

The love shared between a man and a woman leaves both people changed—hopefully, more whole and complete. If he dies, leaving her to go on living without him, she loses everything and nothing, all at once. She loses her companion and friend and a sense of belonging that the union provided. But she continues to be the woman he has helped to shape in their relationship, and that person can never be taken from her. She loses his touch but not the imprint of his companionship. And in her memory and those of their friends and family, he will continue as before.

Outliving Our Partner

Mourning is not forgetting. . . . It is an undoing. Every minute tie has to be untied and something permanent and valuable recovered and assimilated from the dust.

—MARGERY ALLINGHAM

The Tiger in the Smoke

No matter our age, whether we are in our twenties or eighties, losing a partner to death is a horrible shock, rocking the foundation of our lives. Even those women who knew their husbands were terminally ill and had time to prepare for the inevitable experienced his death as unexpected and certainly unplanned.

This was most dramatically illustrated for us when we talked with Paula, a successful businesswoman who, at the age of thirty-three, lost her husband, Andrew, to cancer. The mother of two young children, a son aged nine and a daughter aged five, she was taken completely by surprise when, in a matter of months, Andrew changed from a "big, healthy athlete who was never sick, to a weakening man facing the end of his life."

Going back to when they first met when she was eighteen, Paula told us, "I had graduated from high school and moved to the city to attend college, in defiance of my father who saw me as showing off. I was the first person in my family to graduate from high school. I was not only moving to the big city, I was going to college on a scholarship. In many ways I was lucky that's the form my rebellion took: 'I'll show you, I'll read a book!'

"I moved to the city and got a job working nights at a bank. A friend I met there told me, 'I know a guy who's really funny like you, and you'd really like him.' And so I went on this blind date. It wasn't love at first sight, but I started hanging out with Andrew in a friendly way, not romantic. And when I was twenty, we had become really good friends and we decided to get married.

"We complemented each other. I came from a wild, crazed family—huge and sprawling, loud and argumentative—but there was an emotional availability, whether it was angry or loving. Emotions were always exposed. My husband came from a very repressed family, where he was the only child, so he loved my family and all these things I could bring. Andrew came from a middle-class, stable background. So that was very attractive to me.

"We got married when I was twenty. We had our first child when I was twenty-four and he was twenty-five. We had a nontraditional arrangement in those days. We took turns working and taking care of the kids. At first, I worked while Andrew went to school. Right when Andrew finished his masters' degree—when my daughter was about to go to kindergarten and I was heading back to school—he got sick.

"In February, he went to the doctors, and they misdiagnosed him with hepatitis at first, and we were all worried about that, not realizing how much better that would have been. In June, on the day before our thirteenth wedding anniversary, they did exploratory surgery. The next day, on our anniversary, they told us the cancer was terminal and that he had maybe six months on the outside.

"At first we couldn't believe it. But after a few weeks he had that inner knowledge. He said, 'I think this is it. It's not going to work out,' and he asked if he could go home to die. This was another trauma because they didn't believe in that in those days. This was in 1976. People kept telling us, 'You can't bring him home. You can't let your children see him die.'

"But we had both lost a parent when we were children, and we were both treated as if we couldn't handle it. I was three when my mother died, and I was told that she had gone to be with Jesus, which I interpreted as being on her own volition and which of course made me angry. My husband's father died when he was six years old, and he was told he went to sleep. No one ever spoke of it again. We decided to deal with this in a different way. We believed in our children and in their ability to cope with whatever this turned out to be.

"So he came home. It was very hard for him with the children. He never had that final conversation with our son. They'd get together and talk about sports. Like most men, they did a lot of sporting things together. They'd talk about those things, but they protected each other from having to have that final conversation. That's the only thing I really wanted that didn't happen.

"My daughter was too little to put feelings into words, but they had a nonverbal communication that was very strong. Toward the end, he lost interest in eating because his liver was involved and it's common to lose your appetite. But he would eat for her. She'd sit on his bed, with a little knife and a peach, and cut little pieces off for him. Both of my children spent time with him, and they saw him waste away.

"He died in July. Even though the whole thing only took a matter of months, it seemed very long at the time. And then, all of a sudden, it didn't seem like a very long time at all. Abruptly, everything was changed."

Paula and her family were given a bit of time to prepare for this unexpected devastation. For some there is no warning. Sylvia told us that she had spoken with her parents by phone on a Friday night and the next morning got a call from her mother saying her father was in the hospital. She told us, "I went straight to the hospital and saw him lying there in a coma due to a stroke. He never regained consciousness. I never got to formally say goodbye. None of us did, not even my mother.

"My brothers and sister came in from their various out-of-town homes, and we sat together for four days until he finally died. It was a really unsettling feeling, having him there but not there at the same time. I watched my mother grapple with the fact that there were no more words to be spoken, no more chances to make things right. Bam, it was over."

Losing the spouse that one loves creates hardship at any age. One woman talked about her grandmother, Lucy, who adored her husband to the day he suddenly died, in their sixty-second year of marriage: "Although both my grandparents were in their eighties, it was still inconceivable that one of them should die. When my grandfather suddenly died, my grandmother was lost. He was cremated, but she was unable to bury the ashes for a very long time. When she did, it seemed to help her come to some peace and resolution. It took several years before she had much interest in anything again, because how can you gain equilibrium after losing the man who you were crazy about for over sixty years? Nevertheless, she has recovered somewhat and is back to her social self who goes out to play cards with her girlfriends."

The death of a spouse may be easier to cope with when both parties are at peace with each other prior to the loss. Paula told us, "I always felt that everything was straight between me and Andrew. He had given me so much, in terms of acceptance. From the very beginning, from the first date, he loved me unconditionally. This is something that had never, ever happened to me in my childhood. But Andrew really valued me, and because of his love I learned to value myself.

"I felt that it was reciprocal. We were up-to-date, even though the time together seemed cut short. I gave him back what he needed. I said to someone not too long ago, 'If I died tomorrow, I would feel like I've had a great life.' I have no regrets, no heavy bitterness lying around. I've forgiven my family and hope they've forgiven me. Because of losing my husband, I know all you have is the time you have right now. Your life is just what it is. If you spend your life longing for some faraway future, waiting for something to happen, you have no guarantees that it ever will. Say everything you need to say today, while you still have the time."

Now What?

Proximity was their support; like walls after an earthquake they could fall no further for they had fallen against each other.

—ELIZABETH BOWEN

Friends and Relations

In the immediate wake of the loss of a partner come the urgent demands of how to cope with the present. Everything is suddenly different. Now what? Many women, especially when they don't know what to do, do the one thing they can—turn to a woman friend for support. Girlfriends have proven themselves to be reliable and adept, especially in making immediate decisions, such as funeral arrangements. One woman told us, "I was in shock after my husband died. If it hadn't been for my best friend, who swooped in, took care of all the arrangements, even picked out what I wore to the funeral, I don't know what I would have done. I could barely put one foot in front of the other, let alone make any decisions or phone calls. All I could think of was how different my life was going to be now that he was gone."

The death of a spouse redefines our identities (we're referred to as "widows" henceforth) and redirects our lives. This is especially true if no planning was done prior to the death. Such was the experience of Paula, who had never thought something could happen to Andrew. No health insurance paid the medical bills. No life insurance had been purchased. No savings had been stored away for emergencies. She told us, "By the time he died, I was on welfare. I didn't know what to do, but I was haunted by this image that, if I didn't go back to college, I would end up in a doughnut shop, with the big hanky and the thick-soled shoes. I would be serving coffee to the 'regular,' and I'd know who he was. I saw myself stuck there, on into infinity. I'd have no life.

"So I joined every program I could find. The second year I started a wallpaper-hanging business where I could work the jobs on Mondays and Wednesdays and go to school on Tuesdays and Thursdays. I'd do homework on Fridays and Saturdays. Now I don't know how I kept track of it all. The women at my children's after-school day care became my support group. That helped, but it was still tough.

"I felt very much like the kids were in danger. But

they're doing fine now, and in fact I'm a grandmother. My son has two children. He's thirty and has a job in computer art. My daughter is twenty-five, and she and her boyfriend will be going to graduate school in the fall. Granted, I still have things I could work on, but I feel good about how I've handled life after Andrew died. The years go by. The first three years or so, I thought of myself as a widow. Now I rarely identify myself that way. I feel very attached to my husband in ways that are hard to articulate. He's still very much a part of my life because of all he gave me. He gave me the strength to go forward."

A loss of a spouse frequently results in other changes in our lives. These changes may unfold over several years. Lucy, the eighty-eight-year-old who lost her husband after sixty-one years, decided to move from the small town where she had lived for many years and then moved again a few years later, in an attempt to find a good community "fit" for herself in her altered situation. She has now settled into a comfortable situation in a community she enjoys.

If we are witnessing a woman friend go through this type of loss, we can make a big difference in her life. Chances are she is feeling overwhelmed with all of the changes in her life and the choices she has to make. We may want to offer our help in simple things—taking small children, if she has them, for a day or two while she plans a funeral or deals with legal proceedings, helping her make lists of things that have to be done, listening to her as she processes all the feelings of sadness and anger over her loss, helping her talk through the decisions she has to make. She may not be able to articulate her needs at the time. But our presence and our love may be the best gifts we can give.

Starting Over

The world is round, and the place which may seem like the end may also be only the beginning.

—IVY BAKER PRIEST

Parade

Much is demanded of us in loss. We may feel that there is no point to living in such pain. But the meaning may become clear with time. The suffering that we survive will reshape us once again, starting a new period in our lives. It may challenge our beliefs, bring us face-to-face with our fears, and ferret out who our real friends are. Through this trial by fire, we can emerge stronger and wiser, confident that we are capable of handling whatever life deals us.

Perhaps alone, the loss of a love would be too terrible to survive. But together, we women are up to the task — strong enough to endure the passion, the memories, the final goodbyes, the starting over, even the rebirth that the death of a relationship demands of us.

Letting Go of the Past

The only thing I regret about my past life is the length of it.
If I had my past life over again I'd make all the same
mistakes — only sooner.

—TALLULAH BANKHEAD

The Times

Anyone going through a loss, whether through death or divorce, must be patient with herself. Grief and healing have their own schedule, and, much as we would like to move past them, those processes cannot be forced. Some women may choose to never marry or get seriously involved with men again. They may have too many responsibilities after the death of a spouse or may just feel no desire to try to fill the shoes left empty by the men they loved. Every woman has to decide that for herself.

Those who are thinking about trying again after the loss of a partner, will need time to get back on their feet again. Belinda, who we interviewed a year-and-a-half after her divorce, said, "I'm just getting to the point where I'm feeling something besides pain when I think about him and the marriage. Before, I was just suffering from this huge loss, and it was too soon to say, 'This was the good part and that was the bad part.' Now I'm in the stage of, 'Oh! I'm going to be okay. Oh! It's not the end of the world. Oh! It hurt like hell, and I can get through it.'"

Belinda has ventured back into the dating world, but

she is a long way from jumping into another commitment: "Someone I have been seeing for a few months has been pushing me to move in with him, but I cannot do that right now — commit to someone else, put all my eggs in that basket. If I do it, I want to do it with a sense that this is going to work long-term, and I'm going to do my share to make that happen. I just can't imagine making that kind of commitment at the moment because I'm still disappointed from my marriage not working. I'm not putting the blame on my former husband; I thought it was going to work out and it didn't, and there are a million reasons why it didn't. But I was wrong, and I'm not clear yet why I was wrong or what went wrong in the marriage. I don't yet know what I did right and what I did wrong. I think I have to figure out the lessons from that. I think I still need a little distance before jumping in again."

Giving ourselves some time to figure out what went wrong can help us avoid jumping into another disappointing relationship. Often our sadness over a broken relationship is based on our image of what the relationship *could have been*, not what it really was. We fall in love with the images we have in our minds of what we had hoped the relationship to be. We need to give ourselves time to see the relationship we have left, not as we had hoped it would be, but as it actually was. When we give ourselves some time to collect our thoughts, we can make sure that we avoid the same difficulties in the future. As one woman, married for the second time, said, "I absolutely had different problems in each of the serious relationships in my life. In fact, one thing I said to people when I got married this time was that I was absolutely certain that I was not making the same mistakes I had made before. I wasn't absolutely certain that I wasn't making a new mistake that I had yet to discover, but I was positive that I was not marrying someone who had the characteristics that I wanted to avoid from prior relationships. I think some people do date the same kind of person over and over. I get new problems as I go along."

Joan learned over time and through experience the kind of man she really wanted in her life: "I think these things are very personal, and not true across the board, but the first thing I learned about what I wanted was that I did not want a man who cared about how every little thing in his life was done and thought he knew how to do it and I did not know how to do it. I also didn't want anyone who had a nasty temper.

"The other thing I learned about myself was that I had, for lack of better term, a 'Norman Rockwell' view of what I wanted in life. I wanted to marry someone who was willing to have kids for the first time with me, who was going to grow up with me and grow old with me. As I have gotten to know myself better, I have made better choices. I remember someone saying to me during my first marriage, 'Oh, you got married when you were twenty-one! Well,' she laughed, 'I hope it lasts, but I wouldn't count on it.' She was in her thirties. I was offended at the time, but now I think I was in much better condition in my thirties to find someone. That's not true for everyone, but it was true for me."

Contrary to our culture's messages, life for women is not just a lonely and arid trek from thirty years old to the grave. There are always new possibilities for romance. Witness Stacy, who a few years ago left a dead-end marriage, then had a disappointing relationship with another man after that: "I was in a relationship drought for I can't tell you how long, and healing from all that heartbreak. Once I was healed, which was about last summer, I was ready to start dating, and then I went through months and months of not finding anyone to connect with. I had to go through a lot of frogs! All of a sudden this month I have an embarrassment of riches. I'm finding men who I can have this open communication with. Men with whom I can mix sexual attraction with heart-to-heart talk. One of them is getting me to talk about my life. I spend hours telling him stories about my life because he's interested in knowing them."

So if we are just starting to get back to our feet after being knocked down by our loss, we can start easy. Before we can even think about whether we want to be involved with another man, we first have to get used to a social life again, a life in which we are again single. And who better to help us with that than our friends? If we see a friend who is just emerging from the grief of losing a longtime companion through divorce or death, we can gently bring her out of her cocoon and help her stretch her wings again.

Why Do We Bother with Men Anyway? (Because We Like Them!)

Getting along with men isn't what's truly important. The vital knowledge is how to get along with a man. One man.

—PHYLLIS MCGINLEY

What Women Say About Men

All this talk about the difficulties, the sadness, pain, and struggle, makes us wonder why we bother with all this relationship stuff. Who needs the development and growth anyway? Sometimes it seems just too hard.

But we keep coming back for more. Why? Because we continue to like the company of men, and we hope to share our life with someone whom we respect, admire, and enjoy. When we asked women what they liked about men, the answers came quickly, some flip and facetious, some serious. One thirty-year-old woman, after she asked us laughingly how graphic we wanted her to be, said she liked men because "they look cute in jeans." Another said she liked "the different perspective that men bring."

Amanda, a sixty-five-year-old woman, had this to say: "I like men! I like their posturing and pretenses. I like their willingness to protect, provide, and pander to the women they love. I love their strength and their weaknesses. Did I mention their pliability? Yeah, that too! As a wife, mother, and grandmother I understand that if a woman doesn't like men as they are, she denigrates women. After all, we raised them!"

Several women said that they liked men's directness. Heidi, twenty-seven, said that she appreciated her husband's directness because "when you're upset about something, it makes you see that other side of things — that maybe something isn't a big deal and I should just move on."

Beth, a woman who is starting her own business and trying to raise money for it, said, "I like the directness and the honesty, the 'I'm not playing games here' attitude I get when I am dealing with men. The most recent example that comes to mind is that I am pitching to venture capitalists right now, and there is this sort of swashbuckling, 'show us what you got' attitude. I love it! I can go out there and tell them what we've got. There is none of this 'how are you feeling?' Now, on the flip side, I also need that in my life, god forbid that I don't have it, but I really celebrate that phallic directness. I think its great."

Other women like the physicality of men, that they are comfortable in their own skins and being physically active. Heidi noted, "I like it that my husband is more sports-minded than me. He usually pushes me, makes me take more chances, makes me ride my bike harder and run faster and that sort of thing."

And Gina, an artist with three children, said she liked the confidence that men have in their bodies: "They tend to be very secure with their physical self, which is nice. You don't talk a lot about food with them!"

Obviously there are a lot of reasons why we like men, but as the preceding McGinley quote suggests, we really only need to find one man whom we like. And the reason each woman likes a particular man varies from relationship to relationship. It doesn't really matter what someone else likes, so long as you do!

There has been a lot of male bashing going on in the last quarter century. Some of it is deserved, as women fought to take some control over their own lives. We still see a lot of it in movies where men are portrayed as the Darth Vaders of the Evil Empire. But as we achieve more equality, many women feel that it is time to stop treating men as the enemy.

Sherryl Connelly, in the *New York Daily News*, wrote an article entitled "Is Male-bashing Right? Or Does It Just Keep Them in Their Place?" In the article she says, "We tend to stereotype when we feel a loss of control or where there is an element of unpredictability, which is a good enough definition of the relationship many females have to males. Stereotyping provides us with a ready sense of how to deal in an ambiguous situation."[23] But she goes on to quote other commentators who say that such stereotyping is a form of male bashing. Although it temporarily relieves frustration or anger, it doesn't really serve women all that well in the long run. She quotes Gina Luria Walker, head of social sciences at the New School, who says: "That kind of humor can be corrosive—we're making ourselves angrier. . . . We're feeding each other self-righteousness."

Connelly also cites Wendy Kaminer, author of *True Love Lies*, who says that stereotyping also gives men permission to act in that manner: "We are not saying this is the way [men] choose to be, we are saying this is the way they are. . . . Any sense that something is predetermined becomes, 'It's in my nature to behave this way.'" Accepting "male behavior" indicates that we are approving it!

Further, while stereotyping isn't a good thing for women, it also may not be necessary as a way to reappropriate our power as women. While it may have been more advantageous, socially and financially, to be male in past history, many women agreed that today's women have many advantages men do not enjoy. Perhaps this is most noticeable in the evolving way men and women are portrayed on television. Hope, married for fifteen years, pointed out that "because women have been clamoring for more respect, you can find shows like *Murphy Brown* representing strong women deserving of respect, making her way in the world. In contrast, there is *Men Behaving Badly*. The male actors on these shows are portraying men as jerks, and as my husband, Bart, and I are watching TV, I actually feel sorry for him. He looks at this and is sickened. He comments to me, 'This isn't me.' Even *Home Improvement*, where the lead is basically a nice guy, is still portrayed as the bumbling husband who doesn't do anything right. So his wife ends up saying, 'Oh, honey, why can't you be more sensitive?' I feel sorry for men. There are some really wonderful guys out there that are nothing like these stereotypes."

Many of the women we interviewed agreed with Hope, noting that the men they loved often violated the negative stereotype of today's man. Yvonne told us a beautiful story about how her husband turned their son's bachelor party into a meaningful experience that helped their son start his marriage off on the right foot. She said, "I think there are a group of men who are really trying to be authentic, trying to grow up and not be the little boys with the big toys and all that. Before our son got married, my husband gathered men from our community to share what they've learned about marriage, not only through their successes, but also through mistakes they'd made like having affairs and things like that. Our son sat at each man's feet and, one by one, they instructed him. Then they helped him up and he went to the next man. All the men were in tears because they felt 'I have something of value to pass on.' I really admire these men, and would like to change the image of men so that they can be seen to have integrity and credibility."

Even though her first relationship after divorce did not work out, Stacy had this to say about it: "What I learned in those two years with him was that it was possible to get from a relationship the things that I was looking for—intimacy, nurturing, heart-to-heart communication, sharing lives. That was the first time in my life that someone had just held me when I needed to cry, or touched me all night long. I hadn't had that kind of closeness, even in my marriage. It was a totally new world for me. So I learned that what I was looking for was possible. I learned not to compromise. I didn't have to go out with people who were significantly different from me just in order to have a date. There are enough people out there like me, and I can find them."

We have to be careful what we tell ourselves when we find our relationships have gone south. Our culture tells us repeatedly that the older we women get, the less desirable we are, the fewer men are available, and the more likely we will live alone for the rest of our lives. One woman we spoke with was trying to decide whether she should stay with her boyfriend of three years, and she expressed her fears about giving up this relationship and being alone in the world: "As I'm faced with the prospect of breaking up with my boyfriend, I think 'Okay, here we go.' Now I'm almost forty, nobody is going to want me, and I have some lines on my face now, there a few gray hairs. I know that I am putting up with more than I should because my first thought is that I cannot be alone and that if I give up this connection I will never have another chance."

Every person must have these thoughts when she has disrupted her life (or had her life disrupted). They are normal reactions, but they are not true. As the woman's friend responded to her when she expressed these doubts: "You know what? There are men out there who will find those lines attractive. They have developed lines in their faces, too, over the years." She continued, "What I would like to tell women all over the place is, 'Do not put up with what you don't want, because it ensures that we don't get what we really want. If we don't keep pushing for what we really want, it means that we're not going to get it.'"

For all the talk about women being incurable romantics, we found that most women are realistic, too. We can take what wisdom is available to us from a relationship and move on. Bonnie, in her late twenties, has been living with a man for five years and yet, has known for most of those five years that she will not end up with Larry. However, she finds that it is still a positive relationship because she has learned so much about herself: "Our relationship has let me learn about myself because I've had to explain myself. I have to sit down and say, 'Okay, well, why do I respond a certain way?' In the early years of our relationship, our arguments were the most exciting part of it. It's sounds a little perverse, but we would go through these extremely long, drawn-out, exhausting periods of conversation — but it would be so enlightening. We stayed together because we kept learning all these things in our arguments and because he is a companion, absolutely. We have lived together for just over five years, and we live very well together. We spend our day-to-day time very well together, and he's a great person. He's intelligent. We enjoy doing the same things, but I do not see myself spending the rest of my life with him. There are other things that I want.

"We have talked about marriage and the fact that we would never marry each other. And we have talked about the fact that maybe we're just too young. But I'm ready to be married. I'm ready to find a person that I'm going to spend the rest of my life with."

Asked if she felt that the time together had been a waste, she replied, "I don't think there's one right person. So I don't think I've missed Mr. Right because of some happenstance. I believe that there are people out there that will match me, that I will be happy to be with for the rest of my life. I think there's a lot of them, probably. So I don't feel that I've missed the boat. The past five years have not been a waste. I've learned too much about myself and about what I need and what I want and feel that, had I not been with Larry, I probably would have made these mistakes with someone else. Hopefully it wouldn't have been with someone that I had, at one point, thought would be the right person."

When a relationship is over, we may not seek another

man in our life. If we have been in a long-term relationship, we may come to enjoy the independence and freedom of being alone. Or we may find it too painful to try replacing someone we deeply loved. Is that wrong or a denial of the order of things? No, how we live our lives and with whom is the most personal of decisions, which no one can or should make for anyone else.

Many of us, when a relationship ends, will try again. Are we foolishly optimistic? Perhaps, but if we wish to share our lives with someone, we have no choice! We just need to make sure we give ourselves enough time to heal from the last relationship. Perhaps our optimism just represents a belief that we can have what we want in life. Our experience with talking to women is that it truly is possible to find the man we want. If we are in-between relationships, it may help to know that there are men out there looking for a suitable mate, and it only takes one!

Wisdom from
the Front Lines

The sign of a good marriage is that everything is debatable and challenged; nothing is turned into law or policy. The rules, if any, are known only to the two players, who seek no public trophies.

—CAROLYN HEILBRUN
Writing a Woman's Life

For all of us, by permitting us to see ourselves in the mirror of their affection, friends help to anchor our self-image, to validate our identity.

—LILLIAN B. RUBIN

Having talked with all these women, what do we know, for sure, works with men? Well, some women who considered themselves successful with men were blond, others were redheads, and still others brunette. So hair color isn't a rule. Some women were earth mothers with cookie dough under their fingernails, others were high-powered corporate executives in sleek business suits, and one was even an eccentric artist who showed up for her interview in pajamas. Hmm . . . no hard and fast guideline there.

And what kind of men were the most lovable? Perhaps this conversation, from a group of women we interviewed, will shed some light on the subject of male attractiveness:

Missy: "I like a man who is in shape. A good washboard stomach is appealing."

Hannah: "For me that does not matter. I like it better when my boyfriend has a gut. He's softer then."

Peggy: "I like lots of hair, especially hairy arms."

Hannah: "See, I don't like hairy at all, especially on a man's chest."

Well, that didn't get us anywhere.

So what can we say with any certainty about one of our favorite topics—the men we love and the relationships we share with them? While we can, and will, share some generalities we gleaned from our interviews, we must emphasize that in the same way that every man is unique and interesting and complex, so every relationship between a man and a woman has its own individual rhythm and rhyme. What may be helpful for one couple may prove disastrous for another. What is a hard and fast rule in one household is the subject of ridicule in another. So, as we summarize the wisdom of women, keep in mind that there are only a few "don'ts"—such as, don't stay with a man who physically beats you—and lots of "do's" that you'll have to discover, ultimately, for yourself.

Make It Fun

Humor brings insight and tolerance.

—AGNES REPPLIER

In Pursuit of Laughter

Most women who had long-term mates found that it was important to have fun together. It wasn't a tragedy if two people did not have the same interests, although it helped to have some interests in common. As Stacy told us, "Two people have to have a core of similar interests, but I think it's probably helpful if they each have some separate interests, too. I wouldn't want to marry a clone."

Gina emphasized that commonality is more important in values than in interests: "I think that respect is really important, and sharing a common sense of values. Not sharing a common interest necessarily, but sharing values. I think it is really important to be able to have fun together and to enjoy life together. My husband and I are polar opposites; he is very academic and I am very social. I'm very tactile, he's not. We have some common interests, but not very many. He is very interested in solo activities, like playing the guitar and working with computers, and I am very interested in outdoor activities, with people."

When we asked her how having different interests worked in their relationship, she said, "Well . . . respect. I respect his time with his guitar and his computer, and I love him for it. And I play the fun games on the computer with him, because I have learned to like them. And he respects me for the walks that I go on, and he'll trek along with me now and then, and we give in to each other enough. I'll play golf, but I'll play par three golf instead of eighteen holes. And he'll come shopping with me, which he hates, but he'll do it for an hour before he starts to whine. And so we give in to each other's interests, and we just respect that that person likes it. It is kind of nice to have your own thing to do. Then we try to do a lot of things as a family together."

And Joan told us that having the same interests as her first husband did nothing to make their marriage work: "I was married to someone whose interests could not have been more in sync with mine. It was a joke when we got engaged and got married, that here were two people, who, almost everything they were interested in they could trace together, and almost everything from their past was similar. And yet it didn't work." As we continued to talk to Joan, we found that the man with whom she was with was emotionally abusive and highly critical of her. Unsurprisingly, common interests couldn't save it.

Regardless of how many interests a man and woman have in common, however, most women found it was important to have fun with your spouse. If we can't laugh with the person who can see us when our hair is smashed with one protruding horn and our breath is bad, then we really don't have much hope for the future. One woman did not realize her own playfulness until she was thirty-five and just divorced from her husband of fifteen years. Often, it is fun that attracts us to someone in the first place: How many times would we go out with someone if we did not enjoy ourselves? And how long will we stay with someone if we do not occasionally have a good laugh with our mate?

Obviously, there is a lot in life that it not fun. We spend a significant part of our lives and this book talking about decidedly nonfun things such as laundry, money arguments, and the division of power and labor. The importance of fun often fades as our lives get busier and our responsibilities weigh us down, especially in our hectic society where more is better and the harder you work, the better the person you are perceived to be.

One unmarried woman from North Carolina told this story: "When I was growing up, my parents operated a couple of restaurants—one a diner and one a supper club. Well, in that business, you are there all of the time and there is no time for days off or vacations. There was a lot of emphasis on hard work, and my two sisters and I grew up thinking that if one wanted to make it in life, one had to work all the time, and fun was trivial. Well, it has really affected my relationships with men, because they always get the message that work is the most important thing in my life and that they are a somewhat distant second. That doesn't work very well for a relationship, and I found that I was dating men who understood (and lived) my work ethic. We didn't have much time for each other, and it was hard to build a bond with someone who was always working or always thinking about work. I was reminded of myself when I saw the movie *Baby Boom*, where Diane Keaton was a successful, workaholic ad executive who had a live-in relationship with her equally hardworking boyfriend. When they had sex, it lasted about three minutes, and then they both went right back to work. Of course that is an exaggeration, but it had an uncomfortable ring of truth to it for me."

Another woman who has been with her man for five years has found that fun has played a vital role in maintaining their feelings for each other. She says, "I think we're very lucky that there's still a lot of spark. And I think it has a lot to do with the fact that we just like to have fun together. We're just totally kooky and silly together, and there are times when I'm just overwhelmed by an 'oh-my-God-I-totally-love-this-guy' feeling. It's such a great feeling, and I don't think we've lost it at all. We both continue to feel very much in love. I mean, we're not having sex like rabbits anymore like we did in the first couple of months or anything, but everyone goes through that. But I still very much have this feeling of wanting to be with him, wanting to be near him, missing him when he's gone, all that kind of stuff. And I don't think it's going to quench itself."

Some bonds are created when two people go through serious, difficult times together. A job is lost, a friend or family member gets sick or dies, someone gets into financial or legal trouble. The bonds that are built in those tough situations give you the knowledge that you can stick together in rough times, that both of you are people upon whom the other one can rely. The bonds that are built in happy times, times of fun or silliness, give you the assurance that the other person is the one you want to be with, the person with whom you can laugh and put life in perspective.

Shelley, married for twenty-five years, says she and her husband stay close partly because "we do things together. Every once in a while he likes to get rowdy, but I'm always with him. It may happen every couple of months, especially when we go back to his college town, where he always takes one night to act like he's a child again. But he doesn't go out with the boys and I don't go out with the girls — at least not on a regular basis. I think all that does is cause problems when you start getting your night out once a week separate from each other."

Sometimes fun requires some effort — we may need to share our mate's idea of fun when it isn't necessarily our idea of a good time. This kind of effort can go a long way in creating a sense of appreciation from our mate, and may inspire him to participate in what we as individuals find enjoyable. And who knows? Not only will our shared experience strengthen our bonds with our men, we may be introduced to a new activity that we enjoy!

Accept Change as Inevitable

But people themselves alter so much, that there is something new to be observed in them for ever.

—JANE AUSTEN

Pride and Prejudice

The hallmark of every long-term relationship that we observed was the ability of both parties to adjust to change and to allow the relationship and the roles each person played in it to emerge and evolve. Every woman who was in a long-term marriage or relationship had experienced shifts, many times surprising shifts away from the way the relationship began. None of us are insulated in our lives, and reality has a way of forcing change. We can fight it and allow it to destroy our connections, or we can live through them together, when both parties accept that nothing ever stays the same.

Shelley tells how her marriage has changed: "Well, we couldn't keep up that pace of the early days—being at each other all the time, you know what I'm saying, and trying to please. Now it's more relaxed—I know what he wants and he knows what I want. I think when you're first married you're just so intent on making everything perfect, and later you don't have to worry about that anymore—he knows that you've arrived. It's satisfying and it's easy, but one thing I know, no matter who it is, you have to work at making it exciting."

Paula's advice for surviving losses and change was inspiring. She told us, "Try to participate in whatever life brings you. When my husband was dying, there were people in his own family that, as soon as he lost consciousness, wanted him to go back to the hospital. They said it would be too awful, because they were really afraid. But even though it was difficult, I just felt I had to do keep him at home as he wished. I think that most people do have what it takes to get through it, but sometimes we need a little bit of courage. Believe that you can tolerate intense feelings.

"On the other side of the depth of pain is the height of joy. If you don't ever have the depths, you can't get the heights. In my opinion, if you're somewhere in the middle, you're never going to be really happy. I've had incredible joy and incredible sadness. To me, if I'd refused to experience the sadness, I would have also missed the joy, and it's the joy that I held onto to get me through."

Change is often not enjoyable, as we are faced with new, unfamiliar circumstances to which we are forced to adjust. But it is in times of change that we find we are learning new skills, achieving things which we didn't know we could handle. If we are sharing the challenge of change with another person, whether it is a change in the relationship, such as a person becoming ill, or a change from outside the couple, such as a move cross-country triggered by a job change, we can grow together. We can become sensitive to and support each other in our frailties, and discover and celebrate each other's strengths as we deal with the challenge of change together. Like vines grafted together to produce a stronger plant, we can build a stronger unit, a team better able to face the challenges of life than we can alone.

Be Ready to Forgive (and Say I'm Sorry)

Forgiveness is the act of admitting we are like other people.

—CHRISTINA BALDWIN

Life's Companion: Journal Writing as a Spiritual Quest

Are you a perfect woman in relationship with a perfect man? Didn't think so. That leaves us muddling through life together, continually creating opportunities to say, "Ouch, that hurt!" and "Oh, so sorry!" Without acknowledging hurtful experiences and repairing the breach in trust and safety, even the strongest love will eventually atrophy with resentment.

One woman we spoke with talked about learning to forgive the person, even though the act may rankle for a long time. "There was a time when my husband, Benton, sold my cross-country skis. I had so much pain in my knees at the time and I couldn't do a lot of skiing, but one day I came home and he had sold my skis without asking me. I was really angry that he didn't consult with me first. We had this big argument. The angrier I got, the more the anger built like a volcano. When I decided to forgive *him*, but not necessarily the act that he had done, then it was easier to go on. I learned to forgive the person but take out my anger on the act."

The corollary of the need for forgiveness is the need to apologize when we have hurt someone. Love doesn't mean never having to say you are sorry. Love, at least lasting love, means being able to recognize when you need to say you are sorry. Sometimes it seems that relationships, especially romantic ones, are simply a series of "I apologize" and "You're forgiven."

One woman told us that she watched her parents fight throughout her childhood and then finally divorce when she was eighteen: "It really didn't matter what the fight was about, there was always something to argue or disagree about. But in all the time they were together, I never heard one of them apologize to the other. They would get angry, then ignore each other for a while, then pretend that nothing had ever happened. But all that unresolved stuff—the anger, the lack of forgiveness, the inability to say 'I'm sorry'—it eventually took its toll. Their marriage ended. I didn't realize that this was a problem in a relationship, of course, until many years later. I had to learn as an adult how to swallow my pride and admit when I had done something wrong. Now it is a relief to be able to do that. I can ask for forgiveness and apologize and go on with my life without the burden of guilt and unresolved tension."

Pride is not much of a bed mate, but pride may be what we are left with if we cannot say we are sorry when we are wrong. This is not to say that we should apologize for everything that goes wrong; we do not have control over the universe. And forgiveness is not forgetting or pretending nothing awful happened. Quite the opposite. Forgiveness means responding to an identified wrong, intentional or not, that one person perpetrates on the other. It takes two to forgive — one to admit a failure and ask for a repair in the relationship, and the other to admit hurt and open up once again. Lessons on how to be better lovers, partners, friends, and housemates are byproducts of healthy forgiveness, of somehow making the painful experiences tolerable, redeemable. Without our mistakes, we wouldn't be human. And without forgiveness, we'd all be alone.

Be a Team

If we expect a relationship to be long-term with a man,
we have to act like a team. One aspect of teamwork is
having faith that our spouse is doing something he believes is for the best. When we asked a woman who had
been married for nearly fifteen years what was the secret
to the relationship's longevity, she told us, "We decided
early in the marriage to 'assume good faith.' You know
those moments, sometimes hours or days, in which you
are unable to get a reasonable explanation for what your
spouse has done? Before my husband and I can talk,
and I can fully understand what in the world was going
on in his mind when he did such-and-such, I try not to
draw unsubstantiated conclusions and then act on them
as if they were certainties. Instead, I tell myself, 'He probably had a good reason for doing this. He's acted wisely
in the past,' and then I wait until he can explain just what
that reason, as odd as it might seem to me, actually is.

"This keeps us from having two problems to solve — the original action that is causing the rift between us and the imaginary motivation that I created. And he does the same for me. When I do something stupid, he suspends judgment until I can say, 'Oh, that?' and I can think up a good reason for what I just did."

We also need to be able to prop each other up in time of trouble. Instead of turning on each other when life deals out the unthinkable situation, we have to be each other's friends. Valerie told us about her and her husband Ross's teenage son, who disappeared for over a year and a half. During his disappearance, they each constantly felt guilt and remorse for anything that they had done to cause his disappearance. Like so many parents in that situation, they felt responsible for the situation and were constantly searching their hearts for where they had gone wrong. "I felt guilty, like I wasn't a good-enough mother. I felt like maybe we didn't do something that we should have done."

When we asked how they were able to support each other at that time, she said, "We made an agreement with each other that if we felt like our anxiety or anger or sadness was getting too much, we would not direct it at each other, we would release it together. We would 'blend' our anger together so we were not coming at each other with our feeling. One time I was crying and crying and saying, 'I should not have done my life this way.' I was really upset, as I couldn't understand why there had been no communication from him, and then we had found his abandoned car in Boston. We were so upset.

"I desperately wanted to hear from Ross that I was a good mother, and he wanted to hear from me that he was a good father. So we would say to each other what we wanted the other one to say to us, instead of trying to read each other's minds. We would really be clear about what we wanted. I wanted to cry and let loose, be told that I was a good mother and that it wasn't my fault. I would say, 'This is what I want. I want you to hold my hand right now, don't make solutions right now. I simply want to feel.' And I would ask Ross what he wanted when he would do his little antsy stuff and start to get over-busy. Our agreement was to say what we wanted and to have time to allow ourselves to do that."

Valerie and Ross happily found their son, alive and healthy, a year ago. They were able to come together again as a family, and their marriage has survived the trauma: "It has been a year now since we found him safe and sound, he had run away. What Ross doesn't know is that I am going to fly our son home for Ross's birthday as a surprise. Ross said last week, somewhat tearfully, that he really wanted to go camping with Charlie and really wished he could do that this summer. The fact is, that is what they are going to be doing together, and Ross doesn't know it. I can't wait."

Being able to survive the big things in life starts with thinking of ourselves as part of a team on a daily basis.

Team members play together, but each has specific responsibilities. One of the most important responsibilities each of us has is to take care of our own feelings. We cannot be expected to read each other's minds, and if something is bothering us, it is our responsibility to ourselves and to the relationship to speak up.

Similarly, no one is responsible for making someone else happy, although it would be nice if we could unload that one on someone else, wouldn't it? Many times this is easier said than done, as we look to the man we love to fulfill our dreams for us. But we are perfectly capable of doing that ourselves; we only need him to cheer us on.

Respect Each Other

Like and equal are two entirely different things.

—MADELEINE L'ENGLE

A Wrinkle in Time

Throughout the book, we've quoted from women who adamantly argue that there are no differences between the genders, while others are resolutely convinced that men and women are so different they might be considered different species. The emotion underlying these opinions runs so intensely, that we suspect there is more under the surface here than simply objective observations about the sexes. Perhaps the struggle is rooted in a confusion of sameness and equality.

Women have struggled long and hard for equality in the boardroom and in the bedroom. Unfortunately, sometimes we have traded our uniqueness as women for some semblance of equal power. In order to be equal, this line of thinking goes, we must prove that there are no differences. This might prove successful, to some degree, in the workplace. But in a romantic liaison, insisting on sameness can be the beginning of the end.

Those who can cultivate and enjoy differences of opinion often thrive, whereas couples who insist that both people feel, think, and behave identically crack under the rigidity. The only way couples can allow each other to be different *and* equal is to introduce the experience of respect. By respecting differences, giving both people credit for their thoughts and feelings, perceptions and convictions, a couple grants equal merit to unlike parts.

As couples we are not required to blend into the other person. We each bring something different to the union, and even though those differences may seem inconvenient occasionally, who needs boring? Rene, a minister, told us about one couple who she admired for being able to live with their differences in religious beliefs: "She is what we would have called in the sixties a 'Christian fanatic.' He hasn't been to church probably in thirty years. They don't have children, so they haven't had to deal with their difference in that respect. But in everything else, they are very connected as a couple. He is fine with the fact that she says 'praise the Lord' all the time and has religious stickers all over the refrigerator, as long as she doesn't push him about why he doesn't go to church with her or pray for his salvation. She's careful with that kind of thing."

The benefit to having someone respect us and our beliefs is, not only are we free to think and be in the way that we wish, but we learn to respect ourselves more as well. When someone else reinforces our right to our own opinions and desires, it supports our own sense of self-esteem. Additionally, as we feel autonomy in our own beliefs, we may be even more open to our partner's ideas and beliefs as well. This ability and willingness to consider our partner's opinion's helps our minds stay fresh, allowing us to evolve as individuals. But not only will respect for each other help us mature as separate people, it will increase our loyalty and love for our team. We will have the security of knowing that someone is always on our side, whether or not he agrees with our opinions. In short, sharing respect for each other helps us grow as individuals and as a couple.

Twelve Girlfriend Guidelines

Much advice has been offered and received in this book, and we have gathered here the wise and insightful guidelines of many girlfriends. Hopefully your relationships can be enhanced by heeding these voices of friendship.

1 ∿ Listen to Your Body
Our bodies frequently pick up on feelings faster than our minds do. If you practice paying attention to your interactions with all people you will learn what your own body signals mean to you.

2 ∿ Listen to Your Heart
Once we know in our hearts what is important to us personally, whether it is patience, confidence, intelligence, warmth, the ability to talk about feelings, or other characteristics, then we can figure out what we can let go in a relationship with a man.

3 ∿ Listen to Your Girlfriends
Girlfriends are women who have seen you in more than one relationship and may be more aware of patterns you fall into than you are yourself. They can provide a lot of insight and point out positive and negative aspects of your chosen man.

4 ⤳ Expect to Be Surprised

If you are starting a relationship, get ready to consider someone else's opinion. Once you are coupled, there are few decisions that can be made without taking someone else into consideration.

5 ⤳ Maintain Your Sense of Self

After the first flush of a romantic relationship is the time when a couple struggles with what couplehood means. How much is the individual a part of the couple, and how much is he or she alone, separated from the mate and pursuing other interests?

6 ⤳ Learn to Trust the Process

We suspect everyone who has been in a relationship wakes up one morning and says, "Who is this person lying next to me? I don't know this person." That is the time to sit up and start facing the challenges. Good can come of sticking with the process.

7 ⤳ Recognize That No One is Going to Fulfill All Your Needs

Men and women both benefit from having many loving, supportive relationships, and we gain insight and knowledge from many perspectives.

8 ⤳ Make It Fun

If we can't laugh with the person who can see us when our hair is smashed with one protruding horn and our breath is bad, then we really don't have much hope for the future.

9 ⤳ Accept Change as Inevitable

The hallmark of every long-term relationship that we observed was the ability for both parties to adjust to change and to allow the relationship and the roles each person played in it to emerge and evolve.

10 ∾ Be Ready to Forgive (and Say I'm Sorry)
Without our mistakes, we wouldn't be human. And without forgiveness, we'd all be alone.

11 ∾ Be a Team
Being able to survive the big things in life starts with thinking of ourselves as part of a team on a daily basis.

12 ∾ Respect Each Other
By respecting differences, giving both people credit for their thoughts and feelings, perceptions and convictions, a couple grants equal merit to unlike parts.

Endnotes

1. Margaret Kent, *How to Marry the Man of Your Choice* (New York: Warner Books, 1984), 39.

2. Gregory J.P. Godek, *1001 Ways to Be Romantic* (Boston: Casablanca Press, 1993), 139.

3. Carol C. Wells, *Right-Brain Sex: How to Reach the Heights of Sensual Pleasure by Releasing the Erotic Power of Your Mind* (New York: Avon Books, 1989), 137.

4. Judith Sills, *A Fine Romance: The Psychology of Successful Courtship: Making It Work for You* (New York: Ballantine Books, 1987), 21-22.

5. Ibid., 150.

6. Dave Barry, *Dave Barry's Complete Guide to Guys: A Fairly Short Book* (New York: Fawcett, 1995), 69, 70.

7. Sills, op.cit., 168, 169.

8. Dr. Patricia Allen and Sandra Harmon, *Staying Married . . . And Loving It!: How to Get What You Want from Your Man Without Asking* (New York: William Morrow and Company, 1997), 16, 17.

9. Deborah Tannen, *You Just Don't Understand: Women and Men in Conversation* (New York: Ballantine Books, 1991), 80.

10. Ibid., 80.

11. John Gray, *Men Are from Mars, Women Are from Venus: A Practical Guide for Improving Communication and Getting What You Want in Your Relationships* (New York: HarperCollins, 1992), 37.

12. Tannen, op.cit., 81.

13. Allen and Harmon, op.cit., 3.

14. Gray, op.cit., 245-246.

15. Charles Petit, "Fertility Test Succeeds—Proof's in the Crib" *San Francisco Chronicle*, 26 June 1997, A1.

16. A. Justin Sterling, *What Really Works With Men: Solve 95% of Your Relationship Problems (And Cope With the Rest)* (New York: Warner Books, 1992), 115.

17. Nora Ephron, *Heartburn* (New York: Vintage Books, 1983), 64.

18. Mel White, *Stranger at the Gate: To Be Gay and Christian in America* (New York: Simon and Schuster, 1994), 141-156.

19. Julia Lawlor, "The New Breadwinner" *Working Mother,* June 1997, 12-13.

20. Harriet Lerner, *The Dance of Anger: A Woman's Guide to Changing the Patterns of Intimate Relationships* (New York: HarperCollins, 1989), 134-136.

21. Harville Hendrix, *Getting the Love You Want: A Guide for Couples* (New York: HarperCollins, 1988), 112.

22. Ibid., 3-14.

23. Sherryl Connelly, "Is Male-bashing Right? Or Does It Just Keep Them in Their Place?" *New York Daily News,* in *Wisconsin State Journal,* 11 May 1997, G8.

About the Authors

CARMEN RENEE BERRY is a nationally certified body-worker, former psychotherapist, and the author of ten books including *When Helping You Is Hurting Me, Coming Home to Your Body,* and *Is Your Body Trying to Tell You Something?*. Carmen has an M.S.W. from the University of Southern California and an M.A. in Social Sciences from Northern Arizona University. She resides in Pasadena, California.

TAMARA TRAEDER is a publisher, author, and intellectual property attorney. Tamara graduated from the University of Virginia Law School in 1985, and from the University of Missouri with a liberal arts degree in 1982. She lives in Berkeley, California.

Carmen and Tamara's other *girlfriends* books are *girlfriends: Invisible Bonds, Enduring Ties* and *The girlfriends Keepsake Book: The Story of Our Friendship.* They enjoy a rich and rewarding friendship from opposite ends of California.

WILDCAT CANYON PRESS publishes books that embrace such subjects as friendship, spirituality, women's issues, and home and family, all with a focus on self help and personal growth. Whether a collection of meditations or short essays or a how-to text, our books are designed to enlighten and encourage our readers' hearts and souls. While we insist on a certain intimacy in our authors' writing, we also take responsibility to ensure that their messages are accessible to readers of all levels. Great care is taken to create books that inspire reflection and improve the quality of our lives. Our books demand to be shared and are frequently given as gifts.

For a catalog of our publications, please write:

WILDCAT CANYON PRESS
2716 Ninth Street
Berkeley, California 94710
Phone: (510) 848-3600
Fax: (510) 848-1326
Circulus@aol.com
http://www.ReadersNdex.com/wildcatcanyon